MATCH OF THE ~~DAY~~

TOP 10

of EVERYTHING

OUR ULTIMATE FOOTBALL DEBATES

BBC

MATCH OF THE DAY

TOP 10

of EVERYTHING

OUR ULTIMATE FOOTBALL DEBATES

MICAH RICHARDS	GARY LINEKER	ALAN SHEARER

BBC
BOOKS

1

BBC Books, an imprint of Ebury Publishing
20 Vauxhall Bridge Road,
London SW1V 2SA

BBC Books is part of the Penguin Random House group of companies
whose addresses can be found at global.penguinrandomhouse.com

Penguin
Random House
UK

Compiled by Rory Smith

By arrangement with the BBC
The BBC logo is a trade mark of the British Broadcasting
Corporation and is used under Licence.
BBC logo © BBC 1996

First published by BBC Books in 2021
Paperback edition published 2022

www.penguin.co.uk

A CIP catalogue record for this book is available from the British Library

ISBN 9781785947551

Text design by Seagull Design
Jacket design by Two Associates

Printed and bound in Great Britain by Clays Ltd, Elcograf S.p.A.

The authorised representative in the EEA is Penguin Random House Ireland,
Morrison Chambers, 32 Nassau Street, Dublin D02 YH68

Penguin Random House is committed to a sustainable future
for our business, our readers and our planet. This book is made
from Forest Stewardship Council® certified paper.

CONTENTS

PART 2: CULTURE

PART 3: HALL OF FAME

INTRODUCTION

GARY LINEKER

We spend a lot of time together making *Match of the Day*. Every Saturday during the season, the two guests and I will arrive in the studio a little before lunchtime. We gather, along with the producer, the director and the production staff, in a little office, lined with television screens, and begin a long day doing the really rather pleasant work of watching football.

We start with the early kick-off: we will all watch that one together. Then, when 3pm rolls around, each pundit will be assigned a specific game to monitor: it's not an exact science, but we try to focus on the ones which we think will produce the best stories. In the days before the pandemic, when there might be another four or five kicking off at that time, the director and I would do our best to stay across everything else, keeping a close eye on any game that looked like it might be developing into a real blockbuster. In the edit

1

suites, the team are hard at work, clipping up the most interesting moments from each and every one of the games. When they're over, we'll all gather again to watch the late kick-off.

It doesn't stop there. We still have to pull together the clips of all of the day's fixtures, pull out specific elements of each game for analysis, run through the script and do our best to look vaguely presentable before going on air, live, after the news. The few minutes we spend dissecting each game that you see are the product of an awful lot of work, from an awful lot of people.

Throughout the day, there is plenty of joking and laughing. We cheer when our teams score. We sink with our heads in our hands when they concede. And, in the case of Alan Shearer, whenever his beloved Newcastle are frustrating him, we shout. A lot. Alan has the loudest voice in the world, especially when he's seen his team give away a soft goal or miss an easy chance.

But what we do, most of all, is talk. We debate. We argue. And we tell stories. Every single footballer – or, more accurately, former footballer – has a well of stories from their career: strange incidents and happy memories and bitter regrets from the days when they were playing, all of which they are often happy to share, with their peers, at the drop of a hat. On those long, bustling Saturdays, we tell each other those stories. We compare notes. We contrast experiences. We try to outdo each other, to see who can get the biggest laugh.

It was those bottomless conversations that were the inspiration for what would, eventually, become the *Match of the Day Top 10* podcast, show and, now, this book. It was a chance to tell those stories to a broader audience, to offer a little insight into the way we played the game then and the way we see it now, and perhaps to settle a few of football's ongoing arguments, too. Who was the greatest defender of all time? Was it really harder in mine and Alan's day than it was when Micah Richards was playing? Can you say for sure that Lionel Messi is better than Diego Maradona? And just how many teams did Micah support when he was growing up?

We have tried to cover as many subjects as possible, involving not just the Premier League but the FA Cup, the Champions League, the European Championships and the World Cup, too. We will, occasionally, disappear off down memory lane, just as we do as we sit and watch all of those games in the green room, preparing for *Match of the Day*, thinking about all the players we have faced, the games we have won and the cups – in Alan's case – that we have lost.

As we say at the top of every podcast: these lists are not meant to be definitive. The glory of all of these conversations is that there are no objective answers to them, and we would not pretend to have found them. It is what makes sport – and especially football – special, that so many people can see it in so many different ways.

Please feel free to disagree with our conclusions; they are, after all, no more than personal opinions. I would ask you to let us know exactly where you think we've gone wrong, too, but I know that, when it comes to football, nobody ever needs an invitation to do that. That, after all, is the fun of it.

PART ONE

MOMENTS IN TIME

THE TOP 10
GAMES

GARY LINEKER

The final day of the season in 2012 was a stressful one in the *Match of the Day* office. How we handle that sort of situation is always a tricky editorial decision. Do we do one game first, and then the other? Or do we run the highlights of both simultaneously, cutting between them, to try to tell the story of the day?

We flipped between the two as the day unfolded. Manchester United were playing away, at Sunderland, and Manchester City were at home against QPR, knowing that a win would seal a first title in more than 40 years. Manchester United took the lead first, giving them the edge. By half-time, Pablo Zabaleta had scored for City, meaning the championship was heading for the Etihad.

The second half was chaos. QPR equalised, and then took the lead. The Etihad was silent, and the clock was ticking. The game in Sunderland finished: at that stage, Manchester United were champions. And then, in injury time, Manchester City drew level. They had a few minutes to find another goal. At the last second, Sergio Agüero found it.

Lots of fans of lots of different clubs work on *Match of the Day*, but when Agüero scored, everyone went up: the whole office, delirious with the drama of it all. Well, almost the whole office: there was one United fan who did not quite feel up to joining in the celebrations. It was the same scene at Sunderland. United's players had been on the pitch, getting ready to party, waiting for the final whistle in Manchester, thinking that they'd won it. Then the news came through: the fans heard it in the stands, and someone passed it to Sir Alex Ferguson on the bench, and you could see their heads drop.

So much turned on that single moment. United would recover, of course, going on to win the league in Fergie's final season the next year, but you do wonder what would have happened to City if Agüero hadn't had that chance, if he hadn't scored. It would have been so devastating to choke like that. And though that sounds harsh, that is exactly what it would have been: a choke.

You can make the argument that Liverpool's (first) 4-3 win against Newcastle is the Premier League's greatest ever game, I think. But Manchester City winning the title as they did, the cliffhanger ending of the Agüero goal, is – without question – the defining Premier League moment.

THE CONTENDERS

Liverpool 4-3 Newcastle United (1996)
Newcastle 5-0 Manchester United (1996)
Arsenal 3-2 Manchester United (1997)
Tottenham 3-5 Manchester United (2001)
Liverpool 4-4 Arsenal (2009)

Manchester United 4-3 Manchester City (2009)

Newcastle 4-4 Arsenal (2011)

Manchester City 3-2 QPR (2012)

Crystal Palace 3-3 Liverpool (2014)

Chelsea 2-2 Tottenham (2016)

ALAN SHEARER

It tells you something that there are three Newcastle games on this list, you know. There are happy memories: the 5-0 against Manchester United, of course. That was almost the perfect performance, against the perfect opposition.

And the comeback against Arsenal, from 4-0 down at half-time, showed the power of St James's Park. The crowd had been moaning and groaning at the break. But then, as soon as Arsenal went down to ten men and Newcastle started pulling goals back, they started going mad. It pulls you along, that crowd, and there's not much you can do to resist it.

There was something strange in the air that day. Cheick Tioté was a great player for Newcastle: he spent seven years there, made 139 appearances. But he only scored one goal, and it was the one that completed the comeback that day. If you're going to score just once for a club in all that time, you may as well make sure it's a special game, and a special day.

But then there is, if not a sad memory, then certainly a bittersweet one. The game at Anfield against Liverpool, as Newcastle tried to chase down the title in 1996, had absolutely everything. They'd had a 12-point lead quite late in the season, but Manchester United had been chipping away at it for months.

But what made Kevin Keegan special was that he never wanted to change how his teams played. He never considered altering his approach. It was always, always, all-out attack, whatever the circumstances and whoever the opposition. More than anything else, he wanted to entertain the fans.

That was what made that night so remarkable. Liverpool were still just about in the title race, but that didn't change what Newcastle did. They just kept going at Liverpool: they took the lead twice, but they never thought about sitting back and closing up shop. Instead, they went hammer and tongs for 90 minutes, more than that, until Stan Collymore swept home that winner, and Keegan could do nothing but slump on the advertising board in front of the dugout. That image was so powerful because it seemed to capture what had happened to Newcastle that night: with that one goal, the air had been drawn from its title race.

ALAN'S LIST

1 Manchester City 3-2 QPR (2012)

2 Liverpool 4-3 Newcastle United (1996)

3 Tottenham 3-5 Manchester United (2001)

4 Newcastle United 4-4 Arsenal (2011)

5 Manchester United 4-3 Manchester City (2009)

6 Newcastle United 5-0 Manchester United (1996)

7 Chelsea 2-2 Tottenham (2016)

8 Crystal Palace 3-3 Liverpool (2014)

9 Arsenal 3-2 Manchester United (1997)

10 Liverpool 4-4 Arsenal (2009)

MICAH RICHARDS

I was on the bench for the Agüero game. I wasn't happy that Roberto Mancini had picked Pablo Zabaleta ahead of me, but I was pretty confident I'd get to play. Most of the time, as soon as we went ahead, he'd bring a defender. He's an Italian manager, after all. His first instinct was always to protect the lead.

But when we did score, just before half-time, it was Zabaleta who scored. Zabaleta never scored, and now he'd got one in what was probably the biggest game in City's history. Worse than that was QPR equalising, and then getting a second. Now he couldn't bring a defender on. I knew, as soon as they scored, that I wouldn't play a minute.

I'm not especially proud to admit it but my first reaction was probably a selfish one: when Zabaleta scored, I felt sorry for myself, for what I'd miss out on. That changed with QPR's goals. Suddenly, my own situation didn't matter at all. That was when I realised how big it was. We were going to miss out on winning the Premier League.

You could feel the fans starting to turn. On the bench, you could hear all the comments from the fans sitting near us. 'Typical City.' 'Here we go again.' 'We're going to blow it.' As a substitute, especially as a defender, you feel powerless to help. The gloom that surrounds you starts to envelop you.

At one point, I was warming up with Mario Balotelli. He could see how down I was, how afraid I was, how much it meant to me. 'Don't worry,' he said. 'I'm going to come on, and I'm going to score or assist.' He had that sort of confidence, Mario, but he hadn't always backed it up. He hadn't created a single goal that season.

But he was as good as his word. I always think people forget how crucial Edin Džeko was: he got the goal that gave us the chance to go on and win it. It was Mario, though, who squeezed the ball through to Sergio for the winning goal. I don't really remember what happened next: the whole stadium went nuts. I ran down the touchline with everybody else to meet Sergio, and to celebrate. I was only there, in the end, as a spectator, but it was the most incredible moment of my career. I didn't ever really think I would be able to win the Premier League. I would never have imagined anyone could win it like that.

MICAH'S LIST

1 Manchester City 3-2 QPR (2012)

2 Liverpool 4-3 Newcastle United (1996)

3 Crystal Palace 3-3 Liverpool (2014)

4 Chelsea 2-2 Tottenham (2016)

5 Manchester United 4-3 Manchester City (2009)

6 Tottenham 3-5 Manchester United (2001)

7 Newcastle United 4-4 Arsenal (2011)

8 Newcastle United 5-0 Manchester United (1996)

9 Liverpool 4-4 Arsenal (2009)

10 Arsenal 3-2 Manchester United (1997)

THE TOP 10

1 Manchester City 3-2 QPR (2012)

2 Liverpool 4-3 Newcastle United (1996)

3 Tottenham 3-5 Manchester United (2001)

4 Manchester United 4-3 Manchester City (2009)

5 Newcastle United 4-4 Arsenal (2011)

6 Chelsea 2-2 Tottenham (2016)

7 Crystal Palace 3-3 Liverpool (2014)

8 Newcastle United 5-0 Manchester United (1996)

9 Liverpool 4-4 Arsenal (2009)

10 Arsenal 3-2 Manchester United (1997)

Gary's Verdict: I think we all agree on the top two: the game that maybe best defines the Premier League, and the most memorable conclusion to a season you could possibly hope for. In that situation, with everything on the line, it's hard to think of anyone better to be able to call on than Sergio Agüerooooooooo.

THE DEBATE

Alan: It has to be Manchester City beating QPR, just for the entertainment and excitement of it all: the contrast between the celebrations at the Etihad and the total devastation of the Manchester United players at Sunderland. It was the greatest game, and probably the greatest moment, in Premier League history.

Micah: That image of Keegan against the advertising boards summed up that whole season, didn't it? The excitement and the emotion and then, at the end, he just sort of deflated with the drama of it all. Those games can be really draining: in the derby that we lost 4-3, I remember not being able to press, not being able to get close to anyone, feeling as though I could barely run.

2

THE TOP 10
GOALS

GARY LINEKER

My bar for what qualifies as a beautiful goal is quite high. The best I ever saw on the pitch might well have been the best of all time: Diego Maradona's second against England in the 1986 World Cup.

That goal is, somehow, quite a lot better than people think it is, because that pitch was almost unplayable. They'd relaid it for the tournament, and it was a patchwork of different tufts of grass. Every time you moved, it shifted beneath your feet. It was difficult to stand up, let alone slalom between the whole England team and go round Peter Shilton. All you could do was stand back and admire it. 'My God', I thought, when he scored it. I felt, deep down, like I ought to applaud. But he'd scored the first one, a few minutes before, with his hand, so we weren't in a particularly generous mood.

Whether any of these goals match that one, I'm not sure, but some of them come close. It was hard to narrow it down to just ten: the

Premier League has a knack for producing spectacular goals. There are plenty of iconic ones that have not made the list – David Beckham, Wayne Rooney and Maynor Figueroa scoring from the halfway line, for a start. There's no room for either of Tony Yeboah's iconic goals, against Liverpool and Wimbledon, or the brilliant efforts scored by Luis Suárez, Dalian Atkinson, Michael Essien and all the rest. Even Peter Crouch's volley against Manchester City can't squeeze on.

Other players have made the list, but not quite as often as they might have done. Matt Le Tissier scored some of the greatest goals I have ever seen, and he made it all look so sensible. Rooney, too, has quite a highlights reel: he's on the list for his thunderous volley against Newcastle, but his overhead kick, the one that settled a Manchester derby, is not there. Nor is his first Premier League goal, the swerving, long-range strike for Everton that announced his talent to the world.

That should illustrate just how good the goals from the Premier League era that have made it are. They are all a little different – from the wonderful, flowing passing move that brought Jack Wilshere's goal against Norwich to Trevor Sinclair's gravity-defying overhead kick; some of them stood out for their beauty, like Dennis Bergkamp's finish against Newcastle, and some for their significance, like Vincent Kompany's piledriver to win the title for City. They are all special, though: so special that it will be difficult to choose between them.

THE CONTENDERS

Dennis Bergkamp, Arsenal v Newcastle United
Paolo Di Canio, West Ham v Wimbledon
Thierry Henry, Arsenal v Manchester United
Vincent Kompany, Manchester City v Leicester City
Matt Le Tissier, Southampton v Newcastle United

Wayne Rooney, Manchester United v Newcastle United

Trevor Sinclair, Queens Park Rangers v Barnsley

Andros Townsend, Crystal Palace v Manchester City

Robin van Persie, Manchester United v Aston Villa

Jack Wilshere, Arsenal v Norwich City

ALAN SHEARER

Sometimes, the ball just falls in exactly the right spot. That was the case with the best goal I ever scored – it's a bit disappointing it's not on the list, if I'm honest – a volley against Everton. I knew, as it dropped to me, that I'd hit it; and I knew, as soon as I'd hit it, that I'd caught it just right. It just felt perfect. You could see it going and going, see the goalkeeper start to dive, and know that he wasn't going to get there. It was quite fun.

There's a few like that on this list. It's a very precise technique to get a volley just right; it changes, depending on where the ball is, how it's travelling, your body shape. The one from Andros Townsend against Manchester City is as sweet a connection as you will see. The pass, the run and the finish for Robin van Persie's goal against Aston Villa is all exceptional, a little piece of poetry in motion.

Wayne Rooney's against Newcastle – one of a few too many goals against Newcastle here, I have to say – is another. I was on the pitch for that one. Rooney wasn't having a great game that day. He was running alongside the referee, chuntering away at him, when the ball fell to him from a cleared header. I watched it happen. He was still quite far out. I didn't think he'd try it from there. But it fell perfectly for him, and his finish was brilliant, the ball swerving from outside to in. Shay Given dived, but if I'm honest my first instinct was to wonder why he'd bothered. There was no way he was saving it.

The one that wins it, though, is the sort of goal that doesn't really have a category. It's a true one-off. Unfortunately, this one was against Newcastle, too, and I had a great view of it, again: Dennis Bergkamp's brilliant touch, swivel, control and finish at St James's Park. He'd scored an incredible one against Leicester a few years before, but this one was even better, a true masterpiece.

There is some debate over whether he meant it, but I think that misses the point. I'm sure he did, but even if he didn't, the improvisation was remarkable, to react that quickly and think that coolly. I'm not sure we'd seen a goal like that before. I'm not certain we'll ever see one like it again.

ALAN'S LIST

1 Dennis Bergkamp, Arsenal v Newcastle United
2 Trevor Sinclair, Queens Park Rangers v Barnsley
3 Matt Le Tissier, Southampton v Newcastle United
4 Thierry Henry, Arsenal v Manchester United
5 Paolo Di Canio, West Ham v Wimbledon
6 Jack Wilshere, Arsenal v Norwich City
7 Wayne Rooney, Manchester United v Newcastle United
8 Vincent Kompany, Manchester City v Leicester City
9 Andros Townsend, Crystal Palace v Manchester City
10 Robin van Persie, Manchester United v Aston Villa

MICAH RICHARDS

I'm at a slight disadvantage here when it comes to selecting the best goal I've ever scored: I don't have quite as many to choose from as Alan. I probably should have scored more, to be honest, particularly in the air: I had quite a leap on me. But in the end I only managed a dozen or so and, of those, the one that stands out was at Stoke: a bursting run forward, a little feint, and then slotting the ball into the far corner. I'll have to take what I can get, I suppose.

Thankfully, the best goal I saw on the pitch hasn't made it, either. If you watch the highlights of Wayne Rooney's overhead kick in the Manchester derby in 2011, you can just see my face appear, ready to head the ball away, as he makes contact with it. He just beat me to it. And you can tell from my reaction that I'm not entirely sure how he did it.

I always thought Trevor Sinclair's was better anyway, as it goes. That was an absolutely ridiculous goal. He came to City years after he scored that goal, and I always used to ask him if there was any chance of him doing something similar to that for us. He didn't particularly appreciate it, and I had to stop after a game at West Ham where I'd cost him a goal. He'd had a shot that had been curling into the top corner, but I'd got overexcited and followed it in. I headed it in, trying to claim the goal for myself, and run away to celebrate, only to discover that I was offside. He was raging, and I can sympathise with him.

All these goals are brilliant, obviously, and I've always had a soft spot for the sort of team goal, all intricate build-up and tiki-taka passing, that Jack Wilshere scored against Norwich, but there can only be one winner, really. No matter how important any of them were – goals that won games, goals that won derbies and, in Vincent Kompany's case, goals that won leagues – nobody else could have scored the goal against Newcastle that Dennis Bergkamp scored. It was a true original, and that makes it particularly special.

MICAH'S LIST

1 Dennis Bergkamp, Arsenal v Newcastle United
2 Jack Wilshere, Arsenal v Norwich City
3 Wayne Rooney, Manchester United v Newcastle United
4 Thierry Henry, Arsenal v Manchester United
5 Trevor Sinclair, Queens Park Rangers v Barnsley
6 Paolo Di Canio, West Ham v Wimbledon
7 Robin van Persie, Manchester United v Aston Villa
8 Andros Townsend, Crystal Palace v Manchester City
9 Matt Le Tissier, Southampton v Newcastle United
10 Vincent Kompany, Manchester City v Leicester City

THE TOP 10

1 Dennis Bergkamp, Arsenal v Newcastle United
2 Trevor Sinclair, Queens Park Rangers v Barnsley
3 Jack Wilshere, Arsenal v Norwich City
4 Thierry Henry, Arsenal v Manchester United
5 Wayne Rooney, Manchester United v Newcastle United
6 Paolo Di Canio, West Ham v Wimbledon
7 Matt Le Tissier, Southampton v Newcastle United

> **8** Andros Townsend, Crystal Palace v Manchester City
> **9** Robin van Persie, Manchester United v Aston Villa
> **10** Vincent Kompany, Manchester City v Leicester City

Gary's Verdict: Dennis Bergkamp was not just a beautiful player to watch, he was a scorer of beautiful goals. There are three from his highlights reel that really stand out: one for Holland at the 1998 World Cup, against Argentina; his strike in 1997 against Leicester City; and, top of the tree, the touch, the turn and the finish against Nikos Dabizas and Newcastle at St James's Park. Nobody did it quite like him.

THE DEBATE

Alan: It's not included but there can't have been many more satisfying goals to score than Steven Gerrard's in the FA Cup final. Scoring from that distance to stop your team losing a final, with that sort of power and that sort of placement. It's as pure a strike as you could hope for.

Micah: There's something about the pure team goal that I've always loved, and there haven't been many better examples of it than Jack Wilshere's for Arsenal. All those one-twos, the little interchanges with the ball: that's how football is meant to be played.

3

THE TOP 10
FA CUP MOMENTS

GARY LINEKER

My first FA Cup final was in 1969. I went down to Wembley with my dad, to watch Leicester play Manchester City. It was Leicester's third final in seven years. They didn't win any of them: that day, we lost 1-0 to a goal from Neil Young, and I cried all the way home. That is how much the cup final meant.

That has changed over the last 20 or 30 years, of course, as the league – and Europe – has become the be-all and end-all for most teams. It does not have the same magic as it used to have, when it was the only game televised live and the whole country seemed to stop to watch the final.

But that does not mean it is not still special. Whether it's the tradition or the knockout format or the sense of the whole game coming together – a competition in which a non-league team can go to Old Trafford, or a League Two side host Pep Guardiola and Manchester City – it retains its knack for producing memories.

We have had to be quite selective with which ones we chose for this list, so we decided to limit ourselves to those that we actually remember. No doubt, in an all-time list, things like Bert Trautmann playing in, and winning, a final with a broken neck would feature; so, too, would the Stanley Matthews final, the one in which Stan Mortensen scored a hat-trick.

There are still so many, though, from all stages of the competition. There's Steven Gerrard's inspirational performance in the final in 2006 and Paul Gascoigne's brilliant free-kick in the semi-final of 1991 – Spurs also scored two other goals that day, as it happens, but nobody ever seems to remember who scored them. But there is also Ronnie Radford's iconic strike to help Hereford beat Newcastle in 1972, the game that turned John Motson into a national institution and one of the archetypal shocks that have helped forge the FA Cup's reputation.

They're not pleasant to be involved in, those early games of the FA Cup. I played for Leicester when we lost to non-league Harlow Town. We'd drawn the first game at Filbert Street, and then travelled to Essex for the replay. Our manager was a man called Jock Wallace, and he was absolutely terrifying. I felt awful the day of the replay: I had tonsillitis, but I didn't have the nerve to tell him. As he read the team out, I was praying I wasn't in it. But there I was, and on the right wing. I still couldn't bring myself to admit it to him. So I played, feeling dreadful. We lost, and I was appalling. It's not a happy memory for me, but the fact it happened is what, deep down, makes the FA Cup what it is.

THE CONTENDERS

Ryan Giggs's goal (1999)

The Gerrard final (2006)

Wimbledon's Crazy Gang (1988)

Ricky Villa (1981)

Gazza's free kick (1992)

Crystal Palace 4-3 Liverpool (1990)

Wigan shock Manchester City (2013)

Wrexham defeat Arsenal (1992)

Ronnie Radford (1972)

Sunderland beat Leeds (1973)

ALAN SHEARER

Playing in an FA Cup final is great, but only if you win it. It is no fun at all if you don't, I can tell you that. I lost two finals in a row with Newcastle, in 1998 and 1999, and I don't remember them as great occasions in the slightest. I don't think I cried, but I had this sense of intense disappointment. We'd been playing two really good teams – an Arsenal team going for the double, and Manchester United on their way to the treble – but we hadn't performed, particularly in the latter, and that left a sour taste.

As a fan, though, the cup final used to take up the whole day. The build-up seemed to be on television from about 8am. There would be interviews with the managers as they ate their breakfast, footage of players getting their cup final haircuts, cameras on the coaches as the teams left their hotels, aerial shots of the fans walking down Wembley Way.

I had plenty of experience of the magic of the cup – those difficult away games against lower league teams, the ones where you know you will be in for a real fight – but it is two finals that stand out for me. The first was Wimbledon beating Liverpool in 1988; the Crazy Gang against the Culture Club, as they called it. Wimbledon were horrible to play against. They set out to upset the opposition. They would wreck the dressing room, they would verbally abuse you, and they would smash into you at the slightest opportunity. That was their way, and it was what took them all the way from non-league to the biggest game in the country.

And within 30 seconds or something of it starting, Vinnie Jones had gone into Steve McMahon, kicking him six foot up in the air. McMahon was a tough player himself, but you knew then what Wimbledon were going to try to do. It would have been a straight red card now, obviously, and it wasn't to everyone's tastes, but it worked. They shocked the best team in England that day, one that in terms of talent they didn't get close to.

But the Gerrard final in 2006 just edges it out. That game epitomised everything that made Steven Gerrard great. The game was gone; Liverpool were beaten. It needed something ridiculous to claw it back and, just when his team needed him, he produced it. He was knackered when he took that shot; he's said that if he hadn't been so tired, if he'd had the legs to run, he would have tried to take the ball on, rather than hit it first time. To get the sort of power and accuracy he did, with 90 minutes or so in your legs, and drag your team back from the brink: that's special. And to top it all off, he scored a penalty in the shootout. That was Steven Gerrard.

ALAN'S LIST

1 The Gerrard final (2006)

2 Wimbledon's Crazy Gang (1988)

3 Ryan Giggs's goal (1999)

4 Wigan shock Manchester City (2013)

5 Ricky Villa (1981)

6 Sunderland beat Leeds (1973)

7 Crystal Palace 4-3 Liverpool (1990)

8 Gazza's free kick (1992)

9 Ronnie Radford (1972)

10 Wrexham defeat Arsenal (1992)

MICAH RICHARDS

Winning the Premier League was not something I dreamed about as a kid. Even when I was at Manchester City's academy, it was too distant to be worth thinking about. Maybe it would have been different had I been at Manchester United, or Arsenal, or Liverpool, clubs that seemed to have a realistic chance of winning the title. Before the arrival of Abu Dhabi and the transformation in the club, maybe it wasn't the sort of dream a Manchester City player had.

The FA Cup was different. That felt attainable, somehow, like everyone had a chance. I don't know why that was. Maybe it's because you grow up knowing that giant-killings happen, or because a knockout sort of levels the playing field a bit: we couldn't beat the big boys over the league season, but we could beat them in a one-off game.

At youth level, the big thing was always winning the FA Youth Cup. I played in the final of that for City – our team, which included me, Michael Johnson and Daniel Sturridge, lost to Liverpool in 2006 – so maybe that helped, too: it showed us that we stood a chance. Whatever it was, winning the FA Cup was the first ambition I had in football. People talk about it not being as special as it used to be, but it was special to me.

It is a double-edged sword, though. We won it in 2011, but two years later we were on the other side of the magic of the cup. Wigan were on their way to being relegated from the Premier League, and we'd won the title the year before, so it should have been a huge mismatch: it wasn't quite the same vibe as the 1988 final, when Wimbledon beat Liverpool, because Wigan played good football, but the gulf in quality was probably just as wide.

Looking back, maybe we did not quite have the same urgency as we'd had two years before. We didn't need to win it: we'd already won the cup, and we'd picked up the league, too. In a way, we were the overwhelming favourites but maybe we were not under quite as much pressure as it seemed. They had always been a bit of a bogey team for us, so we would not have been complacent, but we didn't seem to be able to take our chances. And then, late on, Ben Watson scored a header from a corner – a really well-taken goal – and we were done. Well, I say we. I wasn't in the team. I'd probably been bombed or something. So it definitely wasn't my fault.

A couple of days later, Roberto Mancini was sacked, a year to the day after winning the league, and about 48 hours after losing the cup final. It goes to show that maybe the FA Cup does still matter, in certain circumstances, after all.

MICAH'S LIST

1 The Gerrard final (2006)
2 Ryan Giggs's goal (1999)
3 Wimbledon's Crazy Gang (1988)
4 Ronnie Radford (1972)
5 Crystal Palace 4-3 Liverpool (1990)
6 Gazza's free kick (1992)
7 Wigan shock Manchester City (2013)
8 Ricky Villa (1981)
9 Wrexham defeat Arsenal (1992)
10 Sunderland beat Leeds (1973)

THE TOP 10

1 The Gerrard final (2006)
2 Wimbledon's Crazy Gang (1988)
3 Ryan Giggs's goal (1999)
4 Wigan shock Manchester City (2013)
5 Crystal Palace 4-3 Liverpool (1990)
6 Ronnie Radford (1972)
7 Ricky Villa (1981)
8 Gazza's free kick (1992)
9 Sunderland beat Leeds (1973)
10 Wrexham defeat Arsenal (1992)

Gary's Verdict: I didn't like Wimbledon. I don't think I've ever made any secret of that. I didn't like the way they played, I didn't like their manner, and I didn't like the verbal abuse. I don't like them to this day. Anyone who watched the documentary series *The Last Dance* will know what I mean when I say they remind me of the Detroit Pistons, the basketball team that became known as the Bad Boys. But I do recognise that what they achieved, their story, was incredible. Maybe out of revenge for all those nasty tackles, though, I'm glad that Steven Gerrard's inspirational performance in 2006 edged them out.

THE DEBATE

Alan: If there is one player you would not want to gift the ball with a weak pass, it was Ryan Giggs. He glided past one of the most iconic defences in English history in that semi-final at Villa Park, and then beat one of the greatest goalkeepers we've ever seen, too. Then the shirt came off, that hairy chest came out, and a truly great FA Cup moment was born.

Micah: It is long before my time, but the Ronnie Radford goal for Hereford against Newcastle is the perfect FA Cup goal. Look at the pitch – it's a complete mud-bath – and the fans running onto the pitch afterwards. Those are the games and the moments that always made the FA Cup so special.

4

THE TOP 10
BONKERS MOMENTS

GARY LINEKER

There are certain things that happen on a football pitch that you are not meant to want to see. The arguments between teammates. The confrontations between opponents. The occasional beach ball scoring a goal. But while we all know these aren't why we watch the game, they do stick in the memory. Not so secretly, deep down, everyone loves them.

They happen far more often than you would think, too. They certainly did during my career. I remember travelling to Yugoslavia with England for a qualifying game, and standing in the tunnel at the Marakana – Red Star Belgrade's stadium – separated from the Yugoslav team by just a wire mesh fence.

Suddenly, Terry Butcher, was shouting to all of us that we were caged tigers, ready to roar. He just kept shouting 'caged tigers, caged tigers', grabbing hold of the fence. Quite what the Yugoslavs thought he was doing, or talking about, I have no idea. They must have wondered who these strange people were. It worked, though. We were four up inside the first 20 minutes.

I'm not sure how much stuff like that goes on nowadays. It certainly all seems to be very friendly in the tunnel now: players chatting among themselves, holding hands with the mascots. Maybe things are a little more professional. Maybe it's just that everyone knows there are cameras there.

That said, every so often, you do still get a glimpse behind the curtain. Seeing Patrick Vieira and Roy Keane have that simmering exchange before an Arsenal-Manchester United game proved that some of that old enmity is still there. Keane muttering that he would see Vieira on the field was as threatening as anything I'd have heard.

And then, much more occasionally, you get the moments that you just cannot explain. Paolo Di Canio pushing Paul Alcock, the referee, for example, or Eric Cantona's kung-fu kick into the crowd at Crystal Palace. That was in my early days of doing punditry, and I was doing *Match of the Day* that night. I had absolutely no idea what to say. You do get a lot of abuse from fans, but what Cantona did is football's greatest taboo. All I could do was say that it was completely unacceptable: not the most damning indictment, but it was hard to know how else to describe it. I don't know if any of us had ever seen anything quite like it. I know I haven't since.

THE CONTENDERS

Kevin Keegan's 'I would love it' rant

Lee Bowyer and Kieron Dyer fight on the pitch

Luis Suárez bites Branislav Ivanović

Alan Pardew head-butts David Meyler

Sunderland-Liverpool and the beach ball goal

Roy Keane and Patrick Vieira in the tunnel

Martin Keown celebrates at Ruud van Nistelrooy

Eric Cantona's kung-fu kick

Paolo Di Canio shoves Paul Alcock

Temuri Ketsbaia versus the advertising hoardings

ALAN SHEARER

Strangely, I was on the pitch for quite a few of these. I wonder if that's the connection: maybe it was something I was doing?

I remember Temuri Ketsbaia's celebration – if that's the right word – quite well. We were both on the bench that night, and the manager, Kenny Dalglish, had put me on before Temuri. He wasn't happy about that. He came on with a point to prove, and ended up scoring the winner. And then he just went berserk. Off came his shirt. He started taking his boots off. He couldn't quite do it, so he just started booting the advertising boards behind the goal. He was trying to make a point. I'm not sure it worked, though: it took him ages to get his shirt back.

Temuri was a lovely guy, but hard as nails. We went paintballing on one team-bonding trip. He was on the other side to me. At one point, he crept up behind Aaron Hughes, pushed him to the floor, and just emptied his barrel at him. He kept shouting, 'Stay down, stay down!' He was a little bit different, Temuri.

I was there for the night Kieron Dyer and Lee Bowyer got into a scrap, too. It wasn't the first time I'd seen teammates fight: it happened all the time in the tunnel when I was starting out, and there'd been an incident at Blackburn, too, during a Champions League game in Moscow, when David Batty and Graeme Le Saux had a go at each other.

Dyer against Bowyer was something else, though. There had been bits of aggression between the pair of them in training; exchanging choice words at the end of finishing sessions, that sort of thing. They were fighting for the same place in the team, and I guess eventually it just boiled over.

We were being battered by Aston Villa, we were already down to ten men, and there had been a couple of times when Kieron hadn't passed to Bowyer. You could see Bowyer getting more and more angry. The final straw was when he told Kieron to pass the ball, they said something to each other, and it kicked off. I saw it all happening, but there was nothing I could do. They both got sent off. We finished the game with eight men.

When we got back in, I let them both have it. But that was nothing compared to the manager. Graeme Souness was not a man you wanted to cross. He stormed in, looked at them both, and told them in no uncertain terms that if they fancied a fight, he'd take the both of them on, together.

ALAN'S LIST

1 Eric Cantona's kung-fu kick

2 Paolo Di Canio shoves Paul Alcock

3 Luis Suárez bites Branislav Ivanović

4 Alan Pardew head-butts David Meyler

5 Lee Bowyer and Kieron Dyer fight on the pitch

6 Martin Keown celebrates at Ruud van Nistelrooy

7 Kevin Keegan's 'I would love it' rant

8 Roy Keane and Patrick Vieira in the tunnel
9 Temuri Ketsbaia versus the advertising hoardings
10 Sunderland-Liverpool and the beach ball goal

MICAH RICHARDS

I was a well-behaved player, you know. I didn't get a single red card, throughout my career, though I did miss one game for a ban. It was hard to argue with that one. It was a game at Swansea, and their central defender, Federico Fernandéz, head-butted me. I didn't do anything on the pitch, but I wasn't going to let him get away with it.

At full-time, I found him in the tunnel and, though I'm not proud to say it, I cracked him. The problem was that the referee was standing right behind me, and saw it all happen. I got a ban for that, but it was reduced to just one game because of my disciplinary record which, as I may have mentioned, was impeccable.

Most of those incidents happen away from the fans, away from the cameras; as a player, you're so conscious you're being watched that you know that you have to control yourself. Occasionally, and only occasionally, you forget where you are. In the last game of the season after we won the league, in 2013, we played Norwich at home. It was a weird day: there was nothing to play for, and a few days earlier Roberto Mancini had been sacked. Brian Kidd was in charge. Suddenly, I found myself having an argument with Samir Nasri, who was playing ahead of me. I'm not sure what it was about, but we were trading insults and hurling abuse and then we just started walking towards each other.

The game was still going on around us, but we were on course to have a proper confrontation. It was only at the last minute that I snapped back into reality and realised that, yes, the stadium was full and we were on television and that we probably shouldn't have an actual fight. I suppose Kieron Dyer and Lee Bowyer, or even Martin Keown and Ruud van Nistelrooy, didn't have that moment.

The two moments that stand out for me, though, are Kevin Keegan's rant and Cantona's kick. Keegan is one of those iconic Premier League moments; it was the point when the idea of Sir Alex Ferguson's mastery of mind games was born. But there's never been anything like Cantona's kick: it's the sort of thing that, even when you think about it now, it's hard to believe it happened.

MICAH'S LIST

1 Eric Cantona's kung-fu kick

2 Kevin Keegan's 'I would love it' rant

3 Lee Bowyer and Kieron Dyer fight on the pitch

4 Paolo Di Canio shoves Paul Alcock

5 Luis Suárez bites Branislav Ivanović

6 Martin Keown celebrates at Ruud van Nistelrooy

7 Roy Keane and Patrick Vieira in the tunnel

8 Temuri Ketsbaia versus the advertising hoardings

9 Sunderland-Liverpool and the beach ball goal

10 Alan Pardew head-butts David Meyler

THE TOP 10

1 Eric Cantona's kung-fu kick

2 Paolo Di Canio shoves Paul Alcock

3 Lee Bowyer and Kieron Dyer fight on the pitch

4 Luis Suárez bites Branislav Ivanović

5 Kevin Keegan's 'I would love it' rant

6 Martin Keown celebrates at Ruud van Nistelrooy

7 Alan Pardew head-butts David Meyler

8 Roy Keane and Patrick Vieira in the tunnel

9 Temuri Ketsbaia versus the advertising hoardings

10 Sunderland-Liverpool and the beach ball goal

Gary's Verdict: A tricky category to judge, a mixture between the ones that are so shocking they are funny – Paul Alcock stumbling over like he was trying to get Paolo Di Canio sent off – and the ones that are not funny at all. Well, not really. Cantona wins it: he was as eccentric as he was talented.

THE DEBATE

Alan: The Cantona moment was pure chaos. I was watching it on television, and I couldn't believe what I was seeing. You knew he was different – the collar up, the arrogance and the swagger – but that was another level. It was a scandal when it happened, and it is still the strangest moment I have ever seen in football.

Micah: Cantona just edges it, I suppose, but that Keegan speech was incredible. It was one of the great Premier League moments. I was only four when it happened, but you only have to look at how well it is remembered – even by people who did not see it at the time – to see the impact that it had.

5

THE TOP 10
INTERNATIONAL
MOMENTS

GARY LINEKER

Nothing unites the country quite like the summer of a major tournament. Millions of people are glued to their television screens, whatever time of day the games are being played, to watch England, Scotland, Northern Ireland or Wales. The pubs are packed. There are street parties. The newspapers greet every win as a sign of imminent glory, and every defeat as a national shame.

The only group of people who never have any idea about any of that are the players. We're locked away in a hotel or a training camp in another country, another time zone, and we're cocooned from all of the madness unfolding at home. In 1986 and 1990, the two World Cups I played in, it was only after I came home that I realised quite how much it had meant. I hadn't even known, in 1990, that

'Nessun Dorma' was the BBC's theme tune. You're sheltered from all of it.

The semi-final that year is quite a good example. After Paul Gascoigne got booked – a yellow card that would have ruled him out of the final, had we made it – I could see his lip starting to wobble, I could tell he was starting to go. So I signalled to the bench to keep their eye on him, to make sure he was OK, and thought nothing more of it. I didn't realise it was caught on camera. It was much later that I learned it had become quite an iconic moment.

Gazza was incredible in that tournament. Taking him had been considered a bit of a gamble, and he exasperated Bobby Robson, our manager. We were staying in a hotel in Sardinia, where our group games were being held, and one day Gazza had gone off in the blazing sunshine to play golf. For Robson, that was fine. It was less fine when he found out that Gazza was playing topless. Even that was better than the day of either the quarter-final or the semi, when Gazza had ended up playing one of the tourists in the hotel at tennis. On the day of a game! He had to be dragged off the court.

Those summers do not always end happily, of course, and quite a lot of the time they end in penalty shootouts. I always quite enjoyed them, strange as it is to say, and we'd done quite well with penalties in 1990. I'd been the designated penalty taker for England for about five years when we won one against Cameroon in the quarter-final, and it was the first time I'd ever had to take one.

I'd not had ideal preparation: I'd had to change my strategy the day before, because Bobby was convinced there was a Cameroonian spy in the stadium, watching our final training session. I went and practised a few, and put them in the opposite corner to where I would normally go. When we finally got one, I reverted to what I'd been planning to do all along, and it worked. The keeper went the wrong way: the direction I'd put them in training, in front of the alleged spy. At the end of the game – after we'd won, and I'd scored another penalty – Bobby walked on to the pitch, shouting at me: 'See? See? I told you.'

Our luck didn't hold against Germany in the semi. Stuart Pearce and Chris Waddle both missed; Waddle committed the cardinal sin of changing his mind at the last minute. Even that was easier to take, though, than what had happened four years earlier. I didn't see the Hand of God at all. I was on the halfway line. But you could see from the reaction from those who were closer that something strange had happened. They ran to the assistant referee, the referee, and they both said they hadn't seen it. I asked Maradona about it, years later. He was quite cheeky about it: to him, it was cleverness, not cheating. I'm not sure I agree with him. The goal he scored a few minutes later wasn't bad, though.

THE CONTENDERS

On the March with Ally's Army (1978)

Northern Ireland beat Spain (1982)

The Hand of God (1986)

Gazza's tears (1990)

Gazza's Dentist's Chair Celebration (1996)

David Beckham lashes out (1998)

Wayne Rooney sent off against Portugal (2004)

Wales beat Belgium (2016)

England's Iceland humiliation (2016)

England win a penalty shootout (2018)

ALAN SHEARER

I hadn't scored for England for nearly two years by the time Euro 96 rolled around. I should have felt under intense pressure – the number nine, going into a home tournament, in the middle of a goal drought – but Terry Venables managed it perfectly. Before we flew out to Hong Kong and China for our pre-tournament training camp, he called me and said that, whatever happened, whether I scored in any of the friendlies or not, I was going to start against Switzerland. For him to have that much belief in me made me want to perform for him.

It was not necessarily the perfect preparation, that trip. I was there on the night that ended with quite a few of the players having a go in what they called the Dentist's Chair: you had to sit down, with your head tilted back, and have drinks poured down your throat. I left before all of that, but it had been a strange evening before that. We were in the bar and Gazza, Robbie Fowler and Steve McManaman were all ripping each other's shirts. They ripped mine. We were all just standing there with ripped shirts. I don't know why. It was about then that I decided to call it a night.

The pictures of that night were a real scandal, and I think Terry used that to his advantage. We all knew that we had let the country down, and more importantly, we'd let him down, too. We had to put that right. Gazza interpreted it slightly differently, of course. He'd been saying that if he scored in the tournament, he was going to celebrate by mimicking the Dentist's Chair, and making sure that we all knew that whoever was nearest him was going to be tasked with pouring the drinks. He was as good as his word. It's an iconic photograph, but he scored a hell of a goal to do it.

That made him a hero; two years later, at the World Cup in France, David Beckham ended up being cast as the villain. It was a great game – a brilliant goal from Michael Owen, a really clever free kick from Argentina to make it 2-2 at half-time – but it turned on David being sent off, for kicking out at Diego Simeone. Simeone played him fantastically well. There's no way it should have been a red card.

At that point, all I could do was think: 'Help.' We knew it would be tough against a team that good, but we put a real shift in under huge pressure to keep them out. We even thought we'd won it, but Sol Campbell's goal was ruled out for reasons I still don't really understand. Not that I'm bitter, obviously.

There's nothing quite as nerve-wracking as a penalty shootout. From about the 85th minute, you're praying that someone gets you out of the mire, because you really don't want to take a penalty. I always remember asking David Batty, that night in Saint-Étienne, what he was going to do with his. I don't think he'd ever taken, or even practised, a penalty. He said he wasn't sure. That wasn't ideal. I told him to smash it down the middle. That's what I thought he was going to do, but he changed his mind at the last minute. And that, like in 1990, is the worst thing you can do.

ALAN'S LIST

1 The Hand of God (1986)

2 David Beckham lashes out (1998)

3 England's Iceland humiliation (2016)

4 Wales beat Belgium (2016)

5 Northern Ireland beat Spain (1982)

6 On the march with Ally's Army (1978)

7 Gazza's Dentist's Chair Celebration (1996)

8 England win a penalty shootout (2018)
9 Wayne Rooney sent off against Portugal (2004)
10 Gazza's tears (1990)

MICAH RICHARDS

This is a strange thing to admit, but it was always Brazil for me, as a kid. I watched England's games, and I remember running round the house after we were knocked out of Euro 2004 on penalties by Portugal, devastated, but something about those bright yellow shirts drew me in.

The players that stood out to me were, by and large, the ones that stood out to everyone. I loved Ronaldo. I loved Rivaldo. A little later on, I loved Ronaldinho. They were the sorts of players that only Brazil seemed to produce; at Manchester City, I would get to play with a couple who were cut from the same cloth, in Robinho and Elano.

But the one that I really adored was a little different. I was obsessed with Dunga. He wasn't spectacular, by any stretch of the imagination. He wasn't the most skilful. He didn't do tricks to take the breath away, or score goals that captured the imagination. He was a holding midfielder, and quite a slow one. He did the dirty work so that all of the stars could express themselves.

And he did it brilliantly. I was only ten during the 1998 World Cup – when Brazil made the final – but even at that age I could tell that he was dominating the midfield, dictating the tempo, running the game. Nobody grows up dreaming of being a defensive midfielder, but I loved watching him play.

From an English point of view, that summer was dominated, obviously, by David Beckham lashing out at Diego Simeone. The treatment he got at the time was horrific: it was a mistake, obviously, even if getting a red card for it was probably a bit harsh. He shouldn't have kicked out at him, no matter how gently and no matter how exaggerated Simeone's reaction. He lost his cool.

After England were knocked out, though, there were effigies of him hung from pubs. He was public enemy number one. He was blamed, almost alone, not just for England being eliminated but for the country not winning the World Cup. I don't know if any player has ever been subject to quite such a furious response.

Looking back, the way he handled it makes me admire him even more. Can you imagine how mentally strong you would have to be to deal with that? To endure that sort of criticism and go on to become the player he did? Sir Alex Ferguson helped, of course: he gave him his full support, and that seemed to take the sting out of some of it. He kept him in the team at Manchester United, and after a while the fury started to vanish.

But the credit, for the most part, has to go to Beckham. He got through it because of his strength of character. He did not let it affect him. In a way, that period was probably the making of him. He got through something that summer that most players would have struggled to overcome.

MICAH'S LIST

1 The Hand of God (1986)

2 Gazza's tears (1990)

3 David Beckham lashes out (1998)

4 Gazza's Dentist's Chair Celebration (1996)

5 Wayne Rooney sent off against Portugal (2004)

6 Wales beat Belgium (2016)

7 Northern Ireland beat Spain (1982)

8 England win a penalty shootout (2018)

9 England's Iceland humiliation (2016)

10 On the march with Ally's Army (1978)

THE TOP 10

1 The Hand of God (1986)

2 David Beckham lashes out (1998)

3 Wales beat Belgium (2016)

4 Gazza's Dentist's Chair Celebration (1996)

5 Gazza's tears (1990)

6 England's Iceland humiliation (2016)

7 Northern Ireland beat Spain (1982)

8 Wayne Rooney sent off against Portugal (2004)

9 England win a penalty shootout (2018)

10 On the march with Ally's Army (1978)

Gary's Verdict: Diego Maradona produced two of the most memorable moments in the history of international football that day, one to represent each of the two sides to his character. The first, to him, was cunning; to us, it was an outrage. The second, though, was a piece of such brilliance that it almost made up for the first. Only almost, though.

THE DEBATE

Alan: You could guarantee that England would be ready for a penalty shootout in 2018 because of what had happened to Gareth Southgate in 1996. You might be without your first-choice penalty takers by the time you get there, but if you're prepared, it can make all the difference.

Micah: The Iceland game seemed like a nightmare for all the players involved. There were points when it seemed that they were so afraid of what might be about to happen that they couldn't remember the most basic things. They couldn't make simple passes. But even then, it was seen as a stain on so many players' England careers, and I think that's really harsh. It shouldn't overshadow everything else they did for their national team.

6

THE TOP 10
TRANSFER SHOCKS

GARY LINEKER

Being transferred is strange. Leicester City was my team, the one I grew up supporting. I went to every home game, with my dad and my granddad, and for eight years I lived my dream of playing for them. But there came a point when I knew I had to move on, that if I wanted to make the most of my career I had to leave to win trophies, to fulfil my talent, to play at the highest level.

It was an incredibly difficult decision to make, but I made it. My contract at Leicester expired in 1985, and Everton approached me. That was before the Bosman ruling, so there was a tribunal to decide what the fee would be. Both teams had to make a case for what I was worth. It was like being in the dock, but with a twist. Leicester, the team losing me, were determined to talk me up: I was a Golden Boot winner, I'd been leading scorer in the second division, I was destined to play for England.

And Everton, the team signing me, did all they could to talk me down. Howard Kendall, the manager, stood up and said I was a real gamble, that I wouldn't play in the first team this year, that I had talent but nothing more. I left wondering whether I'd made a mistake. But then, as we were walking out, Kendall turned to me. 'Don't worry about all that,' he said. 'We just had to get the price down. You'll be an ever present.'

The strange thing is that, as soon as I joined Everton, my allegiance to Leicester disappeared. It came back, once I'd retired, and it got stronger with time, but at Everton, I hated Liverpool. At Barcelona, I hated Real Madrid. I always checked for Leicester's results, and I was always very civil with them – I never scored against them – but my loyalty to my new club was complete.

That is not always reciprocated. Fans forget that players, at times, are treated as disposable by clubs. I still get stick from Everton fans for leaving, but the truth is that I was really happy there. I didn't want to go. But then one day, before the 1986 World Cup, Kendall told me they'd accepted an offer from Barcelona and, to an extent, that was that.

It took a while to do a deal, and obviously the prospect of playing for Barcelona was a mouth-watering one, but, as a player, I did not really have a vast amount of choice. You start to feel a little unwanted, too. The club were not fighting to keep me, so what reason would there be to stay?

Some transfers, though, are stranger than others. There are a handful that make you sit up and notice: ones that shock you, the ones that seem to leave everyone – managers, players and fans – asking, how, exactly, has that happened?

THE CONTENDERS

Sol Campbell (Tottenham to Arsenal)

Eric Cantona (Leeds to Manchester United)

Andy Carroll (Newcastle to Liverpool)

Andy Cole (Newcastle to Manchester United)

Ashley Cole (Arsenal to Chelsea)

Javier Mascherano and Carlos Tevez (Corinthians to West Ham)

Raheem Sterling (Liverpool to Manchester City)

Carlos Tevez (Manchester United to Manchester City)

Fernando Torres (Liverpool to Chelsea)

Robin van Persie (Arsenal to Manchester United)

ALAN SHEARER

Sol Campbell moving from Tottenham to Arsenal was a sensation, but anyone who understands Sol would know that, if there was one player who simply did not care what other people were thinking, it was him. His attitude was always: 'So what?' He wouldn't have cared that he was moving from one rival to another. It's difficult to have that strength of character, but it worked for him, didn't it? He was one of the final pieces of the jigsaw in that Arsenal team. He picked up three league titles there. Players are always being criticised. Sol did not let the thought of it stop him fulfilling his ambitions.

It's maybe been a little bit forgotten now, but Andy Cole leaving Newcastle for Manchester United was barely believable at the time. He was a hero at St James's Park, part of the first version of Kevin Keegan's entertainers team. He had a wonderful relationship with

Peter Beardsley, and he was scoring bucket-loads of goals. When it emerged that he was going, the whole city was in uproar; it was so bad that Kevin felt he had to go out onto the steps of the stadium and explain to people what was going on.

The money would have been hard to resist, of course – £7 million was a lot of money for a player in 1995 – and Kevin would have known that the club had Les Ferdinand coming in to replace him, but the fans would not have been aware of that. It was an incredible scene: there was so much anger at the thought of Cole leaving, particularly for Manchester United, and Kevin trying to persuade everyone that it would all work out, but not being able to say why.

The thing is that, once an appealing offer has come in and a player has made up their mind they want to go, there is not a vast amount that a manager can do to stop it. Arsène Wenger found that out with Robin van Persie: he wanted to go to Manchester United, to play under Alex Ferguson, and Arsenal did not have any real leverage. He might only have ended up having one season under Ferguson, but that league title justified it.

Sometimes, you get the sense that a club does not really want to stop it. The day that Liverpool sold Fernando Torres to Chelsea, and signed Andy Carroll and Luis Suárez in exchange, was incredible at the time, but looking back you wonder if perhaps Liverpool felt Torres was never going to be the force he had been again, and were quite happy to get a record fee for him.

Kenny Dalglish, who was the Liverpool manager at the time, has always insisted they spent the money they received well. Carroll might have been the bigger shock, and it may not have worked out for him there, but Suárez was an absolute bargain.

ALAN'S LIST

1 Javier Mascherano and Carlos Tevez (Corinthians to West Ham)

2 Eric Cantona (Leeds to Manchester United)

3 Fernando Torres (Liverpool to Chelsea)

4 Andy Cole (Newcastle to Manchester United)

5 Carlos Tevez (Manchester United to Manchester City)

6 Ashley Cole (Arsenal to Chelsea)

7 Raheem Sterling (Liverpool to Manchester City)

8 Andy Carroll (Newcastle to Liverpool)

9 Robin van Persie (Arsenal to Manchester United)

10 Sol Campbell (Tottenham to Arsenal)

MICAH RICHARDS

What was most amazing about the Sol Campbell move was that it was a total secret. There are normally whispers, suggestions, little hints that something might be coming. That one seemed to fall out of the sky. He just appeared at an ordinary, run-of-the-mill press conference. There were only a few reporters there: nobody was expecting it at all.

Sol was a much better player than he's given credit for now. I played with him for England, though it is not a particularly happy memory: it was the night that we lost at Wembley against Croatia, when we failed to qualify for Euro 2008, and Steve McLaren was forever cast as the Wally with the Brolly. It was one of the most difficult experiences of my career. Steve was a great coach, a proper coach, and I was playing with all of these players who had been idols to me growing up. And then, in one night, it all came crumbling down.

In a way, I wonder if the controversy over his move overshadows everything he achieved. He's remembered most, now, for the fact he left Spurs for Arsenal, rather than all of the things he won when he got there. He wasn't the greatest on the ball, but he was a brilliant defender.

You never hold it against a player for being tempted to move. If someone comes along offering you a five- or six-year contract, you're going to want to take it. The money will appeal to you, but so will the guarantee of being paid over such a long period of time. Being a footballer is a very short career, and it is also an extremely delicate one: all you need is one injury at the wrong time, and suddenly everything you have dreamed about and worked towards has gone. If there is an offer that can make you and your family financially secure forever, it is going to be hard to resist.

But even when you look at it like that, the captain of a team leaving to join their fiercest rivals feels like it's not right. Especially given that it was a free transfer, so Spurs did not get anything at all as they watched their best player walk off and join the team they hate more than anyone else. That has to be the most shocking transfer the Premier League has ever seen: I'm not sure how often it can have happened in all of football's history, to be honest.

MICAH'S LIST

1 Sol Campbell (Tottenham to Arsenal)

2 Eric Cantona (Leeds to Manchester United)

3 Andy Cole (Newcastle to Manchester United)

4 Andy Carroll (Newcastle to Liverpool)

5 Fernando Torres (Liverpool to Chelsea)

6 Carlos Tevez (Manchester United to Manchester City)

7 Ashley Cole (Arsenal to Chelsea)

8 Raheem Sterling (Liverpool to Manchester City)

9 Robin van Persie (Arsenal to Manchester United)

10 Javier Mascherano and Carlos Tevez (Corinthians to West Ham)

THE TOP 10

1 Eric Cantona (Leeds to Manchester United)

2 Andy Cole (Newcastle to Manchester United)

3 Fernando Torres (Liverpool to Chelsea)

4 Sol Campbell (Tottenham to Arsenal)

5 Javier Mascherano and Carlos Tevez
(Corinthians to West Ham)

6 Carlos Tevez (Manchester United to Manchester City)

7 Andy Carroll (Newcastle to Liverpool)

8 Ashley Cole (Arsenal to Chelsea)

9 Raheem Sterling (Liverpool to Manchester City)

10 Robin van Persie (Arsenal to Manchester United)

Gary's Verdict: This is a strange one, because Alan has gone for Tevez and Mascherano in first and Sol Campbell in tenth, and Micah is the exact opposite, meaning Eric Cantona sneaks in. I'll have to go for Campbell, though. As a former Spurs player, to leave the club to go to Arsenal is unforgivable. It was such a big story that it made the *News at Ten*. If the criteria here are how much the transfer hurts the fans, then it is the clear winner.

THE DEBATE

Alan: They still call Eric Cantona 'King' at Old Trafford, and that's no bad status to have, but it was clear from the day that Tevez and Mascherano arrived at West Ham that something wasn't right. They just turned up. The manager didn't know a lot about it. And the consequences were huge: a court case from Sheffield United, alleging that West Ham had only stayed up because two players who could not, legally, play for them had made the difference.

Micah: You obviously can't be going from Leeds to Manchester United. There's so much hatred there, and it took Leeds fans a long time to get over it, if they have. But Campbell going to Arsenal, when he was captain of Spurs, just wasn't right. He was an idol of mine, but I lost a lot of respect for him when he went. To go and play for your rivals – and on a free transfer – is the most shocking thing you can do.

7

THE TOP 10
FA CUP FINALS

GARY LINEKER

In my first season at Everton, we were better than Liverpool for most of the year. And in those days, being better than Liverpool tended to mean that you were better than everyone else, too. We beat them 2-0 at Anfield in the February – scoring the second goal that day is one of my happiest memories – and went six points clear. We were flying.

But that Liverpool team weren't that easy to shake off. They basically won every game after that, reeling us in, slowly bringing us back down to earth. They ended up beating us to the title on the final day. But we had a chance for revenge: for the first time, there would be a Merseyside derby in the FA Cup final.

What was strange about that day was the sight of red and blue mixing so happily on Wembley Way. You would see parents with red scarves around their necks carrying kids wearing blue shirts:

there were countless families split down the middle. The cup was still the only circus in town, then, and the atmosphere was fantastic.

We took the lead midway through the first half – I won't mention who scored the goal – and we thought we had them. Jim Beglin and Bruce Grobbelaar were bawling at each other, arguing among themselves, trying to blame one another for the goal. At that point, we were cruising.

And, again, all it took was one mistake. Ian Rush equalised not long after half-time, and it all just seemed to collapse. Craig Johnstone got the second, and then Rushie scored again. Losing a cup final is hideous, but to lose one when you've been leading, and you're the goalscorer, is even worse.

But the real humiliation was still to come. For some reason, they had organised a joint open-top bus parade for when the two teams got back to Liverpool. They would go first in their bus, and then we would follow on behind. It was the most cringeworthy experience of my entire career, I think. There were no Everton fans around at all, obviously: they didn't want to watch their rivals celebrate beating them to win a trophy. But all of the players had to sit on this bus and crawl through tens of thousands of Liverpool fans, jubilant because we had lost. Well, all of us except Peter Reid. I think he refused to get on board the bus. And fair play to him for that.

I had to wait a little longer to win it. I hadn't won much as a player, but to lift the FA Cup in 1991 was magical. It's remembered as the Paul Gascoigne final, though he only played 17 minutes before suffering that terrible knee injury. It was a tragedy, really: he'd dragged us to the final, and he was so hyped for the game. He spent the warm-up trying to kick balls at the musicians in the military band on the pitch. We went to see him afterwards, to make sure he knew how much of a part of it he had been. It was quite emotional for us, but genuinely traumatic for him.

THE CONTENDERS

Liverpool 3-1 Everton (1986)

Coventry City 3-2 Tottenham (1987)

Wimbledon 1-0 Liverpool (1988)

Crystal Palace 3-3 Manchester United (1990)

Tottenham 2-1 Nottingham Forest (1991)

Arsenal 2-0 Newcastle United (1998) and

Manchester United 2-0 Newcastle United (1999)

Liverpool 2-1 Arsenal (2001)

Liverpool 3-3 West Ham United (2006)

Manchester City 1-0 Stoke City (2011)

Wigan 1-0 Manchester City (2013)

ALAN SHEARER

We've only included some of these because we have personal memories of them, but don't expect me to spend too long talking about 1998 and 1999. I can skate past them in about ten seconds: we didn't turn up against Arsenal and Manchester United were a lot better than us. There, all done.

Now, semi-finals. They're great occasions. I've won a couple of those. I lost a couple, too, but even that is nothing compared to falling at the final hurdle. Losing a final is nobody's idea of fun: it had always been my dream to win one, and to fall short like that was painful. We ran into two extremely good sides, of course: it might have been different if we had come up against a Stoke City or a Wigan Athletic. But instead it was Arsenal, chasing a double, and Manchester United, in the hunt for a treble.

Of the two, Arsenal was the more disappointing. The gap between the two teams was not quite as big as it was a year later. I hit the post while it was still 1-0. I could almost see it hitting the post and bouncing in, and it didn't. That might have changed everything, but in the end we had to stay on the pitch and clap as Arsenal were presented with the trophy. Those are excruciating moments. You seem to be there for an eternity, you don't really know what to do, and you are trapped in the last place you want to be.

But, just like Gary, I had to deal with the pain being dragged out, too. That was the first time Newcastle had been in the cup final since 1955, and so an open-top bus had been arranged to take us from Gosforth Park to the Civic Centre in Newcastle when we got back. Tens of thousands of fans were out, on the route, to say thanks to the team. I'm not quite sure what for: thanks for getting beat, maybe.

It just gave us another reminder, though, of what we had missed out on. That was the worst part of it: imagining what that parade would have been like if we'd actually had something to celebrate, rather than something to regret. I would have loved to have seen the reaction if we'd managed to end Newcastle's wait for a trophy. Not being able to do that is the one thing I would change from my career. Losing those games hurt, and hurt a lot. I have no idea where my two medals from those finals are. They are just a reminder that, ultimately, we were just not quite good enough.

ALAN'S LIST

1 Wigan 1-0 Manchester City (2013)

2 Coventry City 3-2 Tottenham (1987)

3 Wimbledon 1-0 Liverpool (1988)

4 Crystal Palace 3-3 Manchester United (1990)

5 Liverpool 3-3 West Ham United (2006)

6 Liverpool 3-1 Everton (1986)

7 Liverpool 2-1 Arsenal (2001)

8 Tottenham 2-1 Nottingham Forest (1991)

9 Manchester City 1-0 Stoke City (2011)

10 Arsenal 2-0 Newcastle United (1998) and

Manchester United 2-0 Newcastle United (1999)

MICAH RICHARDS

Nerves never really troubled me before big games. I always felt quite relaxed before Manchester derbies, for example, even in those years when the gulf between United and City was much bigger than it is now. Those occasions brought out the best in me. The pressure did not bother me.

The FA Cup final in 2011 was different. I couldn't sleep at all the night before. I was sweating all night. I think I lost about four kilograms between going to bed and waking up, just because of the tension of it all. For a kid who had come through Manchester City's academy, the stakes were incredibly high. The club hadn't won the cup since 1969, and hadn't won a trophy at all for 35 years. We knew how much it mattered.

Fortunately, Yaya Touré was completely unfazed by it all. He is a king in the Ivory Coast, and he was probably used to having all of that expectation and all of that pressure on his shoulders. Mario Balotelli was the same. Maybe the occasion meant more to the English players than it did the ones who had arrived over the last couple of years, as City suddenly transformed into this major force, but neither of them seemed to feel it at all. That was probably a good thing that day.

Yaya scored the goal that beat Stoke, and Mario was man of the match.

I don't have many memories of the party that followed, unfortunately. But I'm pretty sure that saying it went on all day is a bit of understatement. That was all down to Yaya and Mario, though, even if the uncompromising right-back played a pivotal role in winning it. City have them to thank for that first trophy of the new era.

That's my favourite FA Cup final, of course, but it was not as dramatic as the Steven Gerrard final in 2006, or even the Michael Owen one a few years earlier. I was an Arsenal fan growing up, but I'm not sure it's bias to say that was daylight robbery. Arsenal absolutely dominated Liverpool, and then Owen popped up to score twice in the last few minutes and win the game.

MICAH'S LIST

1 Manchester City 1-0 Stoke City (2011)

2 Liverpool 3-3 West Ham United (2006)

3 Tottenham 2-1 Nottingham Forest (1991)

4 Crystal Palace 3-3 Manchester United (1990)

5 Wimbledon 1-0 Liverpool (1988)

6 Liverpool 3-1 Everton (1986)

7 Liverpool 2-1 Arsenal (2001)

8 Coventry City 3-2 Tottenham (1987)

9 Arsenal 2-0 Newcastle United (1998) and

Manchester United 2-0 Newcastle United (1999)

10 Wigan 1-0 Manchester City (2013)

THE TOP 10

1 Liverpool 3-3 West Ham United (2006)

2 Wimbledon 1-0 Liverpool (1988)

3 Crystal Palace 3-3 Manchester United (1990)

4 Manchester City 1-0 Stoke City (2011)

5 Coventry City 3-2 Tottenham (1987)

6 Wigan 1-0 Manchester City (2013)

7 Liverpool 3-1 Everton (1986)

8 Tottenham 2-1 Nottingham Forest (1991)

9 Liverpool 2-1 Arsenal (2001)

10 Arsenal 2-0 Newcastle United (1998) and

Manchester United 2-0 Newcastle United (1999)

Gary's Verdict: The Gerrard final, as it became known, is definitely the best final I have ever seen live, even if my personal favourite might be 1991. It's another narrow win for him, just ahead of Wimbledon, and that incredible final in 1990, when Ian Wright came on as a substitute and almost denied Manchester United the trophy that set Alex Ferguson on his way.

THE DEBATE

Alan: It's bad enough to lose any final, but I always felt incredibly sorry for Gary Mabbutt, who was such a devoted player for Tottenham, scoring an own goal in the final in 1987. Fortunately, it's not the goal everyone remembers from that final: it was overshadowed by Keith Houchen's diving header, and I'm sure Gary's grateful for that.

Micah: Yaya and David Silva were capable of special things, of winning a game at any given moment, but only Steven Gerrard could have done what he did against West Ham. He had everything. He didn't have any weaknesses in his game. And he refused to give in, even when everything seemed lost in the last few minutes of a cup final.

8

THE TOP 10
QUOTES

GARY LINEKER

I've been talking about football on television, first as a pundit and then as a presenter, for a quarter of a century, and I have never forgotten that you are always one sentence away from disaster. All it takes is one prediction that doesn't come to pass, or a suggestion that is taken the wrong way, or a claim that, in the fullness of time, is proved wrong. Football will, ultimately, make all of us look like fools.

I was in the *Match of the Day* studio, as a guest, with Alan Hansen the night he declared that Manchester United could win nothing with a team full of kids. It did not seem so unreasonable at the time. An inexperienced United side had just lost 3-1 to Aston Villa. They had sold three really important players over the summer, and everything all of us knew about football suggested not bringing in well-established, ready-made first team players to replace them would be a mistake. It wasn't an off-the-cuff remark, or a former Liverpool player taking the chance to put Manchester United down. He genuinely believed that.

Of course, what Alan did not know was how special the Class of 1992 would turn out to be. That United team proved him wrong in the most spectacular way possible, and that line haunts him to this day. He had a long and illustrious career as a pundit, and he was a respected voice for decades, but to some extent it is that one sentence that everyone remembers.

The strange thing is that, in a way, it made him. I'm not sure he even minded people having a laugh about it, really. It catapulted him to a level of fame that he probably would not have had otherwise. His worst prediction was the one that wrote his name in history.

That goes to show that you can never quite tell what will capture the imagination. There are a handful of quotes from players and, in particular, managers that every football fan knows, whether they were around when they were first uttered or not. The very best of them are now part of the way we talk about the sport: the prawn sandwich brigade, squeaky bum time, parking the bus. They have all become immortal, but they weren't intended to be. They just captured something that everyone instinctively understood, and they caught on. You'd like to think that at some point you'd have an entry on this list, even if it is – like Alan – for something that turned out to be wrong. It's not a bad way to be remembered, is it?

THE CONTENDERS

Rafa Benítez: 'I want to talk about facts.'

Eric Cantona: 'When the seagulls follow the trawlers, it is because they think sometimes sardines will be thrown into the sea.'

Alex Ferguson: 'It's getting tickly now. Squeaky-bum time, I call it.'

Tim Flowers: 'Don't talk to me about bottle, don't talk
to me about bottling it, because that is bottle out there.'
Alan Hansen: 'You can't win anything with kids.'
Roy Keane: 'They have a few drinks and probably the
prawn sandwiches, and they don't know what's
going on out on the pitch.'
Kevin Keegan: 'They've got to go to Middlesbrough and get
something, and I would love it, love it if we beat them.'
José Mourinho: 'I think I am a special one.'
José Mourinho: 'They brought the bus and
parked the bus in front of the goal.'
Nigel Pearson: 'If you don't know the answer to
that question, then I think you are an ostrich.'

ALAN SHEARER

Tim Flowers had been magnificent against Newcastle the night that
he gave that interview about 'bottle'. He'd made a string of brilliant
saves; that was why he won Man of the Match, and that was why he
was on television, giving an interview.

Everyone at Blackburn was extremely tense at that point: we had
one game left, and we knew we were in a position to win – or to
blow – the title. Alex Ferguson had been up to his usual tricks, trying
everything he could think of to put a bit of pressure on us, suggesting
that we might crack in the run-in. Tim, obviously, wanted to put that
idea to bed. He was on a bit of a high from the performance, so he
gave it both barrels.

It didn't matter that we agreed with him. It didn't matter that he'd played brilliantly in the game. The next morning, once all the lads had seen what he'd said, we absolutely hammered him. That's the way it is: if you say something stupid in an interview, you get hammered. It doesn't really matter if you were right or not. Tim knew that. It's safe to say that he gave as good as he got.

The real masters of those moments, though, are the players and the managers who have supreme belief in their abilities. That was true of Eric Cantona, the only player I can think of who would sit in front of the world's press and talk about sardines and trawlers, and it was true of José Mourinho, too, throughout his career in England, and particularly at the start.

It takes incredible self-confidence to declare yourself the Special One. Making that his initial claim when he arrived in England was his equivalent of Cantona's upturned collar: it was his way of showing just how good he was. Make no mistake, though – you have to have the ability to back those sorts of things up.

Mourinho did. His last couple of jobs, at Manchester United and Tottenham, may not have turned out as he would have wanted, but when he first came to Chelsea he wasn't like anything we'd seen before, not really. He was a bit special: cocky and cheeky and charming. It's easy to forget now, almost 20 years on, after he's been sacked twice by Chelsea and once each by Manchester United and Spurs, but people liked what they saw of him then. Declaring himself to be the Special One wasn't greeted with howls of outrage: people laughed. People got Mourinho. They quite liked that arrogance, that self-belief. The fact that, all these years on, we still remember it shows how much of an impression he made.

ALAN'S LIST

1 Kevin Keegan: 'They've got to go to Middlesbrough and get something, and I would love it, love it if we beat them.'

2 Eric Cantona: 'When the seagulls follow the trawlers, it is because they think sometimes sardines will be thrown into the sea.'

3 Alan Hansen: 'You can't win anything with kids.'

4 Roy Keane: 'They have a few drinks and probably the prawn sandwiches, and they don't know what's going on out on the pitch.'

5 José Mourinho: 'I think I am a special one.'

6 Alex Ferguson: 'It's getting tickly now. Squeaky-bum time, I call it.'

7 Rafa Benítez: 'I want to talk about facts.'

8 José Mourinho: 'They brought the bus and parked the bus in front of the goal.'

9 Tim Flowers: 'Don't talk to me about bottle, don't talk to me about bottling it, because that is bottle out there.'

10 Nigel Pearson: 'If you don't know the answer to that question, then I think you are an ostrich.'

MICAH RICHARDS

Players will accept pretty much anything a manager says in a press conference, with one exception: if it is too personal, then it crosses a line. It was the same with other managers, rival players and even pundits. I never objected to anyone suggesting I had done something wrong in a game. I never minded anyone questioning if I had played well, or if there was something lacking in my game, or if I'd made a mistake. It was when it felt like it was a deliberate attempt to get at me that I had a problem.

I think that is probably true of most players. We understand that we are in a business where everyone has an opinion: that is what makes football what it is, and players themselves are no different. That's why so many of us decide to go into punditry after we retire: it is about time people listened to what we think of them, rather than the other way round.

You know, as a rule, what the manager has said to the press. Even before the days of social media, you would find out easily enough. You didn't have to wander down to the shop to buy the papers and scour them for your name: your agent or your friends would tell you, and if they didn't, the other players definitely would. It can be really positive: if you're having a rough time and the manager comes out and backs you, it means the world. It's incredibly reassuring, to know they're on your side. I always cared what was said about me, but I learned after a while to take a lot of it with a pinch of salt. Managers might say something for effect, or they might downplay something if it suits them. What is said in public is not always what is said in the dressing room.

Kevin Keegan was a bit different in that sense. He was a lot more open, a lot more honest than a lot of managers. Every coach I worked with had their own emphasis on what was important. Sven-Göran Eriksson always wanted us to enjoy ourselves. Mark Hughes only ever worked on attack; he never paid any real attention to how we defended. Stuart Pearce was all about heart and passion. But Kevin cared deeply about the way we played. He wanted us to entertain, to express ourselves, to give everything.

You can see that same enthusiasm in that interview. It's easy to say that Sir Alex Ferguson had got to him, but that's what Kevin was like. He expected his players to give everything, because he gave everything, too.

MICAH'S LIST

1 Kevin Keegan: 'They've got to go to Middlesbrough and get something, and I would love it, love it if we beat them.'

2 Eric Cantona: 'When the seagulls follow the trawlers, it is because they think sometimes sardines will be thrown into the sea.'

3 José Mourinho: 'I think I am a special one.'

4 Rafa Benítez: 'I want to talk about facts.'

5 Alex Ferguson: 'It's getting tickly now. Squeaky-bum time, I call it.'

6 Roy Keane: 'They have a few drinks and probably the prawn sandwiches, and they don't know what's going on out on the pitch.'

7 José Mourinho: 'They brought the bus and parked the bus in front of the goal.'

8 Alan Hansen: 'You can't win anything with kids.'

9 Nigel Pearson: 'If you don't know the answer to that question, then I think you are an ostrich.'

10 Tim Flowers: 'Don't talk to me about bottle, don't talk to me about bottling it, because that is bottle out there.'

THE TOP 10

1 Kevin Keegan: 'They've got to go to Middlesbrough and get something, and I would love it, love it if we beat them.'

2 Eric Cantona: 'When the seagulls follow the trawlers, it is because they think sometimes sardines will be thrown into the sea.'

3 José Mourinho: 'I think I am a special one.'

4 Roy Keane: 'They have a few drinks and probably the prawn sandwiches, and they don't know what's going on out on the pitch.'

5 Alan Hansen: 'You can't win anything with kids.'

6 Alex Ferguson: 'It's getting tickly now. Squeaky-bum time, I call it.'

7 Rafa Benítez: 'I want to talk about facts.'

8 José Mourinho: 'They brought the bus and parked the bus in front of the goal.'

9 Tim Flowers: 'Don't talk to me about bottle, don't talk to me about bottling it, because that is bottle out there.'

10 Nigel Pearson: 'If you don't know the answer to that question, then I think you are an ostrich.'

Gary's Verdict: That Keegan speech may be quite hard to watch, now, and it may seem a little cringe with the passage of time, but it's important to remember that it could have gone down in history very differently. Had Newcastle gone on to win the title, it would not have proved that Alex Ferguson was a master of mind games, but that

Kevin's passion and his belief had pulled his team through. A great quote depends on its context.

THE DEBATE

Alan: Only Cantona would have come up with that line about trawlers. He gave another one, not too different, not long ago. You watched it and wondered what on earth he was talking about, but now, because it was him, it kind of makes sense.

Micah: It says something about how surprising Cantona's line was at the time that people remember it better than Nigel Pearson's greatest quote. That was much more recent, and he compared someone to an ostrich. You're doing well to come up with a stranger sentence than that.

THE TOP 10
EUROS GOALS

GARY LINEKER

I try not to mention it, but I scored in two separate World Cups. I won a Golden Boot in one of them. I don't, I'll admit, have quite such happy memories of the Euros. I played in two, in 1988 and 1992. It was a much smaller tournament then than it is now – just eight teams in total – and our stays in both were brief. We lost all three games in 1988, and mustered just a single point in 1992. I didn't even score a goal.

There were mitigating circumstances in West Germany in 1988. I'd started to feel unwell in the final friendly before we headed out for the tournament: nothing major, just a bit lethargic. In our opening game against Ireland, I felt really leggy. By the time we came up against Marco van Basten and the Netherlands, I was really struggling. We were already out before we'd even played the Soviet Union in our last game. I went into training and told Bobby Robson that I wasn't well. There was nothing to play for, I'd not exactly shone in the tournament, and I assumed he'd be happy enough to leave me out of the game.

He didn't: he started me. I don't think he and his coaching staff believed me when I said I was ill. I could barely put one leg in front of the other during that game. I came off at half-time, but by the time we were back on the bus and waiting to head to the hotel, we had got hold of some first editions of the daily newspapers from England. They'd been faxed over to us. In the press conference after we lost to the Soviet Union, Bobby had singled out a few players who had let him down, and I was one of them. I picked up one of the copies of the paper and threw it at him. 'You're out of order,' I said, or words to that effect.

By the time I got home, I was no better. I was admitted to hospital, and diagnosed with hepatitis. I lost a stone and a half in a week. I was there for five days. Three days in, Bobby came to visit. He wanted to check how I was, he said, and he wanted to apologise for what he'd said. That moment meant a lot to me: it was very much the measure of the man.

That, then, at least partly explains why I'm not on this list. There was another striker who had a much better time of it at that tournament, though: Marco van Basten. He scored a hat-trick against us – he turned Tony Adams inside out – but it speaks volumes about how special he was, and how good he was that month, that even that pales into insignificance compared to what he did in the final.

THE CONTENDERS

Antonín Panenka (Czech Republic v West Germany, 1976)

Marco van Basten (Netherlands v Soviet Union, 1988)

Tomas Brolin (Sweden v England, 1992)

Paul Gascoigne (England v Scotland, 1996)
Alan Shearer (England v Netherlands, 1996)
Davor Šuker (Croatia v Denmark, 1996)
Zlatan Ibrahimović (Sweden v France, 2012)
Xherdan Shaqiri (Switzerland v Poland, 2016)
Hal Robson-Kanu (Wales v Belgium, 2016)
Patrik Schick (Czech Republic v Scotland, 2020)

ALAN SHEARER

Let's get one thing clear, right from the start. No matter what Micah says, no matter what Gary suggests, I most definitely did not slice that goal against the Dutch. It wasn't a shank. It wasn't lucky. I picked my spot right down to the exact postage stamp and put the ball there. It was a masterclass of finishing.

I'll admit that I didn't really expect the ball to come to me, though. The move started with Darren Anderton, playing the ball into Teddy Sheringham. I was standing to his right, with my arms in the air, shouting and screaming, but there was no reason for Teddy to pass, particularly. He could have just as easily taken the shot. It tells you all you need to know about what sort of player he was that he passed it. It tells you all you need to know about what sort of player I was that, had the roles been reversed, there is not a chance that I'd have taken a blind bit of notice of him.

I can't put myself top of this list, not ahead of Van Basten, but that was a special night. If you look at England's performances over the last 30 years it would be the game against the Dutch at Wembley and the 5-1 win against Germany in Munich that stand out to people. It was the best atmosphere I ever experienced with England; it was magic just to be a part of it.

There are some games where everything just clicks, and that was one of them. Every player on the pitch had a 10 out of 10 performance. It was a significant moment, too, because the pressure and the expectation on the team to perform was starting to grow. We were hosts, and we'd started off well enough, drawing with Switzerland and beating Scotland. But to produce that kind of display against the Dutch was a real line in the sand for us. It takes a lot of mental strength to play for England at any time, but with that feeling that the whole country was hanging on everything you did, we required real character.

It meant a lot to Terry Venables, too. He'd come up with what was known as the 'Christmas Tree' formation for the tournament, with me playing just ahead of Teddy, and it had been seen as a bit of a risk. We were maybe not used to seeing different systems in England at that point, but for it to pay off so spectacularly – and against a team as good, and as smart, as the Dutch – was his vindication.

Even when we conceded, it was in the perfect way: the Dutch scored late on, to make it 4-1, and with that single goal they ensured that they would reach the quarter-finals, and not the Scots. Absolutely everything went right that night.

ALAN'S LIST

1 Marco van Basten (Netherlands v Soviet Union, 1988)

2 Paul Gascoigne (England v Scotland, 1996)

3 Davor Šuker (Croatia v Denmark, 1996)

4 Alan Shearer (England v Netherlands, 1996)

5 Patrik Schick (Czech Republic v Scotland, 2020)

6 Xherdan Shaqiri (Switzerland v Poland, 2016)

7 Hal Robson-Kanu (Wales v Belgium, 2016)

8 Tomas Brolin (Sweden v England, 1992)

9 Zlatan Ibrahimović (Sweden v France, 2012)

10 Antonín Panenka (Czech Republic v West Germany, 1976)

MICAH RICHARDS

I've been listening to Alan. I've been learning from Alan. He's taught me all you could possibly need to know about how to examine a striker's body language. Thanks to him, I know far more now about how to read a forward's intentions than I did when I was playing. And everything, absolutely everything he has taught me tells me that, when he shaped to shoot against the Dutch at Wembley that night, he was aiming for the other corner. The ball slices off his foot and goes in the opposite direction to where he was intending. No wonder the goalkeeper was wrong-footed.

There were quite a lot of special goals in 1996, though. Not all of them have made this list: Karel Poborský got a move to Manchester United on the back of his clever scooped finish for the Czech Republic. Paul Gascoigne sitting Colin Hendry down was a superb goal, and so was Davor Šuker's incredible chip for Croatia against Denmark. You have to have real presence of mind to attempt something like that, and you need real nerve to try it when the goalkeeper you're up against is Peter Schmeichel. It's among the most spectacular goals on the list, but I'm not sure it can be in the top three or four, just because Schmeichel wasn't set. He couldn't have been because of the opportunism of the strike – there is no way a goalkeeper of his class and his size would have expected Šuker to try something like that – but it means there is something speculative about it. The same goes for Patrik Schick's goal for the Czechs against Scotland in Euro 2020.

You cannot say that for the obvious winner: the goal that is clearly the best one that's ever been scored in the European Championships. I was born the day before Marco van Basten scored for the Netherlands in the 1988 final, but it is one of those goals that everyone just knows, instinctively. It's a masterpiece. Even as a defender, you can only really watch that and admire everything that goes into it: the power, the technique, the precision, the angles. The fact that he thought of it is impressive enough; there cannot have been many players, in any generation, who would have had the ability to pull it off. The best thing about it, without question, is his body shape. You can tell from his body shape, right away, that he has not shanked it. There is absolutely nothing lucky about it.

MICAH'S LIST

1 Marco van Basten (Netherlands v Soviet Union, 1988)

2 Paul Gascoigne (England v Scotland, 1996)

3 Antonín Panenka (Czech Republic v West Germany, 1976)

4 Hal Robson-Kanu (Wales v Belgium, 2016)

5 Xherdan Shaqiri (Switzerland v Poland, 2016)

6 Davor Šuker (Croatia v Denmark, 1996)

7 Patrik Schick (Czech Republic v Scotland, 2020)

8 Alan Shearer (England v Netherlands, 1996)

9 Zlatan Ibrahimović (Sweden v France, 2012)

10 Tomas Brolin (Sweden v England, 1992)

THE TOP 10

1 Marco van Basten (Netherlands v Soviet Union, 1988)

2 Paul Gascoigne (England v Scotland, 1996)

3 Davor Šuker (Croatia v Denmark, 1996)

4 Xherdan Shaqiri (Switzerland v Poland, 2016)

5 Hal Robson-Kanu (Wales v Belgium, 2016)

6 Alan Shearer (England v Netherlands, 1996)

7 Patrik Schick (Czech Republic v Scotland, 2020)

8 Antonín Panenka (Czech Republic v Germany, 1976)

9 Tomas Brolin (Sweden v England, 1992)

10 Zlatan Ibrahimović (Sweden v France, 2012)

Gary's Verdict: Marco van Basten was one of the true greats, and this was his crowning moment. As a forward, he had it all: a beautiful touch, great speed, an ability to turn, wonderful finishing. His place in history is secure, but it is hard not to wonder how much more he might have achieved had an ankle injury not curtailed his career.

THE DEBATE

Alan: I would never have had the nerve to try what Antonín Panenka did in the final in 1976: chipping a penalty when the stakes are that high takes nerves of steel. Of course it is a special moment – if something is named after you, it has to be special – but it was still a penalty. It wasn't a great goal.

Micah: It doesn't matter that it was a penalty – it's one of the most iconic goals of all time. Panenka was not the first player ever to take a penalty like that, but he was certainly the first to try it on such a big stage. That makes him an innovator, an originator. We remember his name because of that penalty, and not many goals lead to that sort of fame.

10

THE TOP 10
EUROS MEMORIES

GARY LINEKER

The team England took to Euro 1992 in Sweden was, it is probably fair to say, one of the weakest we have ever sent to a major tournament. That is not to disrespect any of the players who were in the squad – even Alan – but we were badly lacking in one area in particular: we just did not have any creativity at all.

Injuries had not helped. Paul Gascoigne was still recovering from the damage he had done himself tackling Gary Charles in the FA Cup final the year before. John Barnes had hurt his Achilles. They were the two players we had who might make something happen, and we had to cope without both of them.

But the situation had been made even more complex by some of Graham Taylor's decisions. He'd wanted to ease out some of the older players and start building for the future, which meant that Chris Waddle, Bryan Robson and Peter Beardsley were all missing, too. At the back, Peter Shilton and Terry Butcher had gone. The players who replaced them did not have the experience, naturally, but they also did not have quite that same quality. We'd been within a penalty shootout of making the World Cup final in 1990; two years later, we drew our first two games without scoring – no real surprise, there, given that we couldn't create chances – and then lost, late on, to Sweden, in our final fixture. We were out, yet again, at the group stage.

I went into that last game one goal short of Bobby Charlton's all-time England goalscoring record. It's where, of course, I still am. The truth is that I hadn't looked like scoring and, even if I'd stayed on the pitch, that probably wouldn't have changed. But that is not how strikers think. I was sure, during the game, that I was going to score, that something was going to change for me.

Graham did not see it like that. He took me off after about an hour. I was the captain, and substituting your captain then wasn't something that happened too often, but I was half-expecting it; Graham and I had fallen out a little bit. Even so, there was a real furore about it, because of the significance of removing me before I'd drawn level with Bobby Charlton: it is, sadly, the most significant impact I made on the Euros.

I went and sat on the bench and, at the time, didn't give another thought to the record: I didn't know, then, that it would be my last appearance for England. The only thing I cared about was that someone scored, and we went through. It didn't happen and, in hindsight, Graham probably made me a bit of a martyr. I would have been slaughtered if I had stayed on and not scored. But because he took me off, because he was seen as denying me the record, because it turned out to be my last game, I was spared a lot of that. He was attacked, and I was salvaged. Being knocked out cost me a chance of equalling the record; but being substituted, not drawing level with Bobby, meant that the defeat was not pinned on me.

THE CONTENDERS

Panenka's penalty (1976)

Lineker subbed (1992)

Denmark come off the beach (1992)

Dentist's Chair (1996)

England v Netherlands (1996)

Southgate's penalty (1996)

Trezeguet's Golden Goal (2000)

Wayne Rooney announces himself (2004)

Wales in the semi-final (2016)

England reach the final (2020)

ALAN SHEARER

By the time we reached the semi-final of Euro 96, the whole country seemed to believe we could win it. There was a real energy around the tournament, a genuine excitement that we could get past Germany and make it to England's first major final for 30 years.

We had the best possible start to that game, too: I scored within three minutes. As a striker, that is what you spend your whole life building towards – you work every day so that you can score as many goals as possible. The few seconds after a goal, that immediate rush of delight and joy, is an outrageous feeling. It is the memory of it that makes you want to score again and again, so that you can keep experiencing it.

For all the goals I scored, I am not sure there was ever another one that matched the emotion of that moment. To score a goal for

England, at Wembley, against Germany, that might have set us on a road to the final of the European Championships on home soil? It was an explosion of emotions, not just for me, but for the whole team and the whole stadium. The whole country, maybe.

We know how that game ended. Germany equalised; the game went to extra time, with the added complication that a Golden Goal could have won it – for half an hour, we knew that it was next goal wins. Gazza's miss, just stretching for that cross, is the image that most people have of that game, of how close we came, but it's forgotten too often that Darren Anderton hit the post, too. We were within a couple of inches of getting to the final.

As it was, we had to endure penalties, and the terrible, sinking feeling that followed Gareth Southgate missing. The contrast with what I'd felt earlier in the night could not have been more stark. You want to disappear. You want the ground to swallow you whole. My first instinct was to want to leave the country, as quickly as possible, to go on holiday and forget everything.

First, though, we went back to our hotel, Burnham Beeches. The bus journey was quiet, as though we were haunted by what had just happened. We all went into the bar for a drink, and then another, and then another. I'm not sure any of us could really move. I left at some small hour of the morning, got a couple of hours' sleep, and then came down for breakfast with a stinking hangover. I think some of them were still sat there, with their drinks, just going over what had happened the night before. We'd been so close, and yet now, for us, it wouldn't happen: there would be no final. The nation would, in fact, have to wait for a quarter of a century before its long wait ended. England's run to the final of Euro 2020 was magical; the whole country seemed to stop for a month. That could have been us: we were only inches away.

ALAN'S LIST

1 England v Netherlands (1996)

2 Wayne Rooney announces himself (2004)

3 Dentist's Chair (1996)

4 Denmark come off the beach (1992)

5 England reach the final (2020)

6 Wales in the semi-final (2016)

7 Panenka's penalty (1976)

8 Trezeguet's Golden Goal (2000)

9 Lineker subbed (1992)

10 Southgate's penalty (1996)

MICAH RICHARDS

Gary might never have scored in a European Championship, but I never even managed to play in one. It was during qualification for the 2008 tournament that I broke into the England team: I made my debut in 2006, and played a lot throughout that campaign. It did not end happily: we lost the final game, at home to Croatia, the night that Steve McLaren forever became known as the Wally with the Brolly, and we were out of the tournament.

Not qualifying was really disappointing, but I felt especially bad for Steve. He'd really stuck by me, making me a regular part of the England team, and he was a fantastic coach. People always say that about him and it sounds like faint praise, but he really was: players loved working for him. To see him get so much criticism was hard to take.

I would not have stood a chance of going to Euro 2012 had Fabio Capello been in charge: he ignored me for the 2010 World Cup, and I barely played for England at all while he was the manager. But he left not long before the tournament, and that should have been my chance of a fresh start. Roy Hodgson had other ideas, though: he had to choose between me and Phil Jones for his squad, and he went with Phil. I don't have a problem with that, particularly – managers have to make choices – but I was disappointed that he didn't have the decency to call me himself to break the news. He made Stuart Pearce, who had given me my debut at Manchester City, do it for him. He never really recovered from that in my estimations.

And then, by 2016, the injuries had caught up with me, and I was a long way from the England squad. It's not something I am bitter about, but it is a source of regret. England were not well-stocked with right-backs then; there certainly was not as much competition for places as there was in 2021. There was only, really, Gary Neville. He was a good player and a good pro, Gary, but he did not have more ability than me. I could have made those squads, and it frustrates me that I didn't get into any of them.

MICAH'S LIST

1 Dentist's Chair (1996)

2 England reach the final (2020)

3 Southgate's penalty (1996)

4 Panenka's penalty (1976)

5 Denmark come off the beach (1992)

6 Wales in the semi-final (2016)

7 England v Netherlands (1996)

8 Trezeguet's Golden Goal (2000)

9 Wayne Rooney announces himself (2004)

10 Lineker subbed (1992)

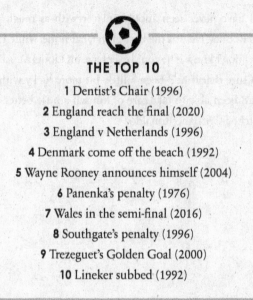

THE TOP 10

1 Dentist's Chair (1996)

2 England reach the final (2020)

3 England v Netherlands (1996)

4 Denmark come off the beach (1992)

5 Wayne Rooney announces himself (2004)

6 Panenka's penalty (1976)

7 Wales in the semi-final (2016)

8 Southgate's penalty (1996)

9 Trezeguet's Golden Goal (2000)

10 Lineker subbed (1992)

Gary's Verdict: It was a brilliant goal and an even better celebration, but there is one thing I have always wondered about the Dentist's Chair, every time I see it, which is fairly often, seeing as it is one of the most iconic Euros moments in history: who put the bottle there? It wasn't one of the goalkeeper's. Did Gazza know he was going to score at that end? Had he planned it out?

THE DEBATE

Alan: Wayne Rooney started as he meant to go on with England. 2004 was his first major tournament, but he was not fazed in the slightest.

He scored four goals in four games, and only the injury he picked up stopped him dominating that tournament entirely.

Micah: I have never seen another player with as much all-round ability as Rooney. He was the best player, bar none, while I was with England. I don't know if he could ever have hit Lionel Messi's heights, but I am sure that if he'd been a little bit more lucky with injuries, and if he'd been able to take care of himself a little better, he could have matched Cristiano Ronaldo.

11

THE TOP 10
WORLD CUP
MEMORIES

GARY LINEKER

England's dressing room after the semi-final in 1990 was almost completely silent. There was nothing much we could say: to miss out on taking the country back to the World Cup final, when we had come so close, was devastating. A few of us offered what words of consolation we could find to the others. Bobby Robson walked round the room, patting players on the shoulders, doing the best he could not so much to lift our spirits, but to show sympathy. Stuart Pearce, one of the two players who had missed penalties, seemed a little bit broken by it. We all were, to some extent. We just sat there with our heads in our hands.

It is forgotten a little bit, now – what people remember are the penalties – but we came incredibly close to winning that game, just as we did in the semi-final of Euro 96 a few years later. I'd equalised quite late on, after Andreas Brehme had put Germany ahead with a deflected free kick, and we'd had chances to avoid the drama of penalties, most notably when Chris Waddle hit the post. In a way, that made it all the more painful.

It took a little while before we left the dressing room that night. There were media duties to fulfil, drug tests to do, and though I think we all probably wanted to leave, none of us quite had the energy to do so. Eventually, we found our way back to the bus, the one that would take us to our hotel and then, the next day, back to England. We'd had this tradition through the tournament that, after games, we would have a couple of beers and a bit of a singalong on the bus on the way back: something silly and childish, like 'Do-Re-Mi' from *The Sound of Music*. Normally, it was a happy thing, a way of celebrating the fact we had made it through to the next round.

That night, the bus did not feel like it was much in the mood for a sing-song. It was pin-drop quiet as we left the stadium, all of us lost in our own thoughts. And then, out of nowhere, someone on one of the back rows started to sing: 'Doe, a deer, a female deer ...' I'm not sure who it was: my guess would be either Waddle or Gazza. And then the next line: 'Ray, a drop of golden sun.' We all started to pick it up: not as raucous as it would have been after Cameroon or Belgium, but a little sad, a little mournful. Suddenly the whole squad was singing it. It was a quite beautiful thing, a lament for what we'd done, and I started to cry.

THE CONTENDERS

Carlos Alberto's goal (1970)

Marco Tardelli's scream (1982)

The Hand of God (1986)

Gazza's tears (1990)

Totò Schillaci (1990)

Ronaldo's breakdown (1998)

Ronaldinho's free kick (2002)

Zidane's head-butt (2006)

Nigel de Jong's boot (2010)

Brazil 1-7 Germany (2014)

ALAN SHEARER

There is something special about travelling to a World Cup with England, knowing that you will be representing your country in the biggest tournament in the world. For me, that would probably have been 1994: I had replaced whoever played up front for England before me by that stage. Sadly, injury meant that I didn't make it, and losing to Holland in a qualifier – with a little help from San Marino – meant England didn't, either.

Instead, I had to wait until 1998. By that time, having watched 1994 on television, I was absolutely desperate to experience it. My first taste of it did not disappoint: beating Tunisia in Marseille, in front of a packed stadium, was unbelievable. To score the opening goal was even better. I knew then that I liked the taste of this.

You are, as Gary's said, a little isolated from everything that is happening at home as a player. You're in your own little world, focusing on training and games, making sure you're ready, and so you don't really know what sort of impact the tournament is having on the country itself. But that doesn't mean you aren't immersed in the tournament. That summer, the whole squad, as well as the staff, gathered in the cinema room at our base in Brittany to watch every single game. If they involved teams in our group, or teams that we might be likely to face in the semi-final, we might have kept a more professional eye on them, seeing where their strengths and weaknesses were, getting to know what they were good at and what we would have to watch for, but, most of the time, we watched them like everyone else did: as fans, enjoying the festival. It was an important chance to build a bit of camaraderie, a way of getting everyone together.

There is a longstanding tradition, with England at major tournaments, of having a bit of a flutter on the games, just to make sure everyone is as involved as they can be as they watch. It's the captain and vice-captain's job to act as bookmaker for each match, setting odds and collecting bets. That summer, it was up to me and Teddy Sheringham. We didn't play for anything major, and I'm not sure anyone won big, in any real sense, but I can tell you one thing for certain: the people that win are not the bookmakers. Not by a long shot.

ALAN'S LIST

1 The Hand of God (1986)

2 Zidane's head-butt (2006)

3 Ronaldo's breakdown (1998)

4 Gazza's tears (1990)

5 Carlos Alberto's goal (1970)

6 Marco Tardelli's scream (1982)

7 Brazil 1-7 Germany (2014)

8 Nigel de Jong's boot (2010)

9 Totò Schillaci (1990)

10 Ronaldinho's free kick (2002)

MICAH RICHARDS

I could have been Theo Walcott, you know. I didn't know it at the time, but Sven-Göran Eriksson had sent some of his staff to keep an eye on me not long after I made my debut for Manchester City; he was, apparently, considering calling me up for the 2006 World Cup. I'd only played a handful of games, then, and barely any in my career at right-back, but he thought I might be a viable option. Normally, your club will let you know if the national team are sniffing around, but nobody mentioned anything to me that time. I suppose they did not want me to get distracted, or to think I had made it. I was still only 17, after all, and it was important for me to keep my feet on the ground. As much as possible, anyway. Or maybe it is a more cynical reason: knowing that I was on the verge of getting an England call-up might have given me a little bit of extra clout in contract negotiations. It wasn't in the club's interests to give me that extra leverage.

In the end, he decided to take someone even younger and less experienced than me to Germany instead. Theo Walcott did not play, but he was there to get to know how a tournament worked. Sven was criticised for it at the time, but it makes sense to me: I would have loved the chance to go, even if I did not play a single minute. Being around all of those players, training with them – especially given that the Manchester City team I had broken into was not quite as full of top-class Internationals as it is today – and seeing what it took to do well in a World Cup. Plus Baden-Baden, the little spa town where England were based, looked like a nice spot. The players and their families definitely seemed to enjoy themselves. Instead, though,

I watched at home, and had to wait until November of that year to make my debut.

If England had had any coach other than Fabio Capello in 2010, I might have stood a chance then, but our relationship was not the best. I barely played for England while he was there, and was not especially sad about it: I don't think I was the only player who found the way he coached a bit off-putting. He was a legend, of course, but he was aloof and awkward, and his intensity made every session quite unpleasant. I remember him interrupting fairly basic crossing drills to scream instructions at me. Plenty of us dreaded an England call-up under him.

That left 2014, under Roy Hodgson, when it was between me, Glen Johnson and Wes Brown for the right-back slots. I had not played much that year, and by that stage I was probably too heavy to be as agile as I had been at my peak. Roy went for Glen instead, who had been playing well for Liverpool, but I still felt a little hard done by: I had played against Glen a couple of times when he played on the left, and always got the better of him. He scored more goals than I did, but I felt I was the stronger player. That he went to two and I missed out on both always struck me as less than I deserved.

MICAH'S LIST

1 The Hand of God (1986)

2 Ronaldo's breakdown (1998)

3 Zidane's head-butt (2006)

4 Brazil 1-7 Germany (2014)

5 Nigel de Jong's boot (2010)

6 Gazza's tears (1990)

7 Ronaldinho's free kick (2002)

8 Carlos Alberto's goal (1970)
9 Marco Tardelli's scream (1982)
10 Totò Schillaci (1990)

THE TOP 10

1 The Hand of God (1986)
2 Zidane's head-butt (2006)
3 Ronaldo's breakdown (1998)
4 Gazza's tears (1990)
5 Brazil 1-7 Germany (2014)
6 Nigel de Jong's boot (2010)
7 Carlos Alberto's goal (1970)
8 Marco Tardelli's scream (1982)
9 Ronaldinho's free kick (2002)
10 Totò Schillaci (1990)

Gary's Verdict: Diego Maradona probably could have taken the top two spots on this list, with both moments coming within a few minutes of each other. That game in 1986 is not one of my happiest memories, but it is probably the most iconic World Cup game of all time.

THE DEBATE

Alan: The controversy and uncertainty of Ronaldo ahead of the 1998 is one of the great World Cup mysteries, but for a player of Zinedine Zidane's level to leave football like he did – head-butting Marco

Materazzi and then trudging past the trophy and down the tunnel – is one of the defining images of the game.

Micah: It's interesting to think what might have happened if Ronaldo had been fully fit before the final in 1998, though. He was unstoppable that year, on his way to being one of the greatest players of all time, and if he had been at his best that day, it's not really a stretch to believe that France would not have won the World Cup.

12

THE TOP 10
SHOCK RESULTS

GARY LINEKER

Liverpool had not lost at home for three years when Leicester went to Anfield in 1981. Under Bob Paisley, they were not only the reigning champions, they would go on to win the European Cup at the end of that season. Leicester, by contrast, were struggling – in vain, it turned out – to avoid relegation. When we won, then, it was against all the odds. That may well have been the biggest shock we recorded during all the time I was at Leicester, and I would love to claim a bit of credit. Sadly, that wouldn't really be right, seeing as I wasn't in the team.

It's what makes football so special that results like that happen. Not all the time – if they did, they wouldn't be special – but regularly enough that the underdog always feels like it has a chance. There is always a possibility, no matter how slim, that a team might be able to grab a lead and hold on, or that an overwhelming favourite might have an off day. It strikes me it happens far more in football than most other sports.

There's no particular recipe for a shock. There are various ingredients: one team having a good day; one team, ordinarily the one with the higher expectations, suddenly lethargic and flat; and probably a healthy dose of luck, even then. Throw those three things together and strange things can, and do, happen. Sometimes that is Watford, threatened with relegation, cutting apart a Liverpool team that had been imperious until that point, or an unheralded Aston Villa sticking seven past the same team, just a few weeks after they had won the title. Sometimes a game between two theoretical rivals is shifted strikingly in favour of one or the other: think of Manchester City thrashing Manchester United at Old Trafford, or Tottenham doing the same, or United scoring an incredible eight against Arsenal.

Sometimes, they are one-offs, and sometimes they are not. No result has shocked me more than Leicester winning at Manchester City in the season they won the league; a game so remarkable that even Robert Huth scored. That was surprising, not because it came out of nowhere, but because it proved that Leicester's form had not been a fluke. If they could win at City, they were to be taken seriously as potential champions, and that was the biggest shock of all.

THE CONTENDERS

Newcastle United 5-0 Manchester United (1996)

Southampton 6-3 Manchester United (1996)

Chelsea 5-0 Manchester United (1999)

Middlesbrough 8-1 Manchester City (2008)

Manchester United 8-2 Arsenal (2011)

Manchester United 1-6 Manchester City (2011)

Norwich City 3-2 Manchester City (2019)

Watford 3-0 Liverpool (2020)
Manchester United 1-6 Tottenham (2020)
Aston Villa 7-2 Liverpool (2020)

ALAN SHEARER

My first game as the most expensive player in the world was a miserable one. Manchester United absolutely battered us in the Charity Shield at Wembley: they won 4-0, and we were nowhere near them. There had been so much excitement when I signed – from the city, and from me, too – and yet when I left that pitch that day, it was hard not to think, 'What have I done?'

Manchester United and Newcastle isn't a derby, of course, but there was a fair bit of animosity between the sides at that point, most of it rooted in what had happened the previous season: the year of Manchester United slowly reeling in Newcastle's 12-point lead, and of Kevin Keegan's meltdown. Losing to them, and losing so heavily, stung.

A couple of months later, they came to St James's Park, and we got our revenge. We more than got our revenge. Newcastle fans always demand a good start: they want their team to be quick out of the blocks, to be assertive, to set the tone. If you do that, the crowd will pull you along with them. It is like a flowing river, washing down the stands, and you can't really help but be swept away.

That is exactly what it was like that night in October, when we dismantled the reigning champions, the mighty Manchester United, humbling Alex Ferguson and his mob. As soon as Darren Peacock scored the first, squeezing a header under Peter Schmeichel, you could feel the atmosphere grab you. Then David Ginola scored the second, Les Ferdinand the third, and I got the fourth. But the one everyone remembers is the fifth: Philippe Albert drifting forward and sending the most delicate chip over Schmeichel. That fifth one made the world of difference to us: we'd beaten them by one more than they had scored against us in the summer.

It doesn't happen very often that you get a game where every player has an absolute 10 out of 10 performance. You might only have one a season, if that, even in a very good team: there's always some flaw, some part of it that is wrong. But we were unplayable that night. Everything clicked: the whole team was perfect. And for it to happen against them, against the side that had taken the league away the previous season, made it even sweeter. Newcastle's fans, as everyone knows, haven't had a trophy to celebrate for a long time. But there are a couple of results that mean almost as much, that still get talked about to this day. Beating Barcelona is one of them. But humiliating Manchester United is right at the top of the list.

ALAN'S LIST

1 Newcastle United 5-0 Manchester United (1996)

2 Manchester United 1-6 Manchester City (2011)

3 Aston Villa 7-2 Liverpool (2020)

4 Manchester United 8-2 Arsenal (2011)

5 Manchester United 1-6 Tottenham (2020)

6 Southampton 6-3 Manchester United (1996)

7 Watford 3-0 Liverpool (2020)

8 Middlesbrough 8-1 Manchester City (2008)

9 Norwich City 3-2 Manchester City (2019)

10 Chelsea 5-0 Manchester United (1999)

MICAH RICHARDS

Sven-Göran Eriksson's reputation is not quite as high as it should be in this country. He's regarded as a failure with England, as the manager who failed to make the most of the golden generation, but to be honest I'm not sure his record in tournaments – three straight quarter-finals – really warrants that. Working with him at Manchester City, I can assure you, it was clear you were dealing with a really good coach. He was warm and personable and caring. Above all, he was nice, and even in an industry as cut-throat as football, you want the nice people to do well.

But nice is not always a strength; nice is not always what you need. On the last day of the season in 2008, we were away at Middlesbrough. We had nothing riding on the game – we'd already qualified for Europe, so it had that relaxed, carefree sort of feeling that you sometimes get when a game doesn't really matter to a team. I was injured, but I travelled up with the team anyway. I want to throw that in there, just so everyone knows that what happened was not my fault.

The cornerstone of our defence that season – for quite a lot of seasons – was Richard Dunne. He is another who is not rated quite as highly as he should be. Unfortunately, that day, he was sent off after about 15 minutes. That would have been hard enough to cope with in any circumstances, especially because I wasn't there to build the team around, but on a day when the players were not quite at it, when the intensity was missing, it proved a disaster.

Middlesbrough absolutely took us apart. Middlesbrough: not the best team in the league, not a side packed full of superstars, just a fairly ordinary Premier League team. We were only two down at half-time, but the second half we were pathetic. It was embarrassing. We ended up losing 8-1. The one flattered us. The result turned Sven into a laughing stock, almost immediately. It was his last game in charge of City, and inevitably it colours the way people remember him. That result was not his fault, particularly, but it is probably fair to say he was not the manager you needed when everything was going wrong. He was too nice, standing on the touchline, trying to shout but not really having the authority to do it. All he could say afterwards was that it was not good enough. There are some things you don't need to be told when you have lost 8-1, and that is one of them.

MICAH'S LIST

1 Manchester United 1-6 Manchester City (2011)

2 Manchester United 1-6 Tottenham (2020)

3 Manchester United 8-2 Arsenal (2011)

4 Aston Villa 7-2 Liverpool (2020)

5 Newcastle United 5-0 Manchester United (1996)

6 Watford 3-0 Liverpool (2020)

7 Norwich City 3-2 Manchester City (2019)

8 Southampton 6-3 Manchester United (1996)

9 Middlesbrough 8-1 Manchester City (2008)

10 Chelsea 5-0 Manchester United (1999)

THE TOP 10

1 Manchester United 1-6 Manchester City (2011)

2 Newcastle United 5-0 Manchester United (1996)

3 Manchester United 8-2 Arsenal (2011)

4 Manchester United 1-6 Tottenham (2020)

5 Aston Villa 7-2 Liverpool (2020)

6 Watford 3-0 Liverpool (2020)

7 Southampton 6-3 Manchester United (1996)

8 Norwich City 3-2 Manchester City (2019)

9 Middlesbrough 8-1 Manchester City (2008)

10 Chelsea 5-0 Manchester United (1999)

Gary's Verdict: One thing that is not a shock, in any way, is Alan and Micah going for results they were involved in to win. Why always them? Manchester City strolling in six at Old Trafford takes it, a result that proved the shifting balance of power in the city and the league, by virtue of Alan being a little more generous than Micah.

THE DEBATE

Alan: It's strange how odd results seem to come along all at once. The week after we beat Manchester United at St James's Park, they went and lost 6-3 at Southampton. Aston Villa scored seven against Liverpool and Tottenham scored six at Old Trafford on the same weekend. But for a real coupon-buster, Liverpool seeing their unbeaten run come to a crashing halt by Watford, battling relegation, takes some beating.

Micah: There are bigger score lines on this list, but newly promoted Norwich beating Manchester City at Carrow Road – a few months after Pep Guardiola's team had retained the Premier League title, and in a season when they were expected to win a third in a row – was remarkable. That defeat was the first hint that Manchester City were not quite at the level to compete with Liverpool that year.

13

THE TOP 10
FIRST IMPRESSIONS

GARY LINEKER

Nerves never really bothered me. Even some of the best players in the world suffer from them before games, but beyond occasionally feeling a little apprehensive on the bus on the way to the stadium, I never found it a problem. I always believed that, if I felt good physically, I would do well. Even when it became obvious that it did not really work like that.

My Leicester debut was not especially auspicious. It was New Year's Day, 1979, and I'd turned 18 a month or so before. We were playing Oldham, and the pitch at Filbert Street was all but frozen. I'd always been a striker, but that day they decided that I would play on the right wing. I don't know why teams do that. I suppose there is a feeling that they've seen something in a young player, and they want to get you in the team, but they also don't want you to do much damage if it doesn't work out, so you go out on the wing.

I was one of three players making their debuts that day, alongside a signing from Hibernian called Bobby Smith and another youth teamer, a striker called Dave Buchanan. It was a perfect start, for both of them: they both scored in a 2-0 win. Out on the right wing, on the other hand, I had an absolutely appalling game. I was dreadful. In my defence, I'd never played there before in my life, but still: it was hardly the introduction I wanted. I was dropped for the next game, and the player I'd replaced, Keith Weller, came back in. He was one of my heroes, Keith, but for some reason he chose to play that game in a pair of bright, white tights. If only I'd played better, I might have been able to save him from that fate.

My first game at Everton, somehow, went even worse. It was, as fate would have it, away at Leicester. It didn't get off to the best possible start when, after arriving at Filbert Street and going out to inspect the pitch, force of habit took me to the home dressing room, and not the away one. Then, when the game started, Mark Bright – the player who'd replaced me at Leicester – scored twice. One of them was a real beauty, too. My new team, Everton, the reigning champions, lost 3-1. Even my family were not exactly sympathetic after that one.

Things went a little better at Barcelona: I had all the pressure not only of the significant transfer fee, but of having arrived as the leading scorer from that summer's World Cup. But I scored within two minutes, and I'd added a second inside 20. The only disappointment from that day was that I'd always thought the second one was one of my very few goals from outside the box, but I saw it back a few years ago and it was just inside. Still, what mattered was that I'd scored, and got off to the start I needed. A good first impression can be priceless.

THE CONTENDERS

Alan Shearer (Blackburn v Crystal Palace, 1992)

Fabrizio Ravanelli (Middlesbrough v Liverpool, 1996)

Jürgen Klinsmann (Tottenham v Sheffield Wednesday, 1994)

Michael Owen (Liverpool v Wimbledon, 1997)

Paulo Wanchope (Derby v Manchester United, 1999)

Wayne Rooney (Everton v Tottenham, 2002)

Federico Macheda (Manchester United v Aston Villa, 2009)

Danny Rose (Tottenham v Arsenal, 2010)

Sergio Agüero (Manchester City v Swansea, 2011)

Marcus Rashford (Manchester United v Arsenal, 2016)

ALAN SHEARER

I suppose I might have got nervous before making my first start as a professional player with Southampton, but I never really had the chance. I was only told I was playing at 11.30 on the morning of the game, when the news came through that Danny Wallace had failed a fitness test. That was it: I was in the team, and I'd be playing a few hours later. That may have worked in my favour. It probably helps not to think about it. It certainly didn't do any harm. I scored a hat-trick. It made me the youngest player in English history to do that, breaking a record Jimmy Greaves had set (until Michael Owen came along and took it off me).

I would have benefitted, too, from the fact that nobody would have had the first clue who I was, unless they'd been watching a lot of games from the South East Counties league. Scouting, then, was not nearly as comprehensive. Promising young players were not tagged as prodigies long before they made it into the first team. I'd come on against Chelsea a couple of weeks beforehand, but other than that, I'm not sure anyone from Arsenal – the team we were playing – would have known what to expect.

It didn't change anything, either. I was still in the next morning, washing the kit, which was one of an apprentice's jobs. It did make Southampton a little bit quicker to offer me a full-time, professional contract, and that was probably a good thing, too: I played another half a dozen games that season, and didn't score again.

But from that point on, debuts never fazed me. I wasn't really the sort to get nervous; if anything, I found the excitement a bonus. It helped that I was quite good at them: I scored twice on my Blackburn debut – my first game in the Premier League – against Crystal Palace, and I scored on my home debut for Newcastle, too. There was added pressure on both games: I was a British record signing for Blackburn, and the most expensive player in the world when I arrived at Newcastle. That could have weighed me down but, to be completely honest, I loved being the world transfer record; I loved the thought that my hometown club had wanted me that much. I was gutted a year or so later when it was broken, though it's a bit of solace that it was for a decent player: Barcelona had to pay more than £15 million to sign Ronaldo from PSV Eindhoven. If you're going to lose your record to anyone, it may as well be him.

ALAN'S LIST

1 Alan Shearer (Blackburn v Crystal Palace, 1992)

2 Fabrizio Ravanelli (Middlesbrough v Liverpool, 1996)

3 Marcus Rashford (Manchester United v Arsenal, 2016)

4 Sergio Agüero (Manchester City v Swansea, 2011)

5 Jürgen Klinsmann (Tottenham v Sheffield Wednesday, 1994)

6 Wayne Rooney (Everton v Tottenham, 2002)

7 Federico Macheda (Manchester United v Aston Villa, 2009)

8 Michael Owen (Liverpool v Wimbledon, 1997)

9 Danny Rose (Tottenham v Arsenal, 2010)

10 Paulo Wanchope (Derby v Manchester United, 1999)

MICAH RICHARDS

The only advice Stuart Pearce gave to me, as I got ready to play in the Premier League for the very first time, was to go and have some fun. There were about five minutes left, and we were losing away at Highbury. I had not long since turned 17, City were mid-table, and that was the Arsenal of Thierry Henry and Robert Pires. There was not much more to do than to try and enjoy myself.

If that seems strange advice to give a defender, you have to remember that I came on upfront. That wasn't a last throw of the dice from Stuart: it was where I had played for most of my career. I'd always been a forward, first at Oldham and then in the academy at Manchester City. A lot of the time, I'd been used as a number 10, because I had the technique to pick passes and score goals. As I got older, I dropped back into midfield more and more, but the coaches felt that my development suffered a bit because of it: it was almost too easy for me there, when I had time and space. The one thing I never really had, the thing that would have held me back, was a large enough passing range.

I only went into defence, at first, because of an injury: we were playing a youth cup game, and one of our central defenders had to go off. I filled in at the back, and did well. I stayed there basically because it meant that I had to get used to playing under pressure, and the staff felt that might be good for me in the long term. It would not be until I was part of Manchester City's first team that I would become a right-back, and that was only because central defence was occupied by Richard Dunne and Sylvain Distin, neither of whom was about to be dropped for a teenager.

That day at Highbury, then, might have been the start of a whole different type of career. I had one shot, one chance to score what would have been a famous equaliser. The ball came across to me, and I shaped to hit it on the volley. If that had gone in, I'd have been a sensation: Manchester City's new teenage striker, a superstar in the making. It was all there. And then I made the connection, and the ball spun off the wrong part of my foot, and came pretty close to hitting the corner flag. It turned out I would have to be a defender after all.

I'd like to think that what people remember from that game is my debut – apart from the shot – but it isn't. Instead, even that seminal moment in football history was overshadowed by the penalty that wasn't: Pires attempting to pass the ball to Henry, rather than shooting himself, but getting it all wrong. On the bench we had no idea what was happening; all I could see was Danny Mills absolutely losing his head at what he had seen. It was only later that we were told what they had tried to do. It would have been brilliant had it come off. But if it doesn't, just like my volley, you have to accept the consequences.

MICAH'S LIST

1 Sergio Agüero (Manchester City v Swansea, 2011)
2 Fabrizio Ravanelli (Middlesbrough v Liverpool, 1996)

3 Wayne Rooney (Everton v Tottenham, 2002)

4 Marcus Rashford (Manchester United v Arsenal, 2016)

5 Federico Macheda (Manchester United v Aston Villa, 2009)

6 Alan Shearer (Blackburn v Crystal Palace, 1992)

7 Michael Owen (Liverpool v Wimbledon, 1997)

8 Jürgen Klinsmann (Tottenham v Sheffield Wednesday, 1994)

9 Paulo Wanchope (Derby v Manchester United, 1999)

10 Danny Rose (Tottenham v Arsenal, 2010)

THE TOP 10

1 Fabrizio Ravanelli (Middlesbrough v Liverpool, 1996)

2 Sergio Agüero (Manchester City v Swansea, 2011)

3 Alan Shearer (Blackburn v Crystal Palace, 1992)

4 Marcus Rashford (Manchester United v Arsenal, 2016)

5 Wayne Rooney (Everton v Tottenham, 2002)

6 Federico Macheda (Manchester United v Aston Villa, 2009)

7 Jürgen Klinsmann (Tottenham v Sheffield Wednesday, 1994)

8 Michael Owen (Liverpool v Wimbledon, 1997)

9 Danny Rose (Tottenham v Arsenal, 2010)

10 Paulo Wanchope (Derby v Manchester United, 1999)

Gary's Verdict: No surprise at all that Alan has put himself top, or that Micah has tried – again – to bask in the reflected glory of Sergio Agüero. That leaves Fabrizio Ravanelli free in the middle to take the crown: it is definitely hard to beat scoring a hat-trick in your first game for a new club, and in a new league.

THE DEBATE

Alan: It was shocking enough to see Middlesbrough sign a Brazilian in 1996, but for them to go and get a Champions League-winning Italian striker in Fabrizio Ravanelli was, if anything, even more incredible. It didn't seem quite right, seeing him there. He fitted right in, though: he scored a hat-trick on his debut, against Liverpool, and they loved him from that moment on.

Micah: Sergio's debut was a hint of things to come: two goals and an assist, all after coming on a substitute. There's a few players here who did not quite deliver on their initial promise – look at Federico Macheda, for example – but for Sergio that was the start of a decade when he basically never stopped scoring goals.

14

THE TOP 10
ENGLISH CHAMPIONS
LEAGUE FINALS

GARY LINEKER

As quite a few of my colleagues in various television studios now never cease to remind me, I never actually played in the Champions League, or even in its predecessor – the tournament that existed while I was playing – the European Cup. It is a regret, of course, but it is something I have come to accept.

In my defence, there were far fewer chances to play in it during my career. You had to be champions to qualify, or hope that the team that beat you to the league title also came out on top in Europe that season. At Barcelona, we finished twice in two of my three seasons there. That would have been enough, had Real Madrid won the European Cup that year. Of course, being Real Madrid, even that was too much of a favour to do us.

111

The one that I rue the most, though, is Everton. They had won the title a few months before I joined, and would have stood a good chance of winning the tournament in my first season. We were a good team, after all, and it was also a time when English teams were dominating, perhaps even more than they are now. Liverpool had won four European Cups in the previous seven years, and there had been victories for Aston Villa and Nottingham Forest, too. I think Everton would have won it, had we taken part, but in the aftermath of the tragedy at Heysel, all English teams were barred from Europe for six years.

All of my memories, then, are of watching the Champions League, rather than playing in it. I was in Barcelona in 1999, watching Manchester United come from behind at the last to beat Bayern Munich. I was sitting behind George Best in Camp Nou, as it happens. He left with about 20 minutes to play – he could not bear seeing United lose, I think – so he missed that incredible conclusion. I am not a Manchester United fan, of course, but I wanted the English team to win, and you could not help but be swept up in the emotion and the drama of it all. I celebrated so wildly when Ole-Gunnar Solskjær scored the winner that I lost my wallet. It was a price worth paying, though, for the privilege of being there at one of the greatest nights of football of them all.

THE CONTENDERS

Manchester United 2-1 Bayern Munich (Barcelona, 1999)

Liverpool 3-3 AC Milan (Istanbul, 2005)

Barcelona 2-1 Arsenal (Paris, 2006)

Manchester United 1-1 Chelsea (Moscow, 2008)

Barcelona 2-0 Manchester United (Rome, 2009)

Barcelona 3-1 Manchester United (Wembley, 2011)

Chelsea 1-1 Bayern Munich (Munich, 2012)
Real Madrid 3-1 Liverpool (Kyiv, 2018)
Liverpool 2-0 Tottenham (Madrid, 2019)
Chelsea 1-0 Manchester City (Porto, 2021)

ALAN SHEARER

I waited all my life to play in the Champions League. It was something that I had always wanted to do, but I had to wait until Blackburn won the league to have a shot at it. There was huge anticipation among the whole squad for who we might get, real excitement at the prospect of welcoming one of the great names – Real Madrid, Juventus, Bayern Munich – to Ewood Park. It would have been a reward for all of the hard work we had put in the previous season.

Except that when the draw was made, we got a group containing Legia Warsaw, Spartak Moscow and Trelleborgs, the Swedish champions. I mean no disrespect to any of those teams when I say it was not quite the glamorous draw we had in mind. It was, it is fair to say, a distinctly underwhelming draw.

Those clubs would be right to say exactly the same to us, of course. Our performances were woeful, even before we get to Graeme Le Saux and David Batty arguing on the pitch in Moscow. It is no excuse to say that we had a lot of players getting their first taste of the Champions League: we had been in Europe the previous year, and the gap then between the UEFA Cup and the Champions League was not quite as big as it is now. And, as you may well be thinking, it was Legia Warsaw, Spartak Moscow and Trelleborgs. We should not have needed to be experienced to give a better account of ourselves.

The bigger issue was that we had not strengthened the squad in the summer after we had won the league. There had been links with Zinedine Zidane and Christophe Dugarry, but ultimately nobody had arrived. That had been a deliberate decision: Ray Harford, who had taken over as manager after Kenny Dalglish became Director of Football, said he wanted to give the squad that had won the title the chance to prove they could do it again. It was a mistake: you should always strengthen when you are on top. I don't think we'd lost our hunger. I don't think it was complacency, but whatever the reason, we did not have the legs or the depth to go again. We struggled in the league, and we let ourselves down in Europe, going out in the group stage.

It was only at Newcastle that I finally had the chance to experience the Champions League at its best. I missed both games against Barcelona through injury – Faustino Asprilla stood in for me in the home game, and I believe he did quite well – but we had games against Inter Milan, Juventus, Marseille and Feyenoord at various points in those years. We were never really serious contenders to win it, or even to reach the final, but those games were everything I had hoped they would be: the noise, the excitement, and the feeling of scoring goals at the very highest level.

ALAN'S LIST

1 Liverpool 3-3 AC Milan (Istanbul, 2005)

2 Manchester United 2-1 Bayern Munich (Barcelona, 1999)

3 Chelsea 1-1 Bayern Munich (Munich, 2012)

4 Barcelona 3-1 Manchester United (Wembley, 2011)

5 Barcelona 2-0 Manchester United (Rome, 2009)

6 Real Madrid 3-1 Liverpool (Kyiv, 2018)

7 Chelsea 1-0 Manchester City (Porto, 2021)

8 Barcelona 2-1 Arsenal (Paris, 2006)

9 Manchester United 1-1 Chelsea (Moscow, 2008)

10 Liverpool 2-0 Tottenham (Madrid, 2019)

MICAH RICHARDS

Not every Premier League game is difficult. Not if you're a top side, anyway, the sort of team that I played for during my latter years at Manchester City, after the Abu Dhabi takeover had happened and once some of the best players in the world started arriving.

That is not to say you don't have to try. It does not mean you can switch off, or coast through 90 minutes. It is, I think, the most intense league in the world. But there are times when the gap in quality is so big that you feel as though you are in complete control: when you are not really tested by the opposition, when you know, deep down, that as long as you concentrate, they cannot realistically hurt you. It never happens against the big teams, obviously, but if you're facing a team that's threatened with relegation at home, and they aren't really set up to attack you, then much of the game can be quite straightforward.

What makes the Champions League different is that there is never, ever a break. The attacks just keep coming. All of the teams can hurt you at pretty much any moment. The technical level is basically flawless, but the real challenge is the speed at which everything is done. Maybe that is the difference: the Premier League is quick, but sometimes the technique lets it down. That is not true of the

Champions League. The players are so good that they get everything right, and if you're not on it, even for a second, you will be punished.

My first game in the Champions League taught me that: up against Bayern Munich, Arjen Robben and Franck Ribéry, you do not get a rest. Often, that is how teams of that quality hurt you: more than anything, they wear you down, relying on the fact that the more tired you get, the more likely you are to slip up. That is not just true of the traditional contenders to win it, though. In 2012, only a few months after we won the Premier League, we went to Amsterdam to play Ajax. We were the reigning English champions, and despite their incredible history in Europe, most would have expected us to be able to beat a Dutch team. Instead, they took us apart: we just could not get near the ball. They were just as good technically, and they outsmarted us tactically. There is no room for error in the Champions League, no matter who you are playing. That's why, I think, it took so long for Manchester City to make a final: they had been in the tournament every year for ten years before they finally got to the biggest game in football, in 2021. You can slip up at any time, against any team. You will be punished for any mistake. And the only way to be ready for it is to learn those difficult lessons, over the course of a few years.

MICAH'S LIST

1 Liverpool 3-3 AC Milan (Istanbul, 2005)

2 Manchester United 2-1 Bayern Munich (Barcelona, 1999)

3 Barcelona 3-1 Manchester United (Wembley, 2011)

4 Chelsea 1-1 Bayern Munich (Munich, 2012)

5 Barcelona 2-1 Arsenal (Paris, 2006)

6 Barcelona 2-0 Manchester United (Rome, 2009)

7 Real Madrid 3-1 Liverpool (Kyiv, 2018)

8 Chelsea 1-0 Manchester City (Porto, 2021)

9 Manchester United 1-1 Chelsea (Moscow, 2008)

10 Liverpool 2-0 Tottenham (Madrid, 2019)

THE TOP 10

1 Liverpool 3-3 AC Milan (Istanbul, 2005)

2 Manchester United 2-1 Bayern Munich (Barcelona, 1999)

3 Chelsea 1-1 Bayern Munich (Munich, 2012)

4 Barcelona 3-1 Manchester United (Wembley, 2011)

5 Barcelona 2-0 Manchester United (Rome, 2009)

6 Real Madrid 3-1 Liverpool (Kyiv, 2018)

7 Barcelona 2-1 Arsenal (Paris, 2006)

8 Chelsea 1-0 Manchester City (Porto, 2021)

9 Manchester United 1-1 Chelsea (Moscow, 2008)

10 Liverpool 2-0 Tottenham (Madrid, 2019)

Gary's Verdict: A close one, this, between two iconic finals. I suspect I would have gone for Barcelona, just ahead of Istanbul, but that may well be because I was at Camp Nou and not in Turkey. If it had been the other way around – if I'd lost my wallet celebrating a Liverpool win – maybe I would have gone for that one.

THE DEBATE

Alan: You could convince me either way on the top two: I played against Manchester United's treble winners just a week before that comeback against Bayern, in the FA Cup final, and they were a special team. But what Liverpool did in Istanbul just shades it, I think, because of the position they were in. Nobody comes back from 3-0 down, never mind in a major final. You can't. It's impossible.

Micah: Only certain clubs can do what Liverpool and Manchester United did in 2005 and 1999. What is remarkable is that it's not even the only time Liverpool have done it: if anything, coming back from 3-0 down to beat Barcelona 4-0 in the semi-final in 2019 is an even more incredible achievement. There is something in the make-up of those clubs that makes those things seem possible.

15

THE TOP 10
WORLD CUP GOALS

GARY LINEKER

The best illustration of just how good Diego Maradona was came on the day I played alongside him. In 1987, the Football League celebrated its centenary. To celebrate, there was a special exhibition at Wembley, with a Football League XI – featuring Bryan Robson and Paul McGrath and Peter Beardsley – playing a Rest of the World team. I was at Barcelona at the time, and so I was selected as the sole Englishman on the visiting side.

It was quite a team. Ruud Gullit and Marco van Basten had not been allowed to take part, but Michel Platini, who had just retired, agreed to play anyway. Paulo Futre was in midfield. Igor Belanov, the guy who had beaten me to the World Player of the Year award in 1986, was there too. And so, despite the fact that he was not exactly popular in England at the time, was Diego Maradona.

There was a lot of concern that, although he had been so kind as to grace us with his presence, memories from 1986 would linger, and his every touch would be booed. Those concerns were, it turned out, well-placed. Maradona was jeered throughout the game, as the Football League team – managed by Bobby Robson – won 3-0.

It is not the score that sticks in my mind, though. What I remember most clearly is before the game, as we were warming up, Maradona spent his time standing in the centre circle, kicking the ball as high in the air as he could. Up and down, up and down. No matter how high it went, it would land straight on his foot and he would boot it straight back up. I don't know how long he was doing it for – a minute, maybe – but he barely had to move.

That sounds simple, but when I went back to Barcelona after the game, I mentioned it to my teammates. We all decided to give it a go, to see whether we could show the same mastery as him. I think the most any of us got was three, and even then we were desperately scurrying around, sprinting to get to the ball before it landed.

Only someone with an extraordinary amount of talent could make it look as simple as Maradona did, just as only he could have scored the goal that, eventually, knocked England out of the World Cup the year before. On a patchwork pitch that made it difficult to stand up, let alone run, he glided past half a team, and then round a goalkeeper, as if he was glued to the floor. And, as ever, he made it all look like it came so naturally to him.

THE CONTENDERS

Carlos Alberto (Brazil v Italy, 1970)

Archie Gemmill (Scotland v Holland, 1978)

Josimar (Brazil v Northern Ireland, 1982)

Diego Maradona (Argentina v England, 1986)

Roberto Baggio (Italy v Czechoslovakia, 1990)

Saeed Al-Owairan (Saudi Arabia v Belgium, 1994)

Michael Owen (England v Argentina, 1998)

Dennis Bergkamp (Holland v Argentina, 1998)

Giovanni van Bronckhorst (Holland v Uruguay, 2010)

James Rodríguez (Colombia v Uruguay, 2014)

ALAN SHEARER

Michael Owen was still just a teenager when he joined up with the England squad for the 1998 World Cup. He had only had one full season at Liverpool. He was already becoming a major star in England, but most of the rest of the world would not have known a vast amount about him. He was not shy at all, though. You could see from the first day of training that he was ready.

For a player that young, surrounded by all of these experienced internationals, he was incredible in training. He was strutting his stuff from the first minute, scoring goals and looking for all the world as though he belonged at that level, even at that age. He had this absolute self-belief in his own ability. He knew what he was about: he was aware of what he was good at, of the sort of talent he had, and he wasn't afraid to show it. He was bursting at the seams.

Glenn Hoddle made him wait. He did not come into the team straightaway: Teddy Sheringham started in both of the first two games, against Tunisia and Romania, and it was only after Michael scored in the latter that he got his first start, against Colombia. He looked assured and composed, totally unfazed by the occasion – playing for his country, at a World Cup, at the age of 18 – but I'd be lying if I said that all of that meant I was expecting him to score the goal he did against Argentina. I was not surprised, exactly, having seen him up close for a couple of weeks, but being capable of something like that is one thing; actually doing it is quite another.

You can see his singlemindedness in the way, when he gets the ball from David Beckham, he shrugs off the first Argentine defender: his head was down, and he only had one thought in his mind. But I think the boyish excitement he must have had to be at the World Cup, to be playing for England, might have helped, too. He made it look like it was something completely natural, the sort of thing he would have done on the playground. I was sprinting to try and keep up with him – although at the speed he was going, I'm not sure I would ever have caught him – but not once did it even occur to me that he might actually pass it.

That game ended in bitterness and regret for us, of course: Beckham being sent off, the goal from Sol Campbell that would have won it for us being ruled out for reasons I still don't understand, and then losing on penalties, but in a lot of ways, too, that game is best remembered as the day Michael Owen announced himself to the world.

ALAN'S LIST

1 Diego Maradona (Argentina v England, 1986)

2 Dennis Bergkamp (Holland v Argentina, 1998)

3 Michael Owen (England v Argentina, 1998)

4 Carlos Alberto (Brazil v Italy, 1970)

5 Roberto Baggio (Italy v Czechoslovakia, 1990)

6 Archie Gemmill (Scotland v Holland, 1978)

7 Saeed Al-Owairan (Saudi Arabia v Belgium, 1994)

8 Giovanni van Bronckhorst (Holland v Uruguay, 2010)
9 James Rodríguez (Colombia v Uruguay, 2014)
10 Josimar (Brazil v Northern Ireland, 1982)

MICAH RICHARDS

James Rodríguez was not stronger than me. He was not quicker than me. But there are not many players who have given me quite such a chasing as he did when we played FC Porto in the Europa League in 2012. We won the game that night in Portugal, and we went through on aggregate a week later, but he took me to the cleaners. It was one of the worst performances of my career.

I'm not sure why, looking back, but I was desperate that night to prove that I was a top-quality attacking full-back. It may have been because it was Europe, and I wanted to show that I could play that sort of football; Manchester City might have been linked with a more offensive full-back, someone to replace me, in the days before. We were being linked with players all the time at that point, and after a while it made you feel distinctly insecure.

Whatever the reason, I spent the evening determined to prove that I was Maicon or Dani Alves or someone. Normally, before games, I would tell myself to keep calm, to do the basics well, to make sure I did my job. Not in Porto: I was busy working myself up, getting ready to show that I was the Chapeltown Cafu.

Nobody had told James. He was not the player we saw at Everton then. In England, he was a sort of drifting playmaker, a number 10 who started out wide but wanted to get into those pockets of space where he could play a pass. For Porto, he was different. He could still come inside, but he was happy to go wide, too.

It wasn't something that I ever discussed while I was playing, but there is a little secret about me: I can't defend on my left-hand side. It was physical, more than anything. I could turn to my right, but my knee just wouldn't let me turn to my left. Every time I tried to do it, it felt like I was trying to move a bus. So I would always show players wide, because that is where I was most comfortable.

James would not let me. Playing against him felt like having two left feet. What made him stand out was his acceleration: he was so quick over those first few yards. I could outsprint him easily, over a distance, but he had this little burst that just left me for dead. He was so sharp that he would have beaten me before I even really knew what was happening.

It was only a couple of years later, with that incredible goal against Uruguay, that he became a proper global star, but you could see that evening in Porto how special he was. Up close, you knew he was going places, and he was getting there ahead of me.

MICAH'S LIST

1 Diego Maradona (Argentina v England, 1986)

2 Carlos Alberto (Brazil v Italy, 1970)

3 Dennis Bergkamp (Holland v Argentina, 1998)

4 James Rodríguez (Colombia v Uruguay, 2014)

5 Giovanni van Bronckhorst (Holland v Uruguay, 2010)

6 Michael Owen (England v Argentina, 1998)

7 Roberto Baggio (Italy v Czechoslovakia, 1990)

8 Archie Gemmill (Scotland v Holland, 1978)

9 Josimar (Brazil v Northern Ireland, 1982)

10 Saeed Al-Owairan (Saudi Arabia v Belgium, 1994)

THE TOP 10

1 Diego Maradona (Argentina v England, 1986)

2 Dennis Bergkamp (Holland v Argentina, 1998)

3 Carlos Alberto (Brazil v Italy, 1970)

4 Michael Owen (England v Argentina, 1998)

5 Roberto Baggio (Italy v Czechoslovakia, 1990)

6 James Rodríguez (Colombia v Uruguay, 2014)

7 Giovanni van Bronckhorst (Holland v Uruguay, 2010)

8 Archie Gemmill (Scotland v Holland, 1978)

9 Saeed Al-Owairan (Saudi Arabia v Belgium, 1994)

10 Josimar (Brazil v Northern Ireland, 1982)

Gary's Verdict: No surprise which goal wins this one. I watched that game back not too long ago, and though the goal still takes the breath away, I noticed that there was a dreadful foul on an England player just before the ball is passed to Maradona. So it is fair to say VAR would have ruled out both his goals that day, and we would have won.

THE DEBATE

Alan: As if scoring two of the greatest goals in Premier League history – against Leicester and against Newcastle – was not enough, Dennis Bergkamp also produced one of the finest to grace the World Cup. His goal in 1998 against Argentina is a work of art: the sort of thing that would make anyone who loves football stand up and applaud.

Micah: Michael Owen had everything. It was not just pace: he had this incredible movement, too, and he was such a composed finisher. It's a tragedy, really, that injuries troubled him so much, because if he'd been fully fit throughout his career, he'd have broken all sorts of records, both for Liverpool and for England.

16

THE TOP 10
TITLE RACES

GARY LINEKER

The day Everton won at Anfield, it looked like the title was won. It was late in February, and that victory put us six points clear of Liverpool. We were the reigning champions, and we had a good, settled side. We knew what we were doing. That day, I'm not sure anyone thought we would be caught. It did not work out like that, of course, and though I can't say for certain that it was because of a missing pair of boots, I can't say for certain that it wasn't, either.

As a rule, if a striker is scoring goals, they will do everything they can not to change anything at all. For me, that always extended to my boots. If you were in a good vein of form with a specific pair, then you certainly wouldn't swap them for another, not least because I always found it took three games or so to mould a boot properly to your feet.

That season at Everton, I scored a lot of goals – I ended up getting 30 that season – and so I rarely changed my boots. By the end of the campaign, they had started to feel like a genuinely lucky pair. They were so special to me that, when it came time to go to the World Cup, I insisted on getting them repaired, rather than replaced. They were flown back to the factory that had made them, stitched back up, and flown back to me. During the tournament itself, they started to fall apart again after the first game, so I had them flown to the United States to be fixed, and flown back to me in time for our second match. By the end of their useful life, they were all but wrecked. But I had to wear them, because they were lucky.

Slowly, over the course of the last couple of months of the season, Liverpool had eaten away at our lead. They won 11 of their final 12 games, and drew the other; at the same time, we started dropping points, just here and there, but enough to give them hope. By the last week, we were only a point ahead. We had to go to Oxford United and win to have any hope of keeping them at bay. But when we arrived, and I looked in the bin where we kept all of our boots, my lucky pair were not there. They'd been left behind on Merseyside. I had to borrow someone else's, a size too small, to play. I missed two or three good chances that night; we lost 1-0. Liverpool won, and went on to win the league.

Maybe it would not have been any different with my lucky boots. Maybe it would. We had two more games left after that defeat at Oxford. I scored five goals. I scored them wearing my lucky boots.

THE CONTENDERS

Blackburn Rovers v Manchester United, 1995

Manchester United v Newcastle, 1996

Arsenal v Manchester United, 1998

Manchester United v Arsenal, 1999

Manchester United v Chelsea, 2008

Manchester United v Liverpool, 2009

Chelsea v Manchester United, 2010

Manchester City v Manchester United, 2012

Manchester City v Liverpool, 2014

Manchester City v Liverpool, 2019

ALAN SHEARER

Kenny Dalglish had been there, and done that. He had won countless titles as a player and as a coach at Liverpool, and in the last few weeks of the season in 1995, he did all he could to convey the message that, for him, this was all business as usual. Outwardly, he was as calm as he could be. Deep down, though, that was probably an act. He must have been nervous, too, because he will have known that what he was on the cusp of doing with Blackburn Rovers was monumental.

None of us ever spoke about being nervous. It was not something anyone felt comfortable discussing. But at the same time, you could feel it in the atmosphere. There was something different to previous seasons. It was a strange mixture of nerves and a giddy kind of excitement. The year before we had been in with a chance, but it felt almost carefree: we were the underdogs, nobody expected anything from us, we were playing without pressure. In 1995, that had gone. We knew, then, that this was our chance, and that we had to deliver.

Few of us in the squad had even been near a title before. Of course you tell yourselves that all that matters is that we do our jobs. You try to switch off from everything and everyone. You try to ignore that there are two teams in a title race, and tell yourself that you are in control, and that nothing else is relevant. But that is not true either, because you are absolutely desperate for the other team – Manchester United, in our case – to mess up. It is a lot easier dealing with that sort of pressure than the other kind, the sort you feel at the bottom of the table, trying to stave off relegation, but still: you feel the intensity of the situation.

For us, it was the penultimate game of the season, at Newcastle, that felt like the moment we made it. We did not play well that night – we owed a lot to Tim Flowers, who produced one of the great goalkeeping displays to keep us in it – but we got over the line. That was, to us, the mark of champions. We still had one game to go, and our margin was still fine: we had to go to Anfield and hope that Manchester United did not win at West Ham.

You know how that went: we took the lead, and then the scale of what we were about to do seemed to hit us all at once. Liverpool equalised, and then scored in the last minute to win the game. A few seconds later, though, the news filtered through that Manchester United had been held at Upton Park, too. We were champions. And, although it was maybe not quite as dramatic as Manchester City managed in 2012, the title went down to the very last kick in 1995, too: had United scored in injury time, they would have been champions.

ALAN'S LIST

1 Manchester City v Manchester United, 2012

2 Blackburn Rovers v Manchester United, 1995

3 Manchester City v Liverpool, 2014

4 Manchester City v Liverpool, 2019

5 Manchester United v Newcastle, 1996

6 Manchester United v Arsenal, 1999

7 Manchester United v Liverpool, 2009

8 Arsenal v Manchester United, 1998
9 Manchester United v Chelsea, 2008
10 Chelsea v Manchester United, 2010

MICAH RICHARDS

I can't remember which player said it. It was the night before the game against QPR in 2012, the one I might have mentioned a couple of times, and the whole Manchester City squad was together, eating dinner, getting ready for what we all knew would be the biggest game of our careers. We knew it so well, in fact, that we did not feel we had to talk about it.

And then, at some point in the evening, someone casually mentioned that all we needed to do to be Premier League champions was win the next day. As soon as it was out of his mouth, the rest of us tried to quiet him. 'Don't say that, don't say that,' we all shouted. That is how superstitious we were. We genuinely did not want anyone to jinx it.

It wasn't a deliberate thing. Roberto Mancini had plenty of superstitions – at one point he took against our club tracksuit because it had purple on it, and he had decided that was an unlucky colour – and there were lots of rules that he brought in to avoid tempting fate, but that was not one of them. It came from the players. At no point in that season did we mention winning the league. We did not talk about becoming champions. We thought about very little else, of course, but we were too worried, I suppose, to say it out loud.

You have to remember that, although it looks like a team of stars in hindsight, it was not at the time. Sergio Agüero and Mario Balotelli were only young. Edin Džeko had won a league in Germany, and Carlos Tevez had won things in Argentina and for that other team he played for in Manchester, but the vast majority of us had won the FA Cup the year before, and that was about it. We were not yet that comfortable with the idea of winning something, and we did not want to take any risks.

The contrast a couple of years later was clear. In 2014, we set out to win the league. We told ourselves that we had to win this game or this run of fixtures to win the league. We talked about it quite openly: it was the difference between expectation and hope. We were not complacent, not at all, but we had got that first one out of the way. By that stage, we knew how to win leagues, and we knew that whether you said it out loud or not did not make any difference in the slightest. But maybe that is what makes the first one special: you are proving to yourself that you can do it.

MICAH'S LIST

1 Manchester City v Manchester United, 2012

2 Blackburn Rovers v Manchester United, 1995

3 Manchester City v Liverpool, 2014

4 Manchester United v Newcastle, 1996

5 Arsenal v Manchester United, 1998

6 Manchester United v Arsenal, 1999

7 Manchester City v Liverpool, 2019

8 Chelsea v Manchester United, 2010

9 Manchester United v Chelsea, 2008

10 Manchester United v Liverpool, 2009

THE TOP 10

1 Manchester City v Manchester United, 2012

2 Blackburn Rovers v Manchester United, 1995

3 Manchester City v Liverpool, 2014

4 Manchester United v Newcastle, 1996

5 Manchester City v Liverpool, 2019

6 Manchester United v Arsenal, 1999

7 Arsenal v Manchester United, 1998

8 Manchester United v Liverpool, 2009

9 Manchester United v Chelsea, 2008

10 Chelsea v Manchester United, 2010

Gary's Verdict: What happened in 1995 was obviously very special to Alan, personally, and it was a wonderfully dramatic title race, but nothing will ever top the sheer drama of 2012, and the Agüero moment. It was a truly extraordinary conclusion to the season.

THE DEBATE

Alan: I might have been involved in 1995, and I might have felt every single twist and turn in that title race, but even I have to give it to Manchester City in 2012, simply for the Sergio Agüero goal. For the season to go to the last kick, and for it to be decided in the way that it was, is absolutely extraordinary.

Micah: What made 2012 so special is that it was decided by the final kick of the season, but a great title race doesn't always go right to the last day. Manchester City and Liverpool pushed each other the whole way in 2019, but by the end it was pretty clear City would win their last game at Brighton, so there would be no drama. In 1996, Newcastle didn't last that long, but the story of Manchester United hauling in their 12-point lead was so dramatic that it did not need to.

PART TWO

CULTURE

1

THE TOP 10
EUROPEAN IMPORTS

GARY LINEKER

What started as a trickle has, over the last 20 years or so, become a flood, carrying hundreds of players from the continent into the Premier League. And change has followed in their wake: our game, our league and our football culture have been transformed by players arriving from Europe.

There is a tendency to focus on the negative, to wonder if the endless influx of players makes it harder for our own young players to earn a chance, but the positive impact has been vast. You only need to look at the way the game is played to see that.

It's not just the style of play, the tactics and the technique, it's the way that players prepare for games, the way they eat, the way they train. Much of that is down to imported managers, of course, people like Arsène Wenger and, more recently, Pep Guardiola, but it is the habits of the players who have come in, too.

It's a world away from the league I played in. There were occasional foreign imports in the 1980s: Jan Mølby at Liverpool, and the Dutch duo of Frans Thijssen and Arnold Mühren at Ipswich, but there were too few of them to influence the way teams played. They were the exception, then. Now they are the rule.

Mostly, they arrive while they are still young: the Premier League is a place that makes stars, rather than buying them ready-made. That is one reason why Cristiano Ronaldo might be further down this list than you would expect. If this was a question of the finest players ever to have graced the Premier League, based on all that they had achieved in their career, then he would be out on his own. Given all that he has gone on to do, there is no question that he is the best player who has ever been in the Premier League. But we are thinking, instead, about what they did while they were here: Ronaldo was created at Manchester United, but he reached the pinnacle of his game at Real Madrid.

The other rule: no goalkeepers. We have limited ourselves to outfield players only. There is no shortage of them, after all. In fact, it's maybe the best measure of how much impact European imports have had on English football that there is no room – not yet, anyway – for Kevin De Bruyne, a player who has won three Premier League titles, and counting.

THE CONTENDERS

Dennis Bergkamp (Arsenal)

Eric Cantona (Leeds United, Manchester United)

Eden Hazard (Chelsea)

Thierry Henry (Arsenal)

N'Golo Kanté (Leicester City, Chelsea)

Roy Keane (Nottingham Forest, Manchester United)

Vincent Kompany (Manchester City)
Cristiano Ronaldo (Manchester United)
David Silva (Manchester City)
Patrick Vieira (Arsenal, Manchester City)

ALAN SHEARER

I always noticed, when I was playing for England, that the teams we faced never seemed afraid to give the ball to a teammate when he was under pressure. It didn't faze them at all: they trusted they had the technical ability to deal with the situation, to get out of trouble. It was something we did not have, in our culture, at the time.

That has changed now. The game here has improved year in, year out, on and off the pitch, thanks to the methods brought in by players we have imported, and the ideas they have brought with them, too. Most teams, now, try to play out from the back, and their players have the talent and the confidence to do it. That is a world apart from the English game you saw when I was first coming through. The more the Premier League has welcomed European players, the more European the league has become.

It's easy to focus on the players who have the extravagant skill: Cristiano Ronaldo's incredible ability just to keep improving, that attitude to get better and better; the way Eden Hazard carried the ball, the ease with which he travelled with it, or Dennis Bergkamp's class. I was on the pitch the night he scored that wonderful goal against Newcastle, the touch, the swivel and the finish. It was such a breathtaking piece of skill that I had to stop myself applauding it, like everyone else in the crowd.

But others stand out for their other gifts. Patrick Vieira could play, but he was as hard as they come, and I have never seen a player cover as much space as N'Golo Kanté. He is just constantly moving, sensing danger, snuffing it out, starting attacks. And he does it all with such ease that sometimes it looks like he's not even sweating.

One name stands out, though, and he's from a little closer to home: Cork, in the Republic of Ireland. Kenny Dalglish almost signed Roy Keane for Blackburn, in 1993, before he moved to Manchester United. He thought he had him at one point. But Sir Alex Ferguson kept at him, and at the last minute Roy changed his mind and went to Old Trafford. It worked out all right for him: he won the Premier League seven times. I'm not sure any European import has had more impact than him.

ALAN'S LIST

1 Roy Keane (Nottingham Forest, Manchester United)

2 Thierry Henry (Arsenal)

3 Eric Cantona (Leeds United, Manchester United)

4 David Silva (Manchester City)

5 Dennis Bergkamp (Arsenal)

6 Patrick Vieira (Arsenal, Manchester City)

7 Cristiano Ronaldo (Manchester United)

8 Vincent Kompany (Manchester City)

9 Eden Hazard (Chelsea)

10 N'Golo Kanté (Leicester City, Chelsea)

MICAH RICHARDS

Everyone thinks David Silva is this quiet, unassuming little guy, but that really couldn't be further from the truth. At Manchester City, David loved a night out. I remember one pre-season, we went to Los Angeles on tour – that's not a great idea – and we were told that we could go out for a bite to eat, as long as we were back in our hotels for midnight.

Midnight? In Los Angeles? That's just when things are getting going.

A few of us decided that we wanted to stay out a little bit later than that. I'd better not name too many names, because some of them are still playing, but me and David were both part of a little group of players who sneaked out of the fire escape and into a fleet of taxis we had waiting for us. Our grand plan was to wear our tracksuits in case we were caught: that way, we could say we were just going out for a bit of a walk. We escaped, though, and had our night on the town. David was the last of us to roll back in, at about 6am.

You wouldn't have been able to tell, though. By the time training started, he was fresh as a daisy, top in sprints, top in shooting, barely misplacing a pass while the rest of us were just trying to get through, hiding at the back, waiting for it to be over. I suppose that's what you can do when you're as gifted as he is.

He goes in just ahead of Cristiano Ronaldo for me. What he went on to achieve at Real Madrid, and then Juventus, was incredible, but he was still on his way while he was at Manchester United. He had two seasons when he was devastating before he left, but to be honest

I never felt like I struggled against him. I saved my best for derbies, and there was at least one when he spent the entire game in my pocket.

I'm not sure any foreign player has ever been as important to English football as Eric Cantona, the King, the signing who helped Leeds win the title and then transformed Manchester United into the dominant force; I think you can make the case that his success opened the door for everyone who followed.

But, despite growing up in Leeds, I was an Arsenal fan as a kid, and a lot of that was down to watching Thierry Henry. He was a beautiful footballer to watch, so elegant but so effective, too. Cantona was just a little bit before my time, so it has to be Thierry, the player who brought a little va-va-voom to the Premier League.

MICAH'S LIST

1 Thierry Henry (Arsenal)

2 Eric Cantona (Leeds United, Manchester United)

3 Roy Keane (Nottingham Forest, Manchester United)

4 Patrick Vieira (Arsenal, Manchester City)

5 Vincent Kompany (Manchester City)

6 Dennis Bergkamp (Arsenal)

7 David Silva (Manchester City)

8 Cristiano Ronaldo (Manchester United)

9 Eden Hazard (Chelsea)

10 N'Golo Kanté (Leicester City, Chelsea)

THE TOP 10

1 Thierry Henry (Arsenal)

2 Roy Keane (Nottingham Forest, Manchester United)

3 Eric Cantona (Leeds United, Manchester United)

4 Patrick Vieira (Arsenal, Manchester City)

5 David Silva (Manchester City)

6 Dennis Bergkamp (Arsenal)

7 Vincent Kompany (Manchester City)

8 Cristiano Ronaldo (Manchester United)

9 Eden Hazard (Chelsea)

10 N'Golo Kanté (Leicester City, Chelsea)

Gary's Verdict: No question that Keane is the greatest captain of the Premier League era: he was a winner and a warrior. But he was not as gifted, or as joyous, as Thierry Henry. That is how I like to think about football: it is designed to bring people joy. If that is the way we are judging it, then I'm not sure any import into English football has brought as much joy as Henry.

THE DEBATE

Alan: None of the players on this list won as much as Roy Keane, or shaped the team around them quite so much. All of those Premier League winners' medals are all the proof you need that he is the best foreign signing we've seen in the last 30 years.

Micah: Keane was the sort of player you would want on your team, but Henry was the sort of player who made you fall in love with football. Every single game he would do something that would make you want to run outside and start pretending to be him. No player has brought more magic into the Premier League than him.

2

THE TOP 10
PLAYERS OUTSIDE
THE BIG SIX

GARY LINEKER

The idea of a Big Six might seem like a fairly recent development. Certainly, the identity of the Big Six as we now know them – Manchester United, Manchester City, Liverpool, Chelsea, Arsenal and Tottenham – is relatively modern: they've only been grouped together for the last decade or so.

But there has always been a group of teams at the very summit of the English game, carving up the trophies and the titles between them. When the Premier League was first formed in 1992, the project was led by six breakaway clubs, only with Everton and Aston Villa taking the places of Chelsea and Manchester City.

For the most part, those teams are the ones who not only collect the honours, they gather together the very best players. The more dominant they have become, the easier it is to assume that to be a truly great player, you have to prove you can cut it at Old Trafford or Anfield, the Etihad or the Emirates.

These players prove that is not quite true. There are plenty of great players out there who spent their whole careers away from the bright lights of the supposed elite. Not all of them have made this list. Rob Lee had a wonderful career at Newcastle; Mark Viduka scored goals wherever he went, too. Wilfried Zaha would, I'm sure, have made it had he not been ineligible: it seems a long time ago, now, and it did not work out quite as he would have wanted it to, but he did have a short spell at Manchester United.

There's one other name missing, too. Striker, played for Blackburn and Newcastle, but never quite made it to any of the teams we know now as the Big Six. Scored plenty of goals. But we decided to rule Alan Shearer out for no other reason than we didn't want to talk about him again.

All of those that did, though, would have graced any team with ambitions of winning the league or competing in Europe. Matt Le Tissier was a brilliant player, and a scorer of brilliant goals. Gary Speed's biggest strength was that he just didn't have any weaknesses. Jay-Jay Okocha might have come to England at the tail-end of his career, but he was still more than talented enough to shine. Gareth Southgate was smart and versatile and dedicated. And then, of course, there's Jamie Vardy, a striker picked up for a million quid who went on to win the league, the ultimate proof that you don't have to be with the elite to get to the mountaintop.

THE CONTENDERS

David Batty (Leeds United, Blackburn Rovers, Newcastle United)

Tim Cahill (Everton)

Paolo Di Canio (Sheffield Wednesday, West Ham, Charlton)

Juninho Paulista (Middlesbrough)

Matt Le Tissier (Southampton)

Jay-Jay Okocha (Bolton)

Kevin Phillips (Sunderland, Southampton,
Aston Villa, West Bromwich Albion)

Gareth Southgate (Crystal Palace, Middlesbrough, Aston Villa)

Gary Speed (Leeds United, Everton, Newcastle United, Bolton)

Jamie Vardy (Leicester City)

ALAN SHEARER

I can't think of a better player I saw than Matt Le Tissier. In terms of his touch, his technique, his shooting, his control there was nobody to hold a candle to him. He was, by some distance, the best penalty taker I've ever seen, too. I think his secret was that he was so laid back. Nothing ever really fazed him, so he felt free to try the spectacular.

Of course, maybe that was what held him back a little. I know he had chances to leave Southampton, but I don't know if he was driven in quite that way. He wasn't the hardest worker – he would tell you himself that he hated running; he was always lagging behind in pre-season training – and he was just so comfortable at Southampton, at a club and in a team that let him express himself, just the way he wanted.

This list is almost split between two types of players. Le Tissier embodies one, along with Jay-Jay Okocha. He was so good on the ball that he just seemed to go past players as if they weren't there; it all came so naturally to both of them.

On the other side are players like Tim Cahill, Paolo Di Canio, Gareth Southgate and David Batty. Cahill came from Australia, via Millwall, and ended up having a long, illustrious career at the top level. Gareth got the best out of himself wherever he went. Di Canio was a maverick, but everyone who played with him said he was a fantastic presence in the dressing room, incredibly dedicated to his work.

David Batty was a curious case. I played with him at Blackburn and at Newcastle and never really got the impression he liked football. He was the last to arrive at training and the first to leave. He did all he could to minimise how much time he was there: he arrived in his kit and went straight off the pitch to his car to leave. You could quite often see him driving away while we were doing extra shooting drills or what have you. He didn't even like stretching: he would turn up for a game and just go straight out and play. But he was a fierce competitor. He put his foot in as hard as anyone. He's not stayed in touch: I'm not even sure he's got a mobile phone.

I don't know of anyone who got more out of themselves than Gary Speed, though. He was an unbelievable trainer, an incredible professional: he wanted to perfect everything about his game. He had a bit of everything, but his main asset was his timing. He arrived in the box at exactly the right moment; you just couldn't mark him. He was as reliable a player as you could hope for. He ended up with 535 Premier League appearances, and he earned every single one of them.

ALAN'S LIST

1 Gary Speed (Leeds United, Everton, Newcastle United, Bolton)

2 Matt Le Tissier (Southampton)

3 Jamie Vardy (Leicester City)

4 Gareth Southgate (Crystal Palace, Middlesbrough, Aston Villa)

5 David Batty (Leeds United, Blackburn Rovers, Newcastle United)

6 Paolo Di Canio (Sheffield Wednesday, West Ham, Charlton)

7 Kevin Phillips (Sunderland, Southampton,
Aston Villa, West Bromwich Albion)

8 Tim Cahill (Everton)

9 Juninho Paulista (Middlesbrough)

10 Jay-Jay Okocha (Bolton)

MICAH RICHARDS

A lot of people don't know that I was the making of Jamie Vardy. I played against him for Aston Villa in the year they won the league. It was early in the season, though, long before anyone would even have thought that was possible. The first half, I kept him nice and quiet: he's quick, but he wasn't going to beat me for pace. At one point, I gave him a little wink, just to let him know I was comfortable.

But the thing about Vardy is that he keeps coming. He never stops making those runs. He never gives up chasing down balls. He doesn't give you a moment's peace. He is always on your shoulder, always looking for something, always asking you questions.

We'd gone in ahead at half-time, and had made it 2-0 early in the second half. I was pretty comfortable, sure I'd got the better of him, until the last 20 minutes, when you're starting to tire and he is just still going. They got it back to 2-2 – he scored the equaliser – and then Nathan Dyer popped up in the last minute with a winner.

Vardy, as he always did that season, had the last laugh: as we walked off, he winked right back at me.

But more importantly, at some point in that game, he claims I broke his wrist. I don't remember it at all, but he said a year or so later that we'd gone into a challenge together and something had broken. That was when he started wearing the cast, the one that he wore even after the injury had healed: players are all very superstitious, so if something seems to be working, you don't change it. Like I say: I was the making of Jamie Vardy.

He's approached his career like he approaches games, I think. He has just never stopped, and that's what's enabled him to come all the way from non-league, via Halifax and Fleetwood, not only to play in the Premier League, but to win it, and get all the way to the England squad, too. There are a lot of players like that on this list – ones who overcame the odds and maximised their talents – but I'm not sure anyone has done it to quite such an extent as Vardy.

MICAH'S LIST

1 Jamie Vardy (Leicester City)

2 Gary Speed (Leeds United, Everton, Newcastle United, Bolton)

3 Juninho Paulista (Middlesbrough)

4 Matt Le Tissier (Southampton)

5 Paolo Di Canio (Sheffield Wednesday, West Ham, Charlton)

6 Jay-Jay Okocha (Bolton)

7 David Batty (Leeds United, Blackburn Rovers, Newcastle United)

8 Tim Cahill (Everton)

9 Kevin Phillips (Sunderland, Southampton, Aston Villa, West Bromwich Albion)

10 Gareth Southgate (Crystal Palace, Middlesbrough, Aston Villa)

THE TOP 10

1 Gary Speed (Leeds United, Everton, Newcastle United, Bolton)

2 Jamie Vardy (Leicester City)

3 Matt Le Tissier (Southampton)

4 Paolo Di Canio (Sheffield Wednesday, West Ham, Charlton)

5 Juninho Paulista (Middlesbrough)

6 David Batty (Leeds United, Blackburn Rovers, Newcastle United)

7 Gareth Southgate (Crystal Palace, Middlesbrough, Aston Villa)

8 Kevin Phillips (Sunderland, Southampton, Aston Villa, West Bromwich Albion)

9 Jay-Jay Okocha (Bolton)

10 Tim Cahill (Everton)

Gary's Verdict: I am slightly biased on this one, and if I was the tie-breaker, it would have to be Jamie Vardy, just ahead of Gary Speed and Matt Le Tissier. Think of all he has achieved for a million pounds: winning the FA Cup and the Premier League with Leicester City. But there's no denying that Speed had a great career, so he makes a worthy winner.

THE DEBATE

Alan: There's something brilliant about Kevin Phillips's story: he was an apprentice at Southampton, but he was released, and had to build his way back through non-league. He ended up playing for England, and winning a Golden Boot at Sunderland. It was similar, in that way, to what happened to Vardy, though obviously without the Premier League title.

Micah: Tim Cahill does not get the credit he deserves, either, having come from Australia, worked his way up at Millwall, and then going on to play in an FA Cup final and having so long at Everton. He had the best timing of any player I have ever seen. The way he found space and made the perfect run, time and again, made him really difficult to defend.

3

THE TOP 10
TOUGHEST GROUNDS

GARY LINEKER

There are some stadiums you dread going to as a player. It can be for all sorts of reasons. Sometimes, the fans are too close to the pitch. Sometimes, the crowd is too hostile. Some grounds always seem to be freezing, no matter what time of year it is when you play. It might be even worse for strikers: there are some places you always seem to score, and some places that you really don't.

That is why I have good memories of playing at Selhurst Park. I probably scored more goals there than anywhere else, just because I played there so often: Crystal Palace, Charlton and Wimbledon all used it as their home ground at various points in my career.

The Victoria Ground, Stoke City's old stadium, was the opposite. I remember going there in the era when managers would grow the grass long in the corners, to hold the ball up: an old trick to help teams who wanted to play direct football. They had grown it so long at Stoke that it cost me a goal – I went round the goalkeeper, clipped the ball toward the goal, and ran off to celebrate. And then I realised that the ball had slowed down in the grass.

But even that was preferable to playing at the Den. I found that harrowing. The tunnel was cramped and narrow. There was this wire-mesh fencing on both sides, with fans within spitting distance outside. Literally within spitting distance. It was the sort of place where you stood there, listening to the abuse – and sometimes wiping some of it off your shirt – and couldn't help but think that this was the sort of stadium where you didn't want to play too well.

Stamford Bridge was a bit like that. Not now, of course: it's become one of the best stadiums in Europe. It's a world away from what it used to be, when there was a car park at one end of the stadium and the pitch was dry and uneven. The goals always seemed to be so far from the stands, but that never seemed to make it less hostile. I remember walking off the pitch after the warm-up and stopping to sign a few autographs for some kids, only to be abused while I stood there by a woman who must have been a grandma. It was not a nice place to go at all.

As a rule, I always found it easier to play in a stadium with a good atmosphere. It didn't matter how intimidating it was. It's one of the reasons why the London Stadium seems such a contrast to Upton Park. Some of the new generation of stadiums have managed to develop an atmosphere of their own: the King Power Stadium can be just as noisy and inspiring as Filbert Street. But West Ham have lost that. Upton Park was a tough place to go because it was so atmospheric. The London Stadium is a tough place to go because it isn't.

THE CONTENDERS

West Ham – Upton Park and the London Stadium

Crystal Palace, Wimbledon, Charlton – Selhurst Park

Stoke City – Bet365 Stadium

Liverpool – Anfield

Manchester United – Old Trafford

Chelsea – Stamford Bridge

Millwall – The Den

Leeds United – Elland Road

Southampton – The Dell

Sunderland – Roker Park

ALAN SHEARER

I loved the Dell. It was where it all started for me. I lived in digs half a mile from the stadium. I'd get up at 7.30am, walk to the ground and do all of the things apprentices used to do: clean the boots, the toilets and the stands. It was where I made my professional debut – a hat-trick, against Arsenal.

But I can see that opposition teams would not have found it a pleasant place to come. It was small, compact, tight. There was no natural light at all in the home dressing room. There were so many times that the manager would be going mad at half-time and one of the apprentices would quietly switch off the lights. All sorts went on in that dressing room: full-on fights, milk bottles thrown.

Elland Road was one of my favourite places to play, too: there was always a great atmosphere, and the fans are hostile and boisterous, but it was a happy hunting ground for me. I always scored there, whether it was for Southampton, Blackburn or Newcastle. It was the opposite of Highbury. I only ever scored there once. I never liked it.

The top two have to be Anfield and Old Trafford. They were tough, first and foremost, because you were always facing such a good team. The atmosphere was always special at Anfield: my Dad took me to stand on the Kop when I was 11, just because he wanted me to experience it, to hear 'You'll Never Walk Alone' before the game. I was in the crowd the night that Liverpool beat Barcelona 4-0 to reach the Champions League final, too. That is the single best atmosphere I have ever heard.

But Old Trafford edges it. Not only was it very rare that we went there and got something, I got dog's abuse off the fans every minute of every game I played there, just for turning the club down. If there was one thing I always wanted to do, it was to score a winner there with about 30 seconds to go: the sort of goal you know has to be the winner. I would have just stood there, looking at the crowd, even when play had restarted. I was that desperate to get my own back. It never happened, though.

ALAN'S LIST

1 Old Trafford

2 Anfield

3 Upton Park / London Stadium

4 Stamford Bridge

5 Roker Park

6 Selhurst Park

7 Elland Road

8 The Dell

9 The Den

10 The Bet365 Stadium

MICAH RICHARDS

You have to remember that when I came through, Manchester City weren't doing very well. We went through one patch where we didn't win at home from January until the end of the season. In that sort of team, every ground you go to is tough.

It was similar at Villa in the season we were relegated. That year, the toughest ground we played at might have been Villa Park: if we weren't winning within 20 minutes, and we quite often weren't winning within 20 minutes, the fans would turn. There were times when you would hear your name being booed when the team-sheets were being read out.

No matter how well we were doing, going to Stoke was always horrible. The stadium was so tight, the fans right on top of you, the long-ball football, the gusts of wind coming through the corners. There's a reason that the test for players coming into the Premier League, for years, was whether they could perform on a cold night in Stoke. There is no other type of night in Stoke. I once told Roberto Mancini not to play me against Stoke. I was happy to sit that one out. He wouldn't have got the best out of me.

But there was never anywhere worse to go than Anfield. As a City player, obviously, Old Trafford meant a lot: coming through the academy, they were always the target. Their youth teams seemed to be arrogant, convinced they were the best. There was plenty of pain there – if you watch the video of that famous Wayne Rooney overhead kick, you can see my face, getting ready to head it clear before he makes contact – but being part of the 6-1 made up for all of it. That was the best day of my career.

It's not like that at Anfield. I don't have a single good memory from Anfield. That tight tunnel, everyone slapping the 'This is Anfield' sign. You'd look at Steven Gerrard as you were waiting to go out and you'd be in awe of him. He'd always set the tempo, make the first tackle, and he would get away with things, too. It was the sort of place that made you feel like you had your legs on back to front.

MICAH'S LIST

1 Anfield

2 Old Trafford

3 The Bet365 Stadium

4 Stamford Bridge

5 The Den

6 Elland Road

7 Upton Park / London Stadium

8 Selhurst Park

9 Roker Park

10 The Dell

THE TOP 10

1 = Anfield

1 = Old Trafford

3 Stamford Bridge

4 Upton Park / London Stadium

5 The Bet365 Stadium

6 Elland Road

7 The Den
8 Roker Park
9 Selhurst Park
10 The Dell

Gary's Verdict: It's equal winners this week, maybe: it would be too difficult to split Anfield and Old Trafford. They both had a different sort of hostility to some of the others on the list. Maybe what made them especially intimidating was not the amount of abuse that came down the stands – with the exception of Alan at Old Trafford – but the quality of the team on the field. Not many visiting players have happy memories of either of them.

THE DEBATE

Alan: Anfield always seemed a little bit more respectful to me. They appreciated seeing a good player, even if they weren't wearing red. I even enjoyed losing there, once: the day that Blackburn won the league despite being beaten by Liverpool on the last day.

Micah: I never found that I got much respect at Anfield. I had to look some of these places up – I don't remember either Roker Park or The Dell – but none of them can have been as bad as Anfield. That was always the worst place to go. It brought me nothing but unhappiness.

4

THE TOP 10
HARD MEN

GARY LINEKER

I'm happy to admit that I wasn't a warrior. In all my years as a player, I don't think I ever hurt anyone. So in a way it's not really a surprise that I was never so much as shown a yellow card: they did not come as easily while I was playing as they do now – you could pretty much do anything. You basically had to commit grievous bodily harm to get booked. And even then, you might get away with it if it was in the first five minutes.

I did what I could to redress the balance. Every time we played that famous Arsenal back four – Tony Adams, Steve Bould, Lee Dixon and Nigel Winterburn – I would pull the referee aside in the tunnel and make sure he knew that, for the first few minutes, they would boot us all over the pitch, and that it would go on all day if he didn't clamp down on it early on. I'm not sure how well it worked, though.

Mind you, I didn't mind playing against Adams or Bould. They were big, heavy centre halves: you could hear them coming. All you had to do was make sure you jumped a little before contact, to make sure your legs were off the ground, and as a rule you were OK. It was a problem if you were rooted.

The problem was with the quick, little nasty ones, the ones who didn't give you any warning. They were much worse. I remember playing for Leicester at Anfield. Our plan was that the defenders would boot the ball up for me to chase. I was meant to stay on the shoulder, trying to use my speed. At one point, the ball didn't quite make it. It was loose in midfield, so I decided to go and get it. That was the moment Graeme Souness came steaming in, right over the top. After that, I decided that it was probably just better to let him have the ball, seeing as he wanted it so much.

Souness was an unbelievably good player, but he was brutal. And like a lot of the players on this list, I'm not sure he could exist in the modern game, not as he was. The balance has shifted so much towards attacking players that someone like him – let alone Vinnie Jones – would be just too much of a disciplinary liability. The quintessential hard man was a fixture of my career, but I think, now, it's a thing of the past.

THE CONTENDERS

Roy Keane

Patrick Vieira

Duncan Ferguson

Vinnie Jones

David Batty

Jaap Stam

Nemanja Vidić

Julian Dicks
Diego Costa
Stuart Pearce

ALAN SHEARER

It's strange for me that it is always the players who make the tackles who are described as hard, rather than the players who have to deal with them. Forwards are not, generally, talked of as being tough. But that is exactly what you have to be, to get scythed down constantly by defenders and to get up, every single time, and go through it again.

There's a difference, too, between being tough and being malicious. I started my career in an era when we were told before we went on the pitch to make sure we got the first dig in. You would always get a couple of free hits before the referee decided you'd done enough to get a yellow card, so you made use of them.

But even then, there were players who went further than most. I played against Julian Dicks a few times. Some of his tackles were designed to hurt. There was intent. Vinnie Jones did brilliantly to make so much of his career: for someone who was working as a labourer when he was 19 to go on and achieve all he did is remarkable. But some of the challenges he put in were pretty disgusting. It is the same with that famous Roy Keane tackle on Alf-Inge Håland. Is that hard? I don't know if it is.

Duncan Ferguson, though, was hard in the truest sense of the word. I played with him and I played against him. His size and his reputation meant he had this aura, this presence. When people say if looks could kill – Duncan had that. You could see the fear in the eyes of defenders as they lined up in the tunnel. People were petrified of going near him, and they were right: he had all the dark arts, but what a player he was, too. You couldn't get near him in the air. His touch was wonderful. And he was as tough as they come, frightened of nothing and of nobody. Going into a game alongside him, me and him upfront, was absolutely magnificent.

ALAN'S LIST

1 Duncan Ferguson

2 Julian Dicks

3 Roy Keane

4 Nemanja Vidić

5 Patrick Vieira

6 Stuart Pearce

7 David Batty

8 Vinnie Jones

9 Jaap Stam

10 Diego Costa

MICAH RICHARDS

First up: what is Diego Costa doing on this list? Diego Costa wasn't a hard man. Not a chance. It was all a façade. I played against him with Aston Villa. All through the first half, he was niggling away at me, so I pulled him in the tunnel at half-time.

I asked him what he thought he was doing, although maybe I didn't put it that politely. I may have made it clear that if he wanted to scrap, though I am not that way inclined, I wouldn't necessarily say no. He smiled, tried to calm me down, backed away. It was all an act. I can think of quite a few players I shared a pitch with who were much tougher than him: Kevin Nolan, Richard Dunne, Joey Barton. Tony Adams should definitely be in there ahead of him.

The way we see players is strange, though. Stuart Pearce had a reputation for being a hard man – you don't get nicknamed Psycho if you're not a psycho – but he was so good to me that it's hard for me to believe it. He was tough, don't get me wrong: if you weren't running, he would be straight into you. But he gave me my debut, gave me his support and his belief.

Patrick Vieira, on the other hand, was the nicest horrible man you could meet. I'd loved Arsenal as a kid, so when he came to Manchester City at the end of his career, I was a little bit star-struck. He could barely move at that stage, but still: it was Patrick Vieira. He arrived and he was so elegant, so intelligent, always smiling. And then we started training. He was disgusting. Raking his studs down your shins, that sort of thing. I told him, that first day, that I had gone from loving him to hating him in the space of one training session.

But Duncan Ferguson has to be the hardest of them all, I'd have said. I've got to know Roy Keane from doing television work with him, and he's perfectly nice with me. But I've seen a video of both him and Jaap Stam backing down in confrontations with Big Dunc. And if he's tough enough to scare Keane and Stam, then that's good enough for me.

MICAH'S LIST

1 Duncan Ferguson

2 Vinnie Jones

3 Jaap Stam

4 Nemanja Vidić

5 Roy Keane

6 Patrick Vieira

7 Stuart Pearce

8 David Batty

9 Julian Dicks

10 Diego Costa

THE TOP 10

1 Duncan Ferguson

2 Roy Keane

3 Nemanja Vidić

4 Vinnie Jones

5 Julian Dicks

6 Patrick Vieira

7 Jaap Stam

8 Stuart Pearce

9 David Batty

10 Diego Costa

Gary's Verdict: It's lovely seeing Duncan now, as a coach at Everton, helping to bring through the likes of Dominic Calvert-Lewin. He always seems to have a smile on his face; how passionate he is about the club shines through. It was much less pleasant seeing him on the pitch, up against you. A defender's nightmare, and a truly tough striker.

THE DEBATE

Alan: Jaap Stam wasn't a hard man, particularly, but he was an extremely good player. I can't remember getting anything from him at all. He was strong and quick and tough, but it would be unfair to characterise him as a hard man and nothing more.

Micah: He had the eyes, though. Those cold blue eyes that seemed to go right through you. He looked scary, and that's a big part of it. He was a really intimidating presence on the pitch, and the fact that he was so good, that he gave nothing away, just added to that.

5

THE TOP 10
BARGAINS

GARY LINEKER

Not every transfer bargain is a cheap one. Nobody would argue that Blackburn didn't get value for money in signing Alan Shearer: he helped them win the Premier League, scored goals by the bucketload, and ended up being sold for a massive profit. He was a bargain, but he was also, at the time, a British record fee.

What he doesn't know was that he wasn't their first choice. Long before they'd started building the team that would go on to win the league, I got a call telling me that they were interested in signing me from Spurs. I wasn't quite sure what to make of it at the time. We didn't know then that they were quite as serious in their ambitions as they turned out to be. I wondered if it was a publicity stunt.

By that stage, though, they were too late. I'd already agreed to sign for Nagoya Grampus Eight in Japan, and I didn't want to renege on the deal. Given the injury problems I had at that point in my career – I had a toe problem that stopped me playing as much as I wanted to in Japan – they probably dodged a bullet. And Shearer turned out to be a decent back-up option.

I always found being involved in transfers quite fraught. I had to go to a tribunal to finalise my move from Leicester to Everton. I only moved from Everton to Barcelona because the club accepted an offer for me: I didn't push to leave. But the most eye-opening was the auction Barcelona held to try and sell me in 1989.

It was all held at the Princess Sofia hotel, just up the road from Camp Nou. They'd invited all of the clubs who were interested in me along, so they could pitch to me on why I should choose them. Fiorentina and Monaco were there, and Tottenham dialled in on the phone. Barcelona were really keen to sell me to Genoa, though, for the very good reason that they had agreed to pay the most money.

When we got there, we found out that Genoa were late. Barcelona told me that they were flying in on a private jet, and it must have been delayed. So we spoke with Monaco and Fiorentina: the former seemed to be bullying my agent, the latter were very amiable. I had a chat with Spurs on the phone. And finally, Genoa arrived, apologising for the wait, blaming Alitalia: they hadn't been on a private jet at all.

We sat down with the chairman and the coach, and they started telling me about the team they were building. They asked if I knew Maradona; I said yes. They said they had a player who wasn't Maradona, but was just like Maradona. Then it was Van Basten: a player who wasn't Van Basten, but was just like him. It went on and on, until I turned to my agent and said: 'You know Mickey Mouse?'

All of the players in this list were more than worth the effort that goes into any transfer. Some of them, like Eric Cantona, cost a considerable sum by the standards of the time. Some of them were signed for a song. And some of them were all but pinched for nothing from clubs who didn't know what they had. But every single one of them was worth every single penny.

THE CONTENDERS

Eric Cantona (Leeds to Manchester United, 1992, £1.2m)

Seamus Coleman (Sligo Rovers to Everton, 2009, £60,000)

Paolo Di Canio (Sheffield Wednesday to West Ham, 1999, £1.5m)

Riyad Mahrez (Le Havre to Leicester, 2014, £450,000)

Lucas Radebe (Kaizer Chiefs to Leeds United, 1994, £250,000)

Andy Robertson (Hull City to Liverpool, 2017, £8m)

Peter Schmeichel (Brøndby to Manchester United, 1991, £505,000)

Kolo Touré (ASEC Mimosas to Arsenal, 2002, £150,000)

Robin van Persie (Feyenoord to Arsenal, 2004, £2.75m)

Jamie Vardy (Fleetwood Town to Leicester City, 2012, £1m)

ALAN SHEARER

I should have been on this list twice: I might have moved to Blackburn for a British record and Newcastle for a world record, but I was a bargain at both. A Premier League title for Blackburn and all those goals over all those years for Newcastle – what more do you want?

The story goes that I chose Blackburn over Manchester United, but that's not quite right. I'd been tipped off by my agent that Blackburn wanted to sign me from Southampton in 1992, and then the club got in touch to say they'd accepted a fee. I went up to the Haydock Thistle hotel for talks not just with Kenny Dalglish, the manager, but his assistant, Ray Harford, and Jack Walker, the owner whose money was transforming Blackburn into a force. It all went very well; I was impressed by all of them. I told them that I wanted to go home, speak to the family and chew it over. I asked them to give me a week to decide, and they said yes.

It was only then that Manchester United got in touch. I was flattered, of course, and I told them that I'd love to speak with them, and that I'd promised Blackburn an answer within a week. That was it; I never heard from them again. It's probably good it worked out like that for Blackburn: can you imagine what would have happened if they'd signed a crocked Gary Lineker instead?

Leaving Blackburn was a little tougher. I'd signed a new contract a month after we won the league, but I'd asked that a clause be inserted that I could leave for a set price if I ever decided to move on. Jack said there was no chance at all of that happening. He said his word meant more than a contract, and because he'd always done the right thing by me, I accepted it.

A year later, we were struggling, and I wanted to look at my options. So I went to see Jack at his magnificent house on Jersey. He said the same thing: no way are you leaving. And because I didn't have the clause in my contract, he wasn't under any pressure to sell me. There was a bit of negotiation, a bit of to and fro, and eventually he backed down. He said I could leave, but only if someone made an offer for £15 million, a world record, and they paid it all upfront. And that if it was Manchester United, it would be a little bit more.

I'm grateful to him for sticking to his word, because transfers can be a ruthless business. Everyone on every side looks after themselves: the agents, the players, the clubs, the chairmen. It's why so many of these deals are so special, and so rare. To get a player like Eric Cantona for £1.2 million, or Jamie Vardy for a million, is a steal.

ALAN'S LIST

1 Jamie Vardy

2 Eric Cantona

3 Peter Schmeichel

4 Seamus Coleman

5 Kolo Touré

6 Robin van Persie

7 Riyad Mahrez

8 Lucas Radebe

9 Andy Robertson

10 Paolo Di Canio

MICAH RICHARDS

I didn't have the best of luck with transfers. Toward the end of my time at Manchester City, my agent got in touch to say that Tottenham were interested in signing me. I knew my chances at City would be limited, so I was quite keen on the idea. City didn't agree: they didn't want to sell me to a potential rival, so they refused to negotiate.

It left me in limbo: not wanted by one club, not able to move to another. That was when Fiorentina came in. Their sporting director was a guy called Eduardo Macià, who'd worked at Liverpool. My agent let me know he was interested in taking me on loan, and I decided to do it. The medical alone took about 12 hours, though, given the state of my knee at the time, it was a bit of a miracle they signed me off.

It struck me as a mistake from the start. They'd booked me into a three-star hotel: not bad, but it didn't really give me the impression they were desperate to sign me. I was a Premier League player! I was used to the finer things in life! More worrying, nobody at the club seemed to speak English. The training ground was small, and a bit dated.

Fortunately, when we started training, Marcos Alonso was there. He's at Chelsea now, but he'd spent time at Bolton, so he spoke English. He took me under his wing, and made it his job to take me out on the town. That was the moment I felt comfortable: even if the football didn't work out, a year in Florence would be a great holiday. I was living in a beautiful flat just off the Ponte Vecchio – it belonged to Luca Toni, the Italy striker – in an amazing city. It wasn't so bad after all.

It went well enough, in fact, for the club to offer me a contract to stay on. My deal at City was expiring, and I'd obviously done something right. But I wasn't sure I wanted to commit there and then, because there might have been other options out there. And because I wouldn't sign the contract, they stopped playing me.

Fortunately, Tim Sherwood called and said he wanted me at Aston Villa, though he made the point that he wasn't signing me on my form for Fiorentina. I had, he said, been 'useless' in Italy. It was great when I arrived at Villa: I was playing well, we started brilliantly, the fans were great. But then the club sacked Sherwood, and it turned into a nightmare.

I think that's what's forgotten about every transfer: that how it works out is dependent on so many things, not just how good a player is. What makes a bargain special is that all of those things come into line unexpectedly. Liverpool picked up Andy Robertson from Hull for a tiny fee in today's market, and it all slotted into place perfectly. Leicester found Riyad Mahrez, this player with a perfect touch, for almost nothing. And more than anyone else, Eric Cantona was the icon Manchester United needed at the time, and all for £1.2 million.

MICAH'S LIST

1 Eric Cantona

2 Jamie Vardy

3 Peter Schmeichel

4 Kolo Touré

5 Robin van Persie

6 Riyad Mahrez

7 Paolo Di Canio

8 Lucas Radebe

9 Seamus Coleman

10 Andy Robertson

THE TOP 10

1 Jamie Vardy

2 Eric Cantona

3 Peter Schmeichel

4 Kolo Touré

5 Robin van Persie

6 Seamus Coleman

7 Riyad Mahrez

8 Lucas Radebe

9 Paolo Di Canio

10 Andy Robertson

Gary's Verdict: You know what I'm going to say. Eric Cantona cost £1.2 million and that, in 1992, was quite a lot of money. He was worth far more, obviously, and he changed Manchester United's history, but I can only put him second. Jamie Vardy plays in the same position as me, and for the club I support. I'm biased, but I don't care. He cost a million pounds and he helped Leicester win the Premier League. That's more than enough in my book.

THE DEBATE

Alan: Eric Cantona was arrogant, but he more than warranted it. I don't think you can overlook what an incredible story Jamie Vardy is. To come from non-league football to be one of the best in the world is phenomenal. It's one thing getting there, but staying there is another. Everyone knows his game, but there's not many able to stop him. It gives hope to every player at that level.

Micah: I'm tempted to say Vardy because he's my era, he's a player I played against, and his rise has been astonishing, but come on: it's got to be Cantona. I grew up in Leeds, and everyone hated Cantona for leaving, and especially for leaving for Manchester United. And yes, way back when, £1.2 million was quite a lot of money. But look what it bought them: an icon.

6

THE TOP 10
CULT HEROES

GARY LINEKER

It's not always the players who win the most who are the most beloved. Sometimes, it's not even the most talented players. Fans are drawn, I think, to players with the most personality. And I'm not sure there has ever been a player with quite as large a personality as Paul Gascoigne.

Gazza was a wonderful player, obviously. He had breathtaking talent. The game came so naturally, so easily to him. But what I remember most of him, from our time together with both England and Tottenham, is that when he was around not a day would go by without something ludicrous happening. He might never have stayed at a club for a long time, but he always left his mark.

There are countless stories I could tell about him: enough to fill a book on their own. He loved nothing more than crossing the line. After he got his first England call-up, he joined up with the squad and we were all taken off for a golf day. There was a dinner afterwards. They tended to be quite stuffy affairs, a meal followed by an address from the chairman of the course we'd just played.

That night, it followed the same pattern: we were all sitting around, the chairman stood up and did about 10 minutes. We clapped politely and were getting ready to leave when Gazza suddenly stood up and started telling jokes and stories. He basically did a 40-minute stand-up comedy set, off the cuff, on his first day in the England squad. He'd get his words a bit muddled, but that just added to the effect. I looked at Bryan Robson and could see him thinking: 'Who on Earth is this fat Geordie kid?' That was Gazza.

At Spurs, we used to have a really dedicated fan, John, who came to the training ground every day, volunteering to do little jobs for the players. The lads were terrible to him, making him do all sorts, but he genuinely seemed happy to do it. We were all waiting for the bus to arrive to travel for an away game, when Gazza appeared. He'd bought his dad a camper van, and he'd parked it up at the training ground.

He walked off, and came back with a parking cone. He shimmied up to the roof of the van, and left the cone there. He went and got in the driving seat, wound his window down and called John over, with this look of mock horror on his face, and told him that someone had left a cone on his van. Could he just nip up and get it?

John was happy to oblige, and duly started climbing up to retrieve it. At that point, Gazza turned the engine on, and started driving around the car park, with John clinging on to the top of the van. It was like something out of a cartoon. It was at that moment that Terry Venables, the manager, came out of his office. He took one look at what was going on and said: 'I don't want to be seeing this, do I?' He turned around, and walked back inside.

THE CONTENDERS

Faustino Asprilla (Newcastle United)

Mario Balotelli (Manchester City)

Eric Cantona (Manchester United)

Paolo Di Canio (West Ham)

Paul Gascoigne (Tottenham Hotspur)

David Ginola (Newcastle United)

Matt Le Tissier (Southampton)

Jay-Jay Okocha (Bolton)

Ole-Gunnar Solskjær (Manchester United)

Chris Waddle (Sheffield Wednesday)

ALAN SHEARER

I have my share of Gazza stories, too. There was a day when Robbie Williams was introduced to the England squad and Gazza just kept punching him in the arm, over and over again, saying, 'Take that, take that,' with this enormous grin on his face, like he'd come up with the best joke in the world.

I only saw him every couple of months, when we met up with England, and that was absolutely fine for me. Everyone has great memories of him everywhere he played, but he must have been a bit of a nightmare to have around every day and every week at your club.

These are all players who were and are revered by their fans. Matt Le Tissier earned that status because of his loyalty to Southampton over all of those years. He had choices to go, at times, and he had the natural ability to play for whoever he wanted, but he loved the club and he loved the area. That means something to supporters.

Some, though, burn much more briefly but no less brightly. They just spark something in the fans. There was a touch of that about Tino Asprilla, when he arrived at Newcastle. He was a brilliant player, and a real bonus for the dressing room. The players loved him as much as the fans did. He was, if this makes sense, a nice lunatic. He loved laughing and joking, even though he never spoke much English. He could take it, as well as give it. We were the last to leave training one day – it must have been in late March – and I told him as he left to remember that the clocks went back the next day, rather than forwards. He nodded, said thanks, and went off.

The next morning, obviously, he turned up two hours late for training. He arrived, saw that everyone was just finishing training before he'd even started, and just kept on walking, cursing at me for the trick. He had that same sense of fun when he played, all arms and legs and bright ideas, and the fans at Newcastle loved him for it, even if he did not stay for long, and even if he never quite got used to the weather.

ALAN'S LIST

1 Eric Cantona (Manchester United)

2 Matt Le Tissier (Southampton)

3 Paul Gascoigne (Tottenham Hotspur)

4 Ole-Gunnar Solskjær (Manchester United)

5 Paolo Di Canio (West Ham)

6 Jay-Jay Okocha (Bolton)

7 Mario Balotelli (Manchester City)

8 Chris Waddle (Sheffield Wednesday)

9 David Ginola (Newcastle United)

10 Faustino Asprilla (Newcastle United)

MICAH RICHARDS

If a cult hero is a player with character, a player with personality, a player that you can't take your eyes off even if they're not the most talented or the most effective or the most reliable, then I am flabbergasted I am not on this list. I tick all of those boxes.

There are a couple of players who I could throw in, too. Gabby Agbonlahor was adored at Aston Villa, a boyhood fan who played for and captained the club. He represented the fans on the pitch; he had that special bond with the crowd. Pablo Zabaleta, at Manchester City, was the other sort of cult hero. He may not have been a City fan as a child, but the way he worked, the effort he put in, meant that the fans could see themselves in him a little, too. He played for City the way they would play for City.

Mario Balotelli is a different case entirely. He was crazy, in a good way, and he was brilliant to have around, but we should also remember that he was very young when he came to Manchester. I was only a couple of years older than him, but at that stage in my career I would have found it hard to move to another city, another country, with all of the pressure he was under.

It was understandable that he struggled at the start. Things improved after his brother came to join him in England; that helped him settle down, and start to play well. But even then there were certain things that only Mario would do. He was always, always late, for a start. His timekeeping was atrocious. As his teammates, we should have been furious, but after a while we realised it was better for us if he was late. He got fined every time, and the fines were £5,000 or £10,000. It all went into a kitty, either for charity or the

Christmas party. He could turn up at whatever time he liked, as far as we were concerned.

And then, of course, there were the fireworks: he did about £40,000 worth of damage to the house he was renting because he had been setting rockets off inside. That was the time there was a fire but, if I'm honest, I'm not sure it was the first time he had done it.

Even the fire didn't stop him, though. After that had happened, he turned up at my house, fireworks in hand, lit them, and started chasing me around the house. I couldn't believe it. I was genuinely scared. It was a completely bizarre situation. There were a lot of those with Mario, but we loved him for it. People still ask me about him. That says a lot: he only ever assisted one goal, as far as I can remember – the one that won the league – but fans are still fascinated by him.

MICAH'S LIST

1 Mario Balotelli (Manchester City)

2 Eric Cantona (Manchester United)

3 Paul Gascoigne (Tottenham Hotspur)

4 Paolo Di Canio (West Ham)

5 Ole-Gunnar Solskjær (Manchester United)

6 David Ginola (Newcastle United)

7 Jay-Jay Okocha (Bolton)

8 Matt Le Tissier (Southampton)

9 Chris Waddle (Sheffield Wednesday)

10 Faustino Asprilla (Newcastle United)

THE TOP 10

1 Eric Cantona (Manchester United)

2 Paul Gascoigne (Tottenham Hotspur)

3 Mario Balotelli (Manchester City)

4 Paolo Di Canio (West Ham)

5 Ole-Gunnar Solskjær (Manchester United)

6 Matt Le Tissier (Southampton)

7 Jay-Jay Okocha (Bolton)

8 David Ginola (Newcastle United)

9 Chris Waddle (Sheffield Wednesday)

10 Faustino Asprilla (Newcastle United)

Gary's Verdict: It feels like there is less place for players like these in the modern game; images are too tightly managed for us to get a feel for their personalities. Nobody had more personality than Gazza, but Cantona definitely came close. The press conference where he talked about the seagulls following the trawler was completely baffling, but completely compelling.

THE DEBATE

Alan: There's no question that Eric Cantona was a little bit bonkers. If you're the sort of player who is going to jump feet first into the crowd, then you have to be a little bit different: that's probably the nice way of putting it. But he was also the leader for that Manchester United team, and he was the player who changed the club, and the face of the Premier League.

Micah: A lot of these are a little before my time, to be honest, so I had to go for Mario: he is the biggest personality I encountered during my career. Who else would think up the 'Why Always Me?' T-shirt he had prepared for the Manchester derby?

7

THE TOP 10
GREAT ESCAPES

GARY LINEKER

Nothing quite illustrates how important confidence is in football than the sight of a team, useless for most of the season, suddenly recording win after win to give itself an unexpected chance of survival. A really great escape can almost seem like a form of magic, leaving you scratching your head and wondering how, exactly, they've managed to do it.

I was relegated as a youngster at Leicester – though I barely played – and came reasonably close a few years later, in my final season with them. But it was only as a fan, when they came so close to going down in 2015, that I fully appreciated how much of a miracle escaping the drop can be.

With just a few games to go that season, they were done. They hadn't played especially badly, and in some ways it would have felt harsh for them to go down, but it looked absolutely certain. And then, all of a sudden, something clicked. They won one game, and then they won another. From nowhere, instead of looking like they couldn't get a point, they looked like they couldn't lose.

How that form suddenly appears is, largely, down to confidence. That first win changes something in you, both as an individual and as a team, and the second one cements it. It can feel like you're playing a different game. Of course, what made Leicester's story all the more special was where that form carried them: they won the title the next year, in no small part because of the confidence and the momentum they'd developed as a group under Nigel Pearson.

Watching it from the outside, as a fan, I realised how special it is. Being in the Premier League means everything to a club: both in terms of the finances on offer and the status it affords you.

It is not necessarily because you hope you can win it, but because it is the biggest show in town. It gives your team a chance to take on the big boys every year, to see if you can claim a scalp or two, to see how much you can grow. No team embodies any of that better than Leicester, and Leicester could not have done it had they not pulled off that great escape.

THE CONTENDERS

Everton (1994)

Bradford City (2000)

West Bromwich Albion (2005)

Portsmouth (2006)

West Ham United (2007)

Fulham (2008)

Wigan (2012)

Leicester (2015)
Sunderland (2016)
Aston Villa (2020)

ALAN SHEARER

It is a damn sight easier playing at the top of the table than at the bottom, I can assure you of that. As a player, I did not have a vast amount of experience of relegation battles, but I walked into one as a manager, when I agreed to take over at Newcastle on – wait for it – April Fool's Day in 2009.

There is always pressure in football. You get used to it, to some extent. But while the pressure at the top can be enjoyable – the stress of being so close to achieving your ambitions or fulfilling your dreams – it is different when you're fighting for survival. You know, as a player or as a manager, that people's livelihoods depend on you. There are real-world effects when a team is relegated. People lose their jobs. That is a tremendous responsibility to have.

The last day of that season was horrific. We needed a point at Aston Villa to try to stay up. I remember not sleeping at all the night before. I was the fourth manager Newcastle had had that season, but I felt responsible for what happened. I did not want to let anyone, or the club I had always supported, down.

But the difference between a player and a manager is that you feel, when you're out on the pitch, that you can do something. You can have an impact on the game. You can make something happen.

The manager does not quite have that power, at least once the whistle has blown. As soon as they are out on that pitch, you're relying on the players to help you out.

It did not end happily: we lost 1-0, and we were relegated. We had tried, but ultimately we weren't good enough, and it hurt. It hurt a lot.

Despite that, I don't regret taking the job. I loved the intensity of it, having to make all of those decisions, and I would never have forgiven myself for not trying to help.

There are things I regret, of course, things I would do differently if I had my time again. I was too concerned with trying to make the players understand what the club meant, too keen to impose the sort of discipline that I had been given during my career. It was the sort of club where the players were in charge. They were always late for training. They didn't give the impression of caring about Newcastle, and I wanted to change that, to make the atmosphere more professional.

In hindsight, perhaps I should have gone in to have a laugh and a joke, to try to lift spirits, to try to keep the mood light and morale high. Maybe that would have worked better. That's why, I imagine, so many teams down there tend to look for managers who have been through it all before, who know what works and what doesn't.

Teams in the mire need the experience of Roy Hodgson, who rescued Fulham, or Alan Curbishley, who got a brilliant run of form out of West Ham in 2007: they won seven of their last nine games and stayed up by winning at Old Trafford on the last day. You need someone who knows what makes a club tick and a team work.

ALAN'S LIST

1 Everton (1994)

2 Aston Villa (2020)

3 West Ham United (2007)

4 Sunderland (2016)

5 Leicester (2015)

6 Wigan (2012)

7 Fulham (2008)

8 Portsmouth (2006)

9 Bradford City (2000)

10 West Bromwich Albion (2005)

MICAH RICHARDS

As a rule, I try not to criticise managers. They do a job that I couldn't. Most of the managers I have worked with have taught me something, or improved me, or had some sort of plan in mind. Even if it didn't work, I could see what they were trying to do. But there is an exception, and that exception is Rémi Garde.

When I signed for Aston Villa, the club had promised me they had plenty of ambition. They were going to build a team around me, Fabian Delph and Gabby Agbonlahor; they were keen to bring in other signings, too. As soon as I arrived, Fabian left: that, maybe, should have been my first warning.

But we started quite well, under Tim Sherwood. I was co-captain with Gabby and, even though my knee was a bit borderline, we were doing fine. Tim was great with me, but it all turned as soon as he got sacked, and Rémi came in. I don't say this lightly, but he brought absolutely nothing to the club.

He ran sessions on controlling the ball: something that, as a Premier League player, even I did not really need to learn. He was awful in the dressing room. Cliques developed, and the squad spirit that had developed under Tim disappeared. Our performances nosedived. I will take my share of the blame – the team was awful, but I was shambolic – but it was a disastrous appointment. We stood a chance of staying up with Tim, but none at all with Rémi in charge.

The consequences were huge. There were pay cuts for the players, but much more importantly, there were staff members who lost their jobs. That's what hurts the most: knowing that you have let those people down.

Team spirit counts for a lot in relegation battles. The teams that pull off a miracle and stay up against all the odds tend to be the ones that are fighting for each other, that understand what it means, that aren't starting to think about themselves. Leicester are the best example of that: they were bottom with ten games to go in 2014, and I think everyone assumed they were finished.

But Nigel Pearson had all his players behind them, and they went on a run that was barely believable. They won seven of their last nine games. In the end, they finished 14th, which makes it look a bit like they were never going to be relegated at all. In truth, they survived by the skin of their teeth: the greatest escape act in Premier League history, and it is only made better by what they went on to do the following season. That's how powerful a great team spirit can be. If you don't have it, you're sunk, and that year at Villa, we definitely did not have it.

MICAH'S LIST

1 Leicester (2015)

2 West Ham United (2007)

3 West Bromwich Albion (2005)

4 Aston Villa (2020)

5 Portsmouth (2006)

6 Everton (1994)

7 Wigan (2012)

8 Sunderland (2016)

9 Fulham (2008)

10 Bradford City (2000)

THE TOP 10

1 West Ham United (2007)

2 Leicester (2015)

3 Aston Villa (2020)

4 Everton (1994)

5 Sunderland (2016)

6 Wigan (2012)

7 Portsmouth (2006)

8 West Bromwich Albion (2005)

9 Fulham (2008)

10 Bradford City (2000)

Gary's Verdict: West Ham's controversial survival, the one inspired by Carlos Tevez, sneaks in to take it, but it will not be a surprise that

I'd say Leicester is the greatest escape of all. They were almost certain to go down that year. They changed their manager in the summer. And still they went on to win the title the following season. I'm not sure anyone can match that.

THE DEBATE

Alan: A lot of these great escapes have led to a lot of controversy. Everton's survival in 1994 – on the last day of the season, facing their first relegation since the 1940s – prompted a major scandal, and there was a court case from Sheffield United after West Ham stayed up.

Micah: I was delighted when Wigan stayed up in 2012: I liked Roberto Martínez a lot, though I think sometimes he overthought things. Roy Hodgson did brilliantly to keep Fulham up, but my experience of him wasn't brilliant: he did not even call me to tell me I wasn't being taken to Euro 2012 with England, after the best season of my career. He got Stuart Pearce to do it. I lost a bit of respect for him after that.

THE TOP 10
MAGICIANS

GARY LINEKER

As a fan, often the players you love most are the ones who can conjure something out of nothing. They are the mercurial talents who can produce a little piece of wonder at any given moment, the ones who seem to be able to turn or settle a game all by themselves.

The same is true of players, obviously. You always want that sort of player on your team, particularly as a striker: someone who can spot a pass or see a gap or find a space that nobody else would spot. But it comes at a price, because it is often the players with the most talent who are the most frustrating to play alongside.

The problem, I think, is that they are playing, ultimately, for fun. They are so good, so gifted, the game comes so easily to them, that they still have that enjoyment of playing we all had as kids. They play to entertain themselves. The professional game is their playground, and they retain a bit of that spirit. And it is here we come, once again, to Gazza.

There were times when Gazza would do things on the pitch that would leave you staring, open-mouthed, with wonder. His talent could leave you speechless. You knew, even at the time, that you were playing in the same team as genuine, timeless brilliance.

And yet we also had so many arguments because, as a striker, I wanted service so that I could score goals. Gazza was more than capable of providing better service than almost anybody else. But often, it never arrived, because he simply would not give you the ball. He was having too much fun keeping it to himself.

Actually, that's not quite true. There were plenty of times when Gazza would dance past three or four players and then lose it to a fifth – all while you were standing there, screaming at him, in acres of space – but there were two specific circumstances in which Gazza could be relied on to pass the ball. The first was when he was tired. And the second was when you were under so much pressure that you basically had no choice but to give it back to him. That is how good he was. He saw all of these elite players around him as little more than walls.

He is not alone in that. Thierry Henry said the same thing was true of Zinedine Zidane, probably the best player of his generation. Henry's memories of Zidane echoed mine of Gazza. You were delighted to call him a teammate. He had all the talent in the world. He could do anything he wanted. But you just wished what he wanted to do was pass the ball a bit more often.

THE CONTENDERS

Dimitar Berbatov (Fulham, Tottenham, Manchester United)

Dennis Bergkamp (Arsenal)

Eric Cantona (Manchester United)

Philippe Coutinho (Liverpool)
Paolo Di Canio (Sheffield Wednesday, Charlton, West Ham)
Georgi Kinkladze (Manchester City)
Matt Le Tissier (Southampton)
Riyad Mahrez (Leicester City, Manchester City)
David Silva (Manchester City)
Gianfranco Zola (Chelsea)

ALAN SHEARER

All players work hard at their technique, to make sure their touch is as good as it can be, but trust me: it comes a lot easier to some players than others. I played five-a-side with Gianfranco Zola not too long ago, and a while after he retired. Even after all that time, it all came ridiculously easy to him.

Zola had to be special, of course, because he wasn't the biggest. He still isn't. But he was incredibly strong, and he had that low centre of gravity that let him twist and turn his way out of blind alleys and dead ends. His legs were something else: his thighs weren't quite at Micah's level, but they weren't far off. For a small man, he could hold his own.

At least Zola had that scurrying, busy style, though. Others do not even have to look like they're trying. Dimitar Berbatov reminded me of Matt Le Tissier in that way: he was so laid back, there was almost an arrogance to him, at least on the pitch. You could not quite tell how bothered he was by what he was doing. He had an effortlessness about him, a natural balance that meant his control was flawless.

That shouldn't be taken for granted. Controlling a ball is hard, especially when it's fired at you at top speed and you're surrounded by defenders, all of them nibbling and jostling and occasionally kicking you. Some players make it look easy. But some genuinely do seem to find it easy. Berbatov was one of those who had that nonchalant air, and so was Le Tissier. He gave the impression that tomorrow was coming, and that there was nothing whatsoever he could do about it, so he might as well enjoy himself. He played with that attitude, and he had all the talent he needed to back it up. He never got stressed, never got worried. He made it look like he wasn't really trying, and that was what made him special.

ALAN'S LIST

1 Dennis Bergkamp (Arsenal)

2 Matt Le Tissier (Southampton)

3 David Silva (Manchester City)

4 Eric Cantona (Manchester United)

5 Gianfranco Zola (Chelsea)

6 Riyad Mahrez (Leicester City, Manchester City)

7 Dimitar Berbatov (Fulham, Tottenham, Manchester United)

8 Paolo Di Canio (Sheffield Wednesday, Charlton, West Ham)

9 Georgi Kinkladze (Manchester City)

10 Philippe Coutinho (Liverpool)

MICAH RICHARDS

Dimitar Berbatov is the only player I could never get anywhere near. I could never quite work out why that was. He wasn't especially quick. He wasn't especially strong. He wasn't the greatest in the air. But he was just untouchable. He had this ability to get his body in between you and the ball, and stop whatever it was you were trying to do.

There was a game against Spurs where I thought I had him as we waited for a long ball. I'd blocked him off; he couldn't move. And then there was little movement – I couldn't tell you exactly what he did, because I had no idea at the time – and he pulled the ball out of the sky with the silkiest piece of control you can imagine. At times, even as a defender, you just have to stand back and applaud.

But you also have to learn, because players like that can make you look very silly. So, to some extent, you start to cheat. Because you don't want to be exposed, you let him have the ball. You don't go and compete for it with him. And if you can, you pass him on to the midfielder. In my case, that was Nigel De Jong: he was our enforcer, so it was his job to help the defence out. Whenever we came up against Berbatov, I made it clear to him that dealing with Berbatov was his problem. I spent most of the game just shouting 'Nigel, Nigel', and pointing at the Bulgarian. Anything to make sure someone else had to deal with him.

Philippe Coutinho has to be on this list too, you know. We played against him in a pre-season game when he was with Inter Milan. He looked tiny, but straightaway you knew you were dealing with something special. He could kill the ball instantly. As soon as you see that, your first thought is: OK, who's this guy?

The rule, as a player, is you look at the boots. Quick players prefer different types of boots to wingers who want to whip crosses in. The main thing, though, is that the more colourful the boots are, the more talented the player is. If you're wearing pink or red, you have to know that you're a player.

I looked at Coutinho's boots that day, almost to see what type of player he thought he was, and they were some lurid colour, as bright as you can imagine. That's when you know you're dealing with someone special.

MICAH'S LIST

1 Dennis Bergkamp (Arsenal)

2 David Silva (Manchester City)

3 Eric Cantona (Manchester United)

4 Gianfranco Zola (Chelsea)

5 Dimitar Berbatov (Fulham, Tottenham, Manchester United)

6 Georgi Kinkladze (Manchester City)

7 Matt Le Tissier (Southampton)

8 Paolo Di Canio (Sheffield Wednesday, Charlton, West Ham)

9 Riyad Mahrez (Leicester City, Manchester City)

10 Philippe Coutinho (Liverpool)

THE TOP 10

1 Dennis Bergkamp (Arsenal)

2 David Silva (Manchester City)

3 Eric Cantona (Manchester United)

4 Gianfranco Zola (Chelsea)

5 Matt Le Tissier (Southampton)

6 Dimitar Berbatov (Fulham, Tottenham, Manchester United)

7 Riyad Mahrez (Leicester City, Manchester City)

8 Paolo Di Canio (Sheffield Wednesday, Charlton, West Ham)

9 Georgi Kinkladze (Manchester City)

10 Philippe Coutinho (Liverpool)

Gary's Verdict: Maybe what made Dennis Bergkamp stand out so much was that he was just as talented, just as magical as all of the players on this list, but he made the right decisions. It's fascinating that Thierry Henry found Zidane frustrating, but referred to Bergkamp as the perfect teammate. That's high enough praise for me.

THE DEBATE

Alan: Eric Cantona did not care a bit about who or what you were. He was the ultimate maverick, with his collar up and that deliberate arrogance about him. But I'd say he only produced those unexpected pieces of magic on and off: he was not quite as consistent with it as Bergkamp. You could rely on Bergkamp to do something special, almost every game.

Micah: David Silva was just like that, too. He was not quite as flashy as someone like Cantona or Paolo Di Canio: he was a very quiet genius, at least on the pitch. He was quite a modern magician in that way: I'm not sure the systems most teams play now have room for a true maverick. But he saw things that other people didn't see, and that made the difference.

9

THE TOP 10
BRAZILIANS

GARY LINEKER

The Brazil teams I played against were not filled with the sorts of names that echo through history. It was just after the era of Zico and Socrates and Falcao, long after Pelé and Jairzinho and Rivellino, and before the likes of Ronaldo, Rivaldo and Ronaldinho came along. I'm not, after all, quite as old as Micah thinks I am.

They still had some fine players, though: they went on to win the World Cup in 1994, so it's not like they were bad teams. I played them three times, in a relatively short space of time, all of the games at Wembley. I scored in two of them. I also missed a penalty in one, with a shot so weak that the goalkeeper almost had to walk out and meet it, but let's not dwell on that.

In fact, I managed to score in one while wearing somebody else's boots. Not even another player: the manager's. I was having some problems with the boots that my sponsors at the time had provided, and so I asked around in the dressing room to see if anyone had any going spare. The closest match to my shoe size was Bobby Robson, and so he was kind enough to lend me a pair. They were a size too big, but they had to do. It would be great to think I scored with one of his boots, but not quite: it was a diving header, so I only managed to score against Brazil in a pair of his boots.

No matter who is in the Brazil side, there is always something special about seeing those yellow shirts: it is, by some distance, the greatest, most iconic kit in football. It conjures up images of samba style and wondrous, inventive players, so it's interesting that so many of the Brazilian imports who have lit up the Premier League over the last few years have been a little bit more defensive.

We have had our fair share of magicians, of course: Philippe Coutinho scored some wonderful goals for Liverpool, while Roberto Firmino – though maybe not quite so spectacular – goes about helping Mohamed Salah and Sadio Mané to shine with a real joy.

But the most successful Brazilians in England have been the ones, like Fernandinho and even David Luiz, who showcase the other side to the Brazilian game: the one that wants to win at all costs, that is not afraid to do the less glamorous elements of the job, that understands that ultimately, football is only fun if you don't lose.

THE CONTENDERS

Philippe Coutinho (Liverpool)

Edu (Arsenal)

Elano (Manchester City)

Fernandinho (Manchester City)

Roberto Firmino (Liverpool)

Gabriel Jesus (Manchester City)

Juninho Paulista (Middlesbrough)

David Luiz (Chelsea, Arsenal)

Gilberto Silva (Arsenal)

Willian (Chelsea, Arsenal)

ALAN SHEARER

The first Brazilian I saw playing in England is not on this list. Partly that is because he came over here before the start of the Premier League, but partly it is because he never really made that much of an impact. Not nationally, anyway. He was called Mirandinha, and he signed for Newcastle in the late 1980s. I'm not sure how good he was, really, but just the fact that there was a Brazilian, with all of the glamour that brings, playing at St James's Park was enough to make him a crowd favourite.

The first Brazilian that really made an impact here was also in the North East: Juninho, at Middlesbrough. It is hard enough to get any player to move up there – Kevin Keegan had to tell Rob Lee that Newcastle was closer to London than Middlesbrough to get him to sign for us – but to get a Brazilian at Middlesbrough? It was unthinkable.

They loved him, though. He was just this scrawny, baby-faced kid who had moved across with quite a lot of his family, but he had the most incredible ability, and he seemed to enjoy himself so much. They got relegated at the end of that season, leaving him in tears on the pitch at Elland Road, but he always had a place in their hearts. There hadn't been many players in England at all at that stage who had his skill and his technical ability, and there certainly hadn't been many at Middlesbrough. They admired him for that as much as where he'd come from.

David Luiz has been in England for far longer than Juninho ever was, but I still don't know if a lot of people know quite what to make of him. He's had incredible success – he's played for Chelsea and Arsenal, as well as Paris Saint-Germain – and all of his clubs have paid a lot of money to sign him. That is because of his ability on the ball: there are not many who can play like him, even now.

But there have always been question marks over how good he is as a defender. He always seems to have a mistake in him; he is the sort of player who gives forwards a bit of hope, and when you have a bit of hope, you always have a chance. I know I would have loved to have played against him, rather than the likes of Tony Adams and Gary Pallister, centre backs who barely ever made a mistake. They could play, too, but at heart they were real defenders, and I'm not sure you can say the same of David Luiz.

ALAN'S LIST

1 Fernandinho (Manchester City)
2 Gilberto Silva (Arsenal)
3 Juninho Paulista (Middlesbrough)
4 David Luiz (Chelsea, Arsenal)
5 Roberto Firmino (Liverpool)
6 Willian (Chelsea, Arsenal)
7 Gabriel Jesus (Manchester City)
8 Philippe Coutinho (Liverpool)
9 Edu (Arsenal)
10 Elano (Manchester City)

MICAH RICHARDS

If only Elano had signed for Manchester City a couple of years later than he did, this list would look very different. He had better technique than almost anyone else I played with. He could strike the ball so sweetly. He could control it so easily. He could drift past players as though they weren't there. Elano was a genius, the sort of player that only Brazil, really, produces.

But he did not arrive in the era of Yaya Touré and David Silva, when City's team was full of players who would have been able to make him shine. He came along not under Abu Dhabi but under Thaksin Shinawatra, into a team that was still very much a mismatch. We had some brilliantly talented young players – Stephen Ireland; Michael Johnson, a young right-back with the world at his feet – but we didn't have the squad to get the most out of Elano. But I'm sure he was as good as if not better than a lot of players who have had more success in the Premier League.

David Luiz has stayed in England far longer than he did, and he's won more than enough trophies to be taken seriously, but I think his main flaw is that he wants to be the star. He wants to define and dictate games. As a defender, that is not your job. When I played at centre back, I would, very occasionally, go off on these long runs deep into the opposition half: there was one goal, scored by Benjani, that came from me bursting past three or four players with the ball at my feet. I shot, the goalkeeper saved it, and he tapped in the rebound. It was the greatest goal I never scored.

But it's not a moment I'm especially proud of, because that was me thinking about what was best for me, not what was best for the team. What would have happened if I'd lost the ball, and we'd been a man short at the back?

Even as an experienced defender, David Luiz still doesn't think like that often enough. He has everything: he is strong, quick, a great reader of the game. He takes a great free-kick. There are times when he is too relaxed, because of his talent, and his concentration slips occasionally. But his biggest problem has always been that he wants to affect the game. The great defenders don't think like that. John Terry, his old partner at Chelsea, was happy organising his defence, keeping things tight, controlling space, doing his job. David Luiz is not content with that. His inability to hold back is, in the end, what has always held him back.

MICAH'S LIST

1 Fernandinho (Manchester City)

2 Philippe Coutinho (Liverpool)

3 Gilberto Silva (Arsenal)

4 David Luiz (Chelsea, Arsenal)

5 Roberto Firmino (Liverpool)

6 Juninho Paulista (Middlesbrough)

7 Gabriel Jesus (Manchester City)

8 Willian (Chelsea, Arsenal)

9 Elano (Manchester City)

10 Edu (Arsenal)

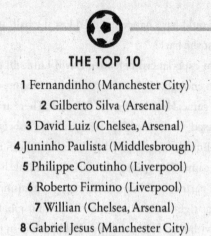

THE TOP 10

1 Fernandinho (Manchester City)

2 Gilberto Silva (Arsenal)

3 David Luiz (Chelsea, Arsenal)

4 Juninho Paulista (Middlesbrough)

5 Philippe Coutinho (Liverpool)

6 Roberto Firmino (Liverpool)

7 Willian (Chelsea, Arsenal)

8 Gabriel Jesus (Manchester City)

9 Edu (Arsenal)

10 Elano (Manchester City)

Gary's Verdict: What makes Fernandinho the Premier League's greatest ever Brazilian is his consistency. We always think of Brazilians as the most technically accomplished players, and he fits that bill – he is a brilliant passer of the ball – but maybe not in the way traditionally associated with Brazilians. We expect samba style. Fernandinho is, more often than not, the one beating the drum.

THE DEBATE

Alan: Coutinho might have been higher up this list if he had stayed at Liverpool for longer. As it was, I wonder if the Premier League only had a couple of years of him at his peak. It was after he left that Jürgen Klopp guided them to the Champions League and the Premier League, too, and Liverpool really hit their stride.

Micah: We had another Brazilian at Manchester City: Geovanni. He'd played for Barcelona, and I was waiting and waiting for him to show me a little bit of that magic. He never did. The best Brazilian imports have been more defensive players: Fernandinho, Gilberto Silva, David Luiz. But Coutinho is probably the most talented attacking Brazilian import we've had.

10

THE TOP 10
TRANSFERS THAT NEVER HAPPENED

GARY LINEKER

As soon as Terry Venables, the manager who had brought me to Barcelona, was fired, I assumed it wouldn't be long before I followed him out of the door. I was not unhappy, particularly, but that is how football tends to work. A new coach does not want to work with the players bought for his predecessor.

Inter Milan were the first team to get in touch. Serie A was the dominant league back then: if they didn't play for Real Madrid or Barcelona, all of the game's stars played in Italy. That was where all of the money, and therefore all of the glamour, was. Even by those standards, Inter stood out. They had a legendary coach, Giovanni Trapattoni, and two of the key parts of the team that would win the World Cup for West Germany in 1990: Lothar Matthäus and Andreas Brehme.

That was enough to sell me on the idea. I flew to Frankfurt for a surreptitious meeting with Trapattoni. He had brought souvenirs to try to persuade me: badges, scarves, an Inter shirt. He explained how keen he was to sign me. I was on board.

There was just one problem. Contrary to all my expectations, Barcelona did not want to sell me. Terry had gone, but they were not budging. It was flattering, of course, to feel wanted, but it was also proof of how fickle football is. The fact I might have liked to sign for Inter did not matter at all. The club wanted to keep me, so that was that. A year or so later, when Barcelona had changed their mind and they held an auction for me in a hotel not far from Camp Nou, nobody really seemed to be concerned with whether I might like to stay or not. Clubs are quick to demand loyalty from their players. They are not always quite so keen to show it to them.

Most players will have a story like that: a transfer that did not quite come off, one that might have changed the course of their careers. For me, Inter will always feel a little bit like the one that got away.

Inter probably do not feel the same. They did just fine without me: they signed Jürgen Klinsmann instead, not a bad second choice, and won three Serie A titles. But it does not always work out like that. There are plenty of transfers that almost happened that have far greater consequences, and a few deals that never quite came off that might have made football look very different indeed.

THE CONTENDERS

Eric Cantona ... to Sheffield Wednesday
Paul Gascoigne ... to Manchester United
Steven Gerrard ... to Chelsea
Kaká ... to Manchester City

Robinho . . . to Chelsea
Roy Keane . . . to Blackburn Rovers
Robert Lewandowski . . . to Blackburn Rovers
Cristiano Ronaldo . . . to Arsenal
Alan Shearer . . . to Manchester United
Zinedine Zidane . . . to Blackburn Rovers

ALAN SHEARER

I was eating dinner with Kenny Dalglish and his wife, Marina, when he got the call. When we sat down at the table, he had been confident that he was about to pull off a deal to sign the most coveted midfielder in English football. It would cost him – or, rather, it would cost Jack Walker – a record fee, but it would be worth it. He was the sort of player who Kenny could build a team around, and he said it was 95 per cent done.

Then the call came and, all of a sudden, the wine was corked. Roy Keane would not be signing for Blackburn. He had chosen to go to Manchester United instead. Kenny was fuming. Sir Alex Ferguson had obviously got to Roy, sold him on the size of the club, persuaded him to change his mind. Keane would have been awesome for Blackburn. And, crucially, without him, Manchester United would have been just a little less awesome.

Whether Blackburn ever came quite that close to signing Zinedine Zidane, I don't know. What I am sure of is that, as players, we were expecting it. The summer after we won the Premier League, we were linked with two of the brightest stars in France: Zidane, who was playing for Bordeaux, and the striker Christophe Dugarry. We were excited. That was the perfect time to strengthen, on the back of all that success, and it would have been an absolute game-changer. As it was, neither of them arrived. Zidane went and signed for Juventus. I wonder how his career turned out. In fact, that summer, Blackburn did not strengthen at all. Nobody came in. Ray Harford, who had taken over from Kenny, said he wanted to give us all a chance to prove we could do it again.

It was a massive mistake. Our form nosedived and, by the next year, I was asking Jack Walker if I could consider my options. There were two on the table: Newcastle and Manchester United. The latter had been in for me before, but it was that year, in 1996, when I came closest. I considered it, seriously, even though Jack had made it clear that because he did not want to sell me to them, they would have to pay more than anyone else.

Ultimately, though, I could not say no to Newcastle, to going home. I felt it was the right thing to do to call Alex and explain my decision. It was nerve-wracking, but I plucked up the courage and dialled. There was no answer. A few minutes later, I rang again. Still no response. I tried a third time, and decided he was ignoring my calls. He must have known I would not be joining. There was no reason for him to speak to me. I didn't ring again.

ALAN'S LIST

1 Alan Shearer ... to Manchester United

2 Roy Keane ... to Blackburn Rovers

3 Zinedine Zidane ... to Blackburn Rovers

4 Paul Gascoigne ... to Manchester United

5 Eric Cantona ... to Sheffield Wednesday

6 Cristiano Ronaldo ... to Arsenal

7 Kaká ... to Manchester City
8 Steven Gerrard ... to Chelsea
9 Robert Lewandowski ... to Blackburn Rovers
10 Robinho ... to Chelsea

MICAH RICHARDS

In those first few months after Manchester City's takeover, the players got used to hearing that they were about to be shunted down the pecking order by some lavish new signing who was about to arrive. The speculation was constant. Ashley Cole was going to sign. The club was going for John Terry. Wayne Rooney was going to come.

You try to avoid it as much as you can – not buying the newspapers was a start – but it seeps through somehow, something made worse by social media. Your friends start texting you asking if one story or another is true. Your agent gets in touch, checking if the rumours are true or if you want them to go to the club to get some reassurances.

It can be really demoralising for a team, and I think it is something we struggled with. We thought we were doing all right but, even if not all of the stories were true, it felt like the club was just biding its time until it could replace us with someone newer, better, more expensive.

I was excited, though, when it came out that Manchester City were trying to sign Kaká. He was the reigning World Player of the Year. He was the star of the AC Milan team that had won the Champions League a couple of years before. He was a signing on another level, and I would have loved to have played with him. I'm sure he'd have been looking forward to playing with me, too.

That one did not come off: Milan convinced him to see out the season and then sold him to Real Madrid the following summer. We had to make do with our own Brazilian, a player we had sneaked in to sign from under the noses of Chelsea: they thought they had completed a deal until they upset Real Madrid by selling shirts with his name on the back before everything was finished. City didn't need a second invitation.

Robinho's biggest problem was that he joined a team that was not ready for a player of that quality. And make no mistake: he had quality. He was effortless. He was not especially quick, but he had this ability to drop a shoulder in almost slow motion and take a player out of the game. He could glide past defenders. He did things I have never seen anyone else do. It was like watching someone play a different sport.

I felt sorry for him, though, because his ability meant that we expected too much of him. Our gameplay basically became: give the ball to Robinho. No matter how good he was, he couldn't win games entirely on his own, but that was effectively what we tasked him to do. If he had come along two or three years later, playing in a team with Sergio Agüero and David Silva, he would have been a legend. As it is, he does not get the credit he deserves. But nobody should underestimate how important he was. Signing a player like Robinho, a genuine star, in the prime of his career, from Real Madrid, put Manchester City on the map. He made it possible to sign everyone who followed. He deserves recognition for that.

MICAH'S LIST

1 Kaká . . . to Manchester City

2 Paul Gascoigne . . . to Manchester United

3 Cristiano Ronaldo . . . to Arsenal

4 Robinho . . . to Chelsea

5 Zinedine Zidane . . . to Blackburn Rovers

6 Roy Keane . . . to Blackburn Rovers

7 Alan Shearer . . . to Manchester United

8 Steven Gerrard . . . to Chelsea

9 Eric Cantona . . . to Sheffield Wednesday

10 Robert Lewandowski . . . to Blackburn Rovers

THE TOP 10

1 Paul Gascoigne . . . to Manchester United

2 Alan Shearer . . . to Manchester United

3 Roy Keane . . . to Blackburn Rovers

4 Kaká . . . to Manchester City

5 Zinedine Zidane . . . to Blackburn Rovers

6 Cristiano Ronaldo . . . to Arsenal

7 Eric Cantona . . . to Sheffield Wednesday

8 Robinho . . . to Chelsea

9 Steven Gerrard . . . to Chelsea

10 Robert Lewandowski . . . to Blackburn Rovers

Gary's Verdict: Alex Ferguson counts not signing Gazza as his greatest regret, but I don't know how different things would have turned out had he joined Manchester United and not Tottenham. Terry Venables managed him as well as anyone could. Fergie won plenty of trophies without him. And Gazza would not have been any different. Gazza could not be any different. He was a one-off. Nobody would have been able to change him, not even Fergie, because he did not want to be changed.

THE DEBATE

Alan: There are a few too many Blackburn players in here. Imagine the team we could have put out: me and Keane and then, a few years later, if it had not been for the eruption of the Icelandic volcano, Robert Lewandowski could have joined and been the second-best striker in Blackburn's history.

Micah: It's almost like every club has a story about a Cristiano Ronaldo near miss. Arsène Wenger thought he had signed him. Liverpool had been told to make an offer. Even Newcastle, under Bobby Robson, had a chance to sign him when he was at Sporting Lisbon. He would have been a superstar anywhere, but I'm not sure missing out on him would have stopped Manchester United winning trophies.

11

THE TOP 10
WORLD STADIUMS

GARY LINEKER

Camp Nou looks big from the outside, but somehow you do not quite appreciate just how big it is until you are inside. My first day there was a Spanish tradition: presentation day, when all of the new signings are put through their paces in a training session open to the public.

I joined at the same time as Mark Hughes, and so we showed up together. You go in, go down the tunnel, past the little chapel on the right-hand side, and then walk up to the pitch. With every step, the stadium just seems to grow taller. The stands keep on rising, up into the sky. It is vast and, to be honest, it is a little overwhelming. There were 70,000 people there that day. To watch a training session.

Barcelona fans have a reputation – particularly now, when they have been so fortunate to watch Lionel Messi for so long – for being difficult to impress. That was certainly my experience. They are all members of the club, socios, and they tend to wait to be entertained. For such a big place, Camp Nou can be extremely quiet, unless it's a monster game.

What makes it special, though, is that when the noise comes, it is deafening, this roar that seems to rush down the stands and swallow you. There is no roof to keep the noise in, but it seems to echo around this vast, old, crumbling bowl. When I scored a hat-trick against Real Madrid, two of the goals came in the first five minutes. I have never heard a roar like it.

I was fortunate enough to play at several iconic stadiums. The Azteca in Mexico City, where we played in the knockout rounds of the World Cup in 1986, has the feel of a proper, gladiatorial arena. It was a world away from the places where we played our group games, in Monterrey. We used two stadiums there. One of them only had stands on two sides, and the rest of the pitch was surrounded by a hedge. It is not what you expect from your first World Cup: playing in front of a privet. It was so hot there that, towards the end of one game, I was pretty sure I wasn't going to make it to the final whistle. I lost a stone or so in weight that day. After that, the altitude of Mexico City was almost a blessed relief.

There is one ground, in particular, that I would love to have to played at. We've limited the list to places where one of us, at least, has been on (or at least near) the pitch, but La Bombonera, where Boca Juniors play, is something else. I watched a game there when I was filming with Diego Maradona, from inside the box he kept at the stadium. He was so excited to be seeing his team play, he was leaning out, over the balcony, his daughter holding on to him to stop him falling. And when he appeared, the stadium itself seemed to shake. Given the state it's in, and the noise the fans make, it probably was shaking. That is an atmosphere.

THE CONTENDERS

Allianz Arena, Munich

Azteca, Mexico City

Celtic Park, Glasgow

Diego Armando Maradona, Naples

Maracanã, Rio de Janeiro

Camp Nou, Barcelona

San Siro, Milan

Santiago Bernabéu, Madrid

Signal Iduna Park, Dortmund

Stade Vélodrome, Marseille

ALAN SHEARER

You rarely get chance to take in a city when you visit as a player. It is a wonderful privilege, obviously, flying around the world to play football, but the trips tend to be so quick that you do not really experience the place: it is the airport to the hotel and on to training, maybe an hour's walk on the morning of a game, back to the hotel for lunch, and then you get ready for the game that night. Where you are does not really matter.

I did make an effort, though, to appreciate the stadiums themselves. There's a few I never made it to: I was injured when Newcastle played at Camp Nou against Barcelona, and we never ran into Real Madrid in our years in the Champions League, so I have not even been to the Bernabéu.

The ones that stand out were the ones that had a reputation for being intimidating. I never objected to a hostile atmosphere: as a rule, fans do not boo bad players. I took it as a mark of respect, as much as anything, that they were singling you out as the biggest threat to their hopes. Newcastle played at De Kuip, Feyenoord's home in the Netherlands, in a Champions League qualifier: it is noisy enough that some people might find it scary, but if I am honest I quite enjoyed it. It helped that we got through that night, of course.

Those are always the stadiums I remember most fondly: the ones I have won at, or at least scored at. Of those, San Siro stands out. It is one of the iconic stadiums in European football: there is a reason people usually describe it as a cathedral.

What made it special to me, though, was the away end. When Newcastle played there, we must have taken 13,000 or 14,000 fans with us. They were all packed in behind one of the goals, the stands towering over them, but they made so much noise that they seemed to fill the place. I have never seen an away end quite like it when I scored: all these Newcastle fans pouring over each other, in one of the greatest stadiums in the world, to celebrate. It would be a real shame, as a player, if you could not stand back and admire that, take it in, and enjoy the fact that all of these people have not only travelled so far to watch you play, but that you have made their whole trip worthwhile.

ALAN'S LIST

1 San Siro, Milan

2 Celtic Park, Glasgow

3 Maracanã, Rio de Janeiro

4 Camp Nou, Barcelona

5 Santiago Bernabéu, Madrid

6 Signal Iduna Park, Dortmund

7 Allianz Arena, Munich

8 Stade Vélodrome, Marseille

9 Diego Armando Maradona, Naples

10 Azteca, Mexico City

MICAH RICHARDS

The sight of the really devoted fans gathered behind the goal in Fiorentina's stadium, the Artemio Franchi, never stopped amazing me. It was not just the noise they made, which was constant, because Fiorentina are not really expected to win all of the time, so they cheer you on no matter what the result is, but the colour: the huge displays they arranged before games, the flares, the banners.

The scenes after we beat Tottenham in the Europa League are something I will never forget. I had been desperate to play in that game: I wanted to prove I could still cut it against a Premier League team, maybe remind a few clubs back home that my contract at Manchester City was about to expire, just keep myself fresh in people's minds. Vincenzo Montella, the manager, didn't pick me at White Hart Lane, but I pushed and pushed myself to be fit for the return. I told him how much I wanted to play, and I started. We played brilliantly that night, knocked a supposedly superior Premier League team out, and the celebrations were wild.

The stadiums were one of the best things about playing in Italy: going to San Siro and Juventus's stadium and all of these other iconic grounds. The toughest, by far, was Napoli's: the one that has now been renamed after Diego Maradona. It is a horrible place, in need of more than a lick of paint. The dressing rooms, back then, were old and dark. The walk to the pitch is intimidating. And once you are out there, the noise hits you like a wall. It is the most hostile place I have ever played. It didn't help that it was boiling hot, and we could not get the ball off Napoli.

But there is something special about a big Champions League night at one of the big Champions League stadiums, so the Allianz Arena, home of Bayern Munich, comes out top for me. It is a spectacular place, sitting like a spaceship outside the city, different colours rippling around its shell. And once you get in, the noise is something else. As soon as there is a chance, you hear this enormous roar. It is ridiculous. I made my Champions League debut there: in the Allianz Arena, against Bayern Munich. I am not sure there is any tougher place to start.

MICAH'S LIST

1 Allianz Arena, Munich

2 Camp Nou, Barcelona

3 Diego Armando Maradona, Naples

4 Signal Iduna Park, Dortmund

5 Celtic Park, Glasgow

6 Santiago Bernabéu, Madrid

7 San Siro, Milan

8 Maracanã, Rio de Janeiro

9 Azteca, Mexico City

10 Stade Vélodrome, Marseille

THE TOP 10

1 Camp Nou, Barcelona

2 Celtic Park, Glasgow

3 San Siro, Milan

4 Allianz Arena, Munich

5 Signal Iduna Park, Dortmund

6 Maracanã, Rio de Janeiro

7 Santiago Bernabéu, Madrid

8 Diego Armando Maradona, Naples

9 Stade Vélodrome, Marseille

10 Azteca, Mexico City

Gary's Verdict: You've reached the correct decision again. You're getting good at this. They are a demanding crowd at Camp Nou: they're used to the finer things in football, having seen so many of the greatest teams and the greatest players. When they are with you, the noise spurs you on. But when they are against you, when you are not living up to their expectations, they are quick to get the white handkerchiefs out.

THE DEBATE

Alan: After I retired, I made a point of going up to an Old Firm game in Glasgow for the first time. It was something I really wanted to experience, just as a spectator, just to feel what the atmosphere is like. The animosity between Celtic and Rangers, as an outsider, is unlike anything else in the world, I think. The atmosphere was loud and intense, but it is rooted in undiluted hatred of each other.

Micah: I played at Celtic Park once, but only in a charity game, for James Milner's foundation. It probably wasn't quite the same atmosphere as you'd get at an Old Firm game but, even for an exhibition match, Celtic Park was glorious. It's a brilliant stadium, one of those places you can feel the history in the walls.

12

THE TOP 10
PANTOMIME VILLAINS

GARY LINEKER

There are some underdogs you do not want to win. Wimbledon, as you may have guessed, fell into that category for me. Looking back, you can admire all that they achieved. You can appreciate the romance of their story, rising through the divisions to win the FA Cup, and you can respect the fact that every single one of their players managed to get as much out of their talent as was humanly possible. But I just could not bring myself to like them.

This category is devoted to those players that opposition fans – and sometimes players – loved to hate, the ones who relished their status as cartoon villains. In the 1980s, Wimbledon had a whole team of them. There was a huge element of pantomime to them. They were nasty. They were horrible. And they played up to it as much as they could.

It got results. We played at Plough Lane when Peter Shreeves was caretaker manager at Spurs, and we got absolutely battered: we were three or four down at half-time, I think. We were playing terribly. Peter was a soft-spoken, gentle man, but as we went into the dressing room I was thinking even he would give us both barrels for the performance we'd just put in. Any manager would have been fuming. Any manager except Peter. Once we were all inside, he turned to us and said: 'Well, boys, it appears that we are not exactly singing from the same hymn sheet.' And that was it.

Eventually, I got my chance to have a bit of revenge. Playing Wimbledon, you would hear them constantly urging each other to 'put it in the mixer'. They would roar it and growl it and shout it throughout the game. Once they'd left Plough Lane, we played them at Selhurst Park, and I ended up scoring four. By the time the fourth had gone in, I'd started to feel brave. So as I ran back to the halfway line, I turned to them all and shouted: 'Where's your mixer now, lads?' I think we were 5-1 up at the time. It seemed safe. And then they got it back to 5-3, and I started to get a little bit worried.

But there were players in that team who could play, not least Dennis Wise. He was a cheeky, chirpy little Cockney, and he was always great company when we were away with England, but he had a craftiness on the pitch that gave him a bit of a dark side. That may not have appealed to his opponents – or quite a few fans – but all of his teammates will have appreciated not just how talented he was, but the dark side that made him so effective.

THE CONTENDERS

Joey Barton (Manchester City, Newcastle United, QPR)
Dennis Wise (Wimbledon, Chelsea, Leicester)

Robbie Savage (Leicester, Blackburn Rovers,

Birmingham City, Derby County)

Diego Costa (Chelsea)

Craig Bellamy (Norwich, Coventry, Newcastle, Blackburn,

Liverpool, West Ham, Manchester City)

Emmanuel Adebayor (Arsenal, Manchester City)

Lee Cattermole (Sunderland)

El Hadji Diouf (Liverpool, Bolton)

Ben Thatcher (Wimbledon, Tottenham,

Leicester, Manchester City)

Mike Dean (Referee)

ALAN SHEARER

Quite often, the players who seem the most unpleasant on the pitch are the complete opposite off it. I played with Francis Benali at Southampton. He is the nicest guy in the world, as he proved by doing so much fantastic work for charity after he retired. But on the pitch he would break your leg without so much as thinking about it.

I'd put Lee Cattermole in the same category. He was a bit of a lunatic as soon as he crossed the white line. I've had a round of golf with him since, though, and you wouldn't have guessed that he would spend most of a game going round the pitch trying to kick people.

Those sorts of players can be helpful to have on your team. You have to accept them for what they are, but there are times when they are useful to have in your dressing room. Craig Bellamy was just the player I needed alongside me at Newcastle when he arrived: it was towards the end of my career, and I was slowing down a little, so we became one of those traditional strike partnerships, a big man and a little man, doing most of the running. It worked perfectly for us.

He was a very, very good player, but having Craig around wasn't always easy. He does not really have an off switch: back then, at least, he was angry all of the time. There was no shortage of rows at the training ground. He could, at times, be annoying. But then it is important not to try to change players like that. You don't want to curb their personality if, as was true of Craig, that is part of what makes them the player they are. As much as anything, the rest of the team had to learn to cope with it.

And then, of course, there are the ones who enjoy the notoriety. Robbie Savage was one of those. He enjoyed the tension. He was attracted to it. He revelled in it. He was the one who, quite often, caused it. He was, basically, a bit of a troublemaker. Even with a player like that, though, most of his teammates would have respected that what he was doing could help the team, and that is what matters. You had him in your corner, and that was no bad thing.

ALAN'S LIST

1 Joey Barton (Manchester City, Newcastle United, QPR)

2 Robbie Savage (Leicester, Blackburn Rovers, Birmingham City, Derby County)

3 El Hadji Diouf (Liverpool, Bolton)

4 Craig Bellamy (Norwich, Coventry, Newcastle, Blackburn, Liverpool, West Ham, Manchester City)

5 Mike Dean (Referee)

6 Dennis Wise (Wimbledon, Chelsea, Leicester)

7 Lee Cattermole (Sunderland)

8 Diego Costa (Chelsea)

9 Emmanuel Adebayor (Arsenal, Manchester City)

10 Ben Thatcher (Wimbledon, Tottenham,
Leicester, Manchester City)

MICAH RICHARDS

When Emmanuel Adebayor scored that goal against Arsenal, not long after he'd moved to Manchester City, I thought he was running towards me. We got on well, the two of us, and when I saw him sprinting, full pelt, away from the goal I just assumed he'd decided we should celebrate together. Maybe we'd do a little dance or something.

But then, of course, he went straight past me. He didn't even look at me. He was heading for the other end of the pitch, to celebrate in front of all of the Arsenal fans. The reaction he got was extraordinary. It is one of the most disrespectful things I've ever seen, but even now, I have to admit: it was quite funny. You could tell how much it meant to him by the fact that it was, quite comfortably, the fastest he moved all season.

He regretted it afterwards, I think. It was his way of letting all of that emotion out: he'd had a lot of abuse from Arsenal's fans for the way he left, and that affects you. It is impossible to ignore it. But once it was out, and he'd done it, he understood that he had gone too far. I think he apologised after the game. He had, with that sprint, said what he needed to say.

That was a one-off, from Adebayor; Joey Barton made mistakes much more often. He was a curious character, Joey. Most of the time, he was absolutely fine: smart, thoughtful, interesting. But every so often, something would happen and it was as if he couldn't quite control himself. There were so many things that happened on the training ground: only a fraction of them ever made it into public knowledge. That final ten per cent was always Joey's problem. It was as if he was always fighting against his demons.

I don't know where it came from, but I know he could be different. He was the big player at Manchester City, before the money arrived, but I was called up for England before he was. When he did eventually get the nod, in 2007, we were in the squad together. He was new, and by that stage I was a bit of an old hand. So it was him coming to me for advice, to ask questions about what he should do and how he should be, rather than the other way round. He was quiet, all that week, surrounded by those big stars from Manchester United and Liverpool and Chelsea, not quite as loud or as domineering as he was at club level. He was not quite as quiet as a mouse – that wasn't really Joey's style – but he was subdued. Being like that more often might have helped him.

MICAH'S LIST

1 Joey Barton (Manchester City, Newcastle United, QPR)

2 Robbie Savage (Leicester, Blackburn Rovers, Birmingham City, Derby County)

3 Diego Costa (Chelsea)

4 El Hadji Diouf (Liverpool, Bolton)

5 Craig Bellamy (Norwich, Coventry, Newcastle, Blackburn, Liverpool, West Ham, Manchester City)

6 Ben Thatcher (Wimbledon, Tottenham,
Leicester, Manchester City)

7 Dennis Wise (Wimbledon, Chelsea, Leicester)

8 Lee Cattermole (Sunderland)

9 Mike Dean (Referee)

10 Emmanuel Adebayor (Arsenal, Manchester City)

THE TOP 10

1 Joey Barton (Manchester City, Newcastle United, QPR)

2 Robbie Savage (Leicester, Blackburn Rovers,
Birmingham City, Derby County)

3 El Hadji Diouf (Liverpool, Bolton)

4 Craig Bellamy (Norwich, Coventry, Newcastle,
Blackburn, Liverpool, West Ham, Manchester City)

5 Diego Costa (Chelsea)

6 Dennis Wise (Wimbledon, Chelsea, Leicester)

7 Mike Dean (Referee)

8 Lee Cattermole (Sunderland)

9 Ben Thatcher (Wimbledon, Tottenham,
Leicester, Manchester City)

10 Emmanuel Adebayor (Arsenal, Manchester City)

Gary's Verdict: It's in football's tribal nature that fans hate some clubs, and because of that they hate some individuals. But there are some players that play up to that reputation, and even use it to drive them on. It can be quite powerful motivation, and it can, at times, even help a team, if used correctly.

THE DEBATE

Alan: You accept a lot of things on a pitch: players will do almost anything they can to win. But to a lot of players, spitting is the one thing that crosses a line: it's a vile act in so many ways. It may not hurt as much as a bad tackle, but it is always, always deliberate. That was what made El Hadji Diouf so unpopular, and it is impossible to have any sympathy.

Micah: I like Robbie Savage off the pitch, but I didn't have any time for him on it. He spent most of his time trying to wind other players up. He wasn't going into a game to focus on his team or how he played; he was focusing on irritating the opposition as much as possible.

13

THE TOP 10
UNSUNG HEROES

GARY LINEKER

Our team at Everton was so predictable that I can still name it now, more than 30 years on, from Neville Southall in goal to me and Graeme Sharp upfront. If everyone was fit, Howard Kendall did not even have to think about it. He knew, too, who he would turn if almost anyone was missing: Kevin Richardson.

Kevin could basically play anywhere: either full-back position, and right across the midfield. He might have been regarded as a jack of all trades, but a master of none, but to me that undersells quite how gifted you have to be to play in so many different places. Kevin had mastered all of those roles; that was what made him so important.

Versatility is hugely important for a team, but it can be a disadvantage for an individual. If you do not carve out a specific role for yourself, a specialism, then you can be condemned to being seen as a square peg in a round hole. From the outside, at least: I think inside a squad, everyone knows how valuable a utility player like that can be. There are not as many of them now as there used to be – because squads are bigger and rotation more common, and because roles are now so tightly defined, managers tend to prefer specialists – but those that are still around tend to be revered, especially by their managers: look at James Milner at Liverpool.

There are two more classic unsung heroes that stand out to me, alongside Kevin. One would be Peter Beardsley. He played in two World Cups for his country, and won league titles with Liverpool, so it is hard to say he did not get the credit he was due, but perhaps because he had someone playing ahead of him, scoring all of the goals and taking all of the glory, he was not appreciated quite as much as he should have been.

The other was Gary Mabbutt, my teammate at Tottenham and, occasionally, for England. I roomed with him for Spurs: as a diabetic, he had to jab himself with insulin four times a day, including waking up in the night to do it. He was an example of sheer perseverance, of absolute dedication to his career. He was a giant of a player, a total warrior, but one of the most pleasant men you could hope to meet. He was an inspiration, on and off the pitch, and all of the players who played alongside him would say the same.

THE CONTENDERS

Gareth Barry (Aston Villa, Manchester City, West Ham)

Sylvain Distin (Manchester City, Everton, Portsmouth)

Richard Dunne (Everton, Manchester City)

Denis Irwin (Manchester United)

Rob Lee (Newcastle)

James Milner (Leeds United, Aston Villa,
Newcastle, Manchester City, Liverpool)

Kevin Nolan (Bolton, Newcastle, West Ham)
Emmanuel Petit (Arsenal)
Nolberto Solano (Newcastle, Aston Villa, West Ham)
Tugay (Blackburn Rovers)

ALAN SHEARER

There are players in every team who do not quite get the credit they deserve: they will certainly be appreciated by their own teammates, and they are often adored by their own fans, but maybe people who do not watch them regularly do not quite realise how much they bring to the team.

We had plenty of those at Newcastle. Rob Lee is probably the most obvious example: he was one of the signings that made everything that followed possible; he was almost the first part of the team that became known as the Entertainers. It was a close-run thing, too. Middlesbrough had wanted to sign him, and he only plumped for Newcastle because Kevin Keegan told him it was closer to London than Teesside. If you know Rob, you will know that story has him written all over it. His terrible geography worked out for everyone, though. I don't think he has any regrets.

Newcastle is quite a lot further from Peru than it is London, but that did not stop Nolberto Solano becoming an idol in the North East. He fell in love with the area, and it fell in love with him: he loved nothing more than going for a pint, and he took his trumpet with him wherever he went. But what is lost, just a little, is what a brilliant player he was. He was only a little guy, but he was technically magnificent. His crossing was fantastic. His set-pieces were as good as anyone's: if you think about the reputation James Ward-Prowse has for his delivery now, Nobby's was every bit as precise. He was a hugely important part of that Newcastle team for years: to do that so far from home, in a culture that must have been so distant to him, takes not only talent but incredible courage.

Kevin Nolan would be the other name I would throw in: he arrived at Newcastle after my time as a player, but he was part of the team that I managed, very briefly, to try and avoid relegation in 2009. I am absolutely sure that he is appreciated as much as he should be at all the clubs he played for: Bolton and West Ham, as well as Newcastle, but maybe because of his physical style, or maybe because those teams were not all that fashionable, he was never really given the respect he should have been outside of those teams. But he was a fantastic professional, a really talented player, and the sort of figure that you can build a side around. They don't always get all of the attention, but you need players like that in every team.

ALAN'S LIST

1 Nolberto Solano (Newcastle, Aston Villa, West Ham)

2 Rob Lee (Newcastle)

3 Denis Irwin (Manchester United)

4 Gareth Barry (Aston Villa, Manchester City, West Ham)

5 Tugay (Blackburn Rovers)

6 Emmanuel Petit (Arsenal)

7 James Milner (Leeds United, Aston Villa,
Newcastle, Manchester City, Liverpool)

8 Sylvain Distin (Manchester City, Everton, Portsmouth)

9 Richard Dunne (Everton, Manchester City)

10 Kevin Nolan (Bolton, Newcastle, West Ham)

MICAH RICHARDS

There is a simple rule whenever footballers go out for a night out together: you leave the ball at home. Whatever you do talk about – it might be cars or watches or girlfriends or whatever – you do not talk about football. There is zero tolerance on shop talk.

Gareth Barry was always one of the best value on those sorts of occasions. Nobody took their career more seriously: he was the perfect professional, but he was also good value on a night out. You'd have maybe expected him to be one of the first to arrive – punctual and sensible and all that – but he was also always among the last to leave. He was quite a quiet, shy sort of person most of the time, but he opened up after he'd had a drink. Not that you would ever see him drunk: alcohol never really seemed to affect him. He'd just get more and more chatty, more and more fun.

He was also, obviously, a proper player. I think in some eyes he never really recovered from what happened at the 2010 World Cup, when Mesut Özil left him scrambling to keep up as England lost to Germany, but to allow everything else he achieved to be overshadowed by one game is ridiculous. That happens too often in football: that a player is defined by one moment, by one mistake, that people cannot see past. It's a real shame. Gareth played for three massive clubs, won a load of major trophies, played for his country, and seemed to go on forever. He is one of the most underrated players of my era, without question.

In the days before the Abu Dhabi takeover, there were quite a few players at Manchester City who fitted that bill. Richard Dunne was our player of the year four years in a row, and yet you never really hear him mentioned as one of the defining Premier League defenders. Did he make our top 10 list? Of course he didn't. He should have done, though.

The same can be said for Sylvain Distin. At first, I found Sylvain a little patronising: he always seemed to be treating me like a kid, criticising things I did, telling me that I had to do the same things he did. At 18, when you're in great shape, you sometimes do not like to be told that you're not all that you might think you are. I realised after a while, though, that it came from a good place: he believed in my ability, and he wanted to make sure I got the most out of it. There was no better example of that than him: he had drained every last drop from his talent. He was in incredible shape. He looked after himself perfectly. He barely ever had any injuries. His attitude and his dedication allowed him to get the best out of what he had. He just wanted the same for me.

MICAH'S LIST

1 Sylvain Distin (Manchester City, Everton, Portsmouth)

2 Denis Irwin (Manchester United)

3 Gareth Barry (Aston Villa, Manchester City, Everton)

4 Tugay (Blackburn Rovers)

5 James Milner (Leeds United, Aston Villa, Newcastle, Manchester City, Liverpool)

6 Richard Dunne (Everton, Manchester City)

7 Nolberto Solano (Newcastle, Aston Villa, West Ham)

8 Emmanuel Petit (Arsenal, Chelsea)

9 Rob Lee (Newcastle)

10 Kevin Nolan (Bolton, Newcastle, West Ham)

THE TOP 10

1 Denis Irwin (Manchester United)

2 Gareth Barry (Aston Villa, Manchester City, West Ham)

3 Nolberto Solano (Newcastle, Aston Villa, West Ham)

4 Tugay (Blackburn Rovers)

5 Sylvain Distin (Manchester City, Everton, Portsmouth)

6 Rob Lee (Newcastle)

7 James Milner (Leeds United, Aston Villa,
Newcastle, Manchester City, Liverpool)

8 Emmanuel Petit (Arsenal)

9 Richard Dunne (Everton, Manchester City)

10 Kevin Nolan (Bolton, Newcastle, West Ham)

Gary's Verdict: Denis Irwin takes it, thanks to both Micah and Alan reserving first place for someone they experienced first-hand. Irwin was a mainstay of two of Alex Ferguson's great Manchester United sides, and he was a bit of a set-piece specialist, too, at least until David Beckham emerged and his chances to take them started to dwindle.

THE DEBATE

Alan: It is easy to watch a player like Gareth Barry and assume that he is not the most talented on the pitch, or to dismiss him as a destroyer, someone who gets by on work rate and industry alone. But you need to be really good to have the sort of longevity he did, to play for the teams he did, and to win everything he did.

Micah: Tugay was absolutely ridiculous. He could do anything with the ball that he wanted – his passing was impeccable. He seemed to dictate games just by strolling around the centre circle. That is maybe what prevented him playing for one of the truly elite teams in the Premier League, his lack of athleticism, but in terms of talent, he had it all.

14

THE TOP 10
DERBIES

GARY LINEKER

I played in two of the great traditional English derbies – on Merseyside and in North London – and have happy memories of both of them, winning at Anfield and beating Arsenal at Wembley, but there is no question about the biggest club fixture I ever experienced: Real Madrid against Barcelona, just edging out Leicester against Nottingham Forest.

Of course, technically, Real and Barcelona is not a derby. The cities are hundreds of miles apart. But still, that is what everyone in Spain called it. At least until the word *clásico* caught on, it was known as the *derbi*. I think the word has been adopted, in Spanish, as a synonym for monster game.

My memories of those games are of noise, and of the lack of it. Because it's so much larger than England, there is no real tradition of Spanish fans travelling to other cities for league games. Nowadays, you might get a few hundred visiting fans inside a stadium, but certainly while I was there, Barcelona's games with Real Madrid were strictly home supporters only.

It made our visits to the Bernabéu very strange. Whenever we scored, you would be greeted by complete, crushing silence, the sort of deathly hush in which you can hear a pin drop. My first assumption would always be that the goal had been ruled out, and that was why nobody was celebrating. It always took a second to remember that there was nobody there who wanted to celebrate, and the goal stood.

It was exactly the same when Real Madrid scored at Camp Nou. My favourite *clásico* memory will be no surprise at all: the day that I scored a hat-trick, the game that sealed my reputation in Spain as the scourge of Barcelona's great rivals. I have never heard a noise like the one that greeted each of my goals in my life. It was like an explosion: 120,000 Barcelona fans screaming in delight at the idea of the old rival being beaten. The thought of it still gives me goose bumps.

The part of that story that I don't mention too often is that Real quickly pulled a couple of goals back. And, just as was the case with our goals at the Bernabéu, all you heard was nothing. Total quiet. On those occasions, the flutter of anxiety was replaced with a little ray of hope, that perhaps their goal had been ruled out, only to realise that, no, there just weren't any Real fans there to enjoy it and that, yes, we really did have to hold on, or risk the wrath of the entire stadium, furious at throwing away a lead in the biggest game in the world.

THE CONTENDERS

Arsenal v Tottenham
Aston Villa v Birmingham City
Chelsea v Tottenham
Everton v Liverpool

Liverpool v Manchester United
Manchester City v Manchester United
Newcastle United v Sunderland
Southampton v Portsmouth
Tottenham v West Ham United
Wolves v West Bromwich Albion

ALAN SHEARER

Hatred is a strong word to use, but there is no other way of describing it, not really: games between Newcastle and Sunderland are full of genuine loathing. I remember one game, in Sunderland, which was supposed to have only home fans in attendance. We scored, and the Newcastle fans who had sneaked in, sitting among their enemy, could not help themselves. They all went up, and all hell broke loose.

The North East derby gave me one of the worst moments of my career. We were losing 2-1 to Sunderland at St James's Park, with a few minutes to go, when Niall Quinn fouled Rob Lee in the box: penalty. We had a chance to save our blushes and to spare our fans the embarrassment of losing to that lot. I stepped up, and missed. Thomas Sørensen saved it. We lost the game, and it was my fault. I came out and apologised, but that is not the same as getting over it. That missed penalty haunted me for years. From that point on, I wanted not just to score against Sunderland, but to score a penalty against them: that was the only way to lay the ghost to rest.

The chance finally came six years later, in another derby, this one at the Stadium of Light. We were one down at half-time, but Michael

Chopra drew us level, and then, a minute later, Charles N'Zogbia won a penalty. I had my chance. I had been practising all week, putting them in the top corner, just in case we got one: I was not going to make the same mistake again. Thankfully, I didn't.

That was my 260th Premier League goal, and my 379th in all competitions, and it proved to be my last. More than that, it was my last ever touch of a football as a professional. A few minutes later, before I could be involved again, my knee gave way, and I had to come off. That was my season done. I was scheduled to retire at the end of the year anyway, but I had no choice but to bring it forward.

I suppose I could have been disappointed – not having a chance to say goodbye to St James's Park, to retire on my own terms, or to add a couple more goals to the tally – but I didn't see it like that. I am a believer in fate, and it seemed just perfect to me that my last ever touch should have been to score against Sunderland, rectifying the mistake I had made six years earlier, the miss I regretted more than any other. It felt to me like it was meant to be that way.

ALAN'S LIST

1 Liverpool v Manchester United

2 Newcastle United v Sunderland

3 Liverpool v Everton

4 Manchester United v Manchester City

5 Southampton v Portsmouth

6 Arsenal v Tottenham

7 Aston Villa v Birmingham City

8 Chelsea v Tottenham

9 Wolves v West Bromwich Albion

10 Tottenham v West Ham United

MICAH RICHARDS

The rivalry between Birmingham City and Aston Villa runs deep. Although I was born in Birmingham, I did not realise quite how deep until I played for Villa. I'd always assumed that Manchester City against Manchester United was the most passionate local derby in England. In hindsight, that's probably wrong.

That passion caught me out on at least one occasion. In 2018, after I had missed an entire season for Villa through injury, I went to Ibiza on holiday. A guy came up to me and told me that he had launched a brand of hats, and asked if I'd be kind enough to have a picture with him to promote it. He asked me to join my hands together in a sort of 'Z' shape – that, he said, was the company's logo. I didn't want to refuse, so I did it, and thought no more of it. And then, after a few minutes, my phone started going wild, with all these Villa fans abusing me. My first thought was: 'What have I done now?' The guy had obviously posted the picture straightaway: he'd tricked me into making a sign associated with the Zulus, Birmingham's old hooligan firm. I had no idea, but the damage was done: Villa fans were furious that this player who was always injured seemed to be mocking the club.

It didn't help that one of my rare stormers came in a Birmingham derby at Villa Park. I'd always done quite well in derbies in Manchester; something about the sense of occasion seemed to bring out the best in me. That was the same after I moved to Villa. My first taste of the Birmingham derby came in a league cup game in 2015. Birmingham were in the Championship then, and we were in the Premier League, though not for long. They came at us in the first half, and me and Joleon Lescott had to keep them at bay. We played really well, and eventually Rudy Gestede scored to knock them out. The place went wild.

There was something really vicious about the atmosphere, a real hatred in the air. I didn't know it was that heated, but experiencing it left you in no doubt about how much it meant to fans on both sides. I think the fact that it doesn't happen all that often – unlike with the Merseyside or Manchester derbies, Villa and Birmingham are not always in the same league, so you don't automatically get two meetings a season – adds to that. There is a lot of spite and animosity saved up for when they do meet.

MICAH'S LIST

1 Liverpool v Manchester United

2 Manchester United v Manchester City

3 Aston Villa v Birmingham City

4 Liverpool v Everton

5 Newcastle United v Sunderland

6 Arsenal v Tottenham

7 Tottenham v West Ham United

8 Chelsea v Tottenham

9 Southampton v Portsmouth

10 Wolves v West Bromwich Albion

THE TOP 10

1 Liverpool v Manchester United

2 Manchester United v Manchester City

3 Newcastle United v Sunderland

4 Liverpool v Everton

5 Aston Villa v Birmingham City

6 Arsenal v Tottenham

7 Southampton v Portsmouth

8 Chelsea v Tottenham

9 Tottenham v West Ham United

10 Wolves v West Bromwich Albion

Gary's Verdict: There is no question that Liverpool against Manchester United is the biggest game this country has to offer, but I would question whether it's truly a derby. That, surely, has to be reserved for games between teams from the same city, or near enough. Maybe it would be more straightforward if we borrowed from the Spanish, and just called it the English *clásico*.

THE DEBATE

Alan: Manchester United and Liverpool might not be a traditional, one-city derby, but it is the defining game in English football. And, crucially, it is bigger for both of those clubs than their games against their more local rivals, even now that Manchester City are a far bigger threat to Manchester United than they have been at any point before.

Micah: I still think about my worst performance in a Manchester derby. It came in the game we lost 4-3 at Old Trafford, with Michael Owen scoring a late winner. I regret it because it was my fault: he was my man, my problem, but I was trying to pass him on to Shaun Wright-Phillips so I wouldn't have to deal with him. I was cheating a little bit, and I got found out.

15

THE TOP 10
FEUDS

GARY LINEKER

Management is an intensely pressurised job. They may be well paid, but the people in charge of the biggest clubs in the game live under the most unbearable scrutiny. One false move, they know, and it could all come tumbling down. The line between success and failure is so fine. Everything is so fragile. It should not be a surprise, then, that they are prone to the occasional emotional outburst; it certainly should not be a surprise that they are susceptible to the jibes of one of their peers.

Often, the real target of one manager's acerbic comment is not his opposite number at all, of course: the message is for the referee. A manager commenting on another team's striker diving is not hoping to enrage his counterpart; he is hoping to sow a seed of doubt in the official's mind that what might look like a penalty is, in fact, a trick.

Whether they work or not is a different matter. My usual response to them, I have to admit, is just to laugh: whenever José Mourinho is up to his usual tricks or a couple of coaches are trading barbs through the media, it does not strike me as particularly likely to influence the results of a game; it is all just for show. I suspect most players can tune it all out, if they even hear it at all.

Sometimes, though, the occasional comment does get through. Managers, as I say, are not always the most rational creatures. That is why we were treated to Rafa Benítez responding in such spectacular fashion to Alex Ferguson when Liverpool and Manchester United were locked in a title race, or Kevin Keegan's remarkable outburst as Newcastle ran out of steam in 1996. Ferguson always seemed to come out on top in those mind games, as we call them, though I've always thought that the quality of his teams made more difference than his ability to get under his opponents' skin.

I never had a particular rival as a player; there was only one who I did not get on with especially, and that was Tony Adams. It never turned into a feud, but there was always a little bit of an atmosphere when we joined up with England together. I'm not sure why it was: perhaps I was a little too ambitious at a time when Tony, like many other players, took the off-field culture of football just as seriously as he did the on-pitch business. But he has changed, and I have changed, and we get on great now. We have talked about it, and ironed out whatever differences there may have been. That's the thing with football: what happens in the heat of battle has to be left behind when the struggle is over.

THE CONTENDERS

Rafa Benítez v José Mourinho

Rafa Benítez v Alex Ferguson

Andy Cole v Teddy Sheringham

Kenny Dalglish v Alex Ferguson
Alex Ferguson v Kevin Keegan
Alex Ferguson v Arsène Wenger
Pep Guardiola v Jürgen Klopp
Roy Keane v Alan Shearer
Roy Keane v Patrick Vieira
José Mourinho v Arsène Wenger

ALAN SHEARER

Nothing between me and Roy Keane was ever personal. It may not always have looked that way: neither of us were the sort to give an inch, and neither of us objected to going head to head if it was necessary, but that was not because – and I can only speak for myself, here, I suppose – we didn't like each other.

From my point of view, what mattered was what Keane represented. He was a symbol of Manchester United, most of the time the best team in the country and, for a while at both Blackburn and Newcastle, the biggest rival we had if we were to fulfil our ambitions. They were, in their eyes, the biggest club in the world, and the only way to overcome them was to stand up to them. I did not look forward to playing against him because I wanted to get one over on him; I looked forward to playing against him because I wanted to get one over on them.

I think that is true for most of the best players: you relish the days you come up against your peers and your equals, because it's on those occasions that you really test yourself. Those sorts of meetings always brought the best out of me, and it's probably fair to say that they brought the best out of Roy, too.

That respect extends to the managers. Kevin Keegan might have been the most famous victim of Alex Ferguson's mind games, but he and Kenny Dalglish wound each other up constantly, both when Kenny was at Blackburn and then again when he was at Newcastle. Neither of them would miss an opportunity to get under the other's skin; we were always aware, as players, of precisely what Fergie was saying, and how Kenny was responding. That is part of the game: their job is to find whatever advantage they can, and try to make the most of it. Whether they liked each other or not was not really relevant: what mattered was that they were both unapologetic winners.

But if you listen to both of them talk now, long after their battles have stopped, it is obvious how much they admire each other. They may have butted heads, but they did so because that was what they thought would help their teams at the time; there is no animosity between them, no spite, that lingers to this day. They can see themselves in each other; they were both just doing what they had to do.

ALAN'S LIST

1 Alex Ferguson v Arsène Wenger

2 Alex Ferguson v Kevin Keegan

3 Kenny Dalglish v Alex Ferguson

4 José Mourinho v Arsène Wenger

5 Pep Guardiola v Jürgen Klopp

6 Rafa Benítez v José Mourinho

7 Rafa Benítez v Alex Ferguson

8 Roy Keane v Patrick Vieira

9 Roy Keane v Alan Shearer

10 Andy Cole v Teddy Sheringham

MICAH RICHARDS

Throughout Manchester City's rise, Alex Ferguson always had something to say. I think until the takeover happened, and the club's fortunes were completely transformed, he'd never really thought that City were worth bothering with. He might throw a jibe in our direction before a derby, but he always had bigger fish to fry: he reserved his comments for teams that he felt were rivals, and we were not his rivals.

That started to change under Mark Hughes. Although he'd played for Manchester United under Ferguson, I'm not sure they had the easiest relationship when Hughes started coaching. The thing about mind games, though, is that whether they are thought to have worked or not is decided by the team that wins the trophy at the end. Take the famous 'noisy neighbours' comment, from 2009. That was Ferguson responding to the billboard that City had put up, right in the middle of Manchester, celebrating the signing of Carlos Tevez.

Now, because City did not go on to win anything that year, that was seen as another brilliant put-down from Ferguson. But look at it in another way and you could easily say that it was City who came out on top: the billboard had clearly had its desired effect, and got under the skin of the dominant team in the city.

The rivalry went up another level when Roberto Mancini took over. Mancini was not inclined to keep the peace, as Mark Hughes had been. He respected Ferguson and all that he had achieved, of course, but he had no particular loyalty to him. I loved that side of it: the little wars of words, the thinly veiled insults, the attempts to turn the screw. That's how it should be. Everyone is too nice, too respectful, now. Mancini knew he had an added incentive to try to seek whatever advantage he could, because by that stage City were not only catching United, we were starting to overtake them.

You could tell something had changed, by the year we won the title, because the little digs stopped having an effect. I think a comment from an opposing manager only really makes a difference if it touches a nerve: the truth hurts, after all. Ferguson did it better than anyone else, exposing the insecurities of his rivals.

The problem, for him, was that by 2012 we knew our squad was just as good as theirs. Of course we didn't have the history, but that didn't matter there and then. We were aware of it, whenever he said something – you would see it in the paper, or read it on social media, or your friends would let you know – but none of it fazed us at all. We knew, to an extent, that we had already won the mind games: if he felt it was worth trying to get under our skin, then he clearly knew we were a threat.

MICAH'S LIST

1 Alex Ferguson v Arsène Wenger

2 José Mourinho v Arsène Wenger

3 Rafa Benítez v Alex Ferguson

4 Alex Ferguson v Kevin Keegan

5 Pep Guardiola v Jürgen Klopp

6 Rafa Benítez v José Mourinho

7 Roy Keane v Patrick Vieira

8 Kenny Dalglish v Alex Ferguson

9 Andy Cole v Teddy Sheringham

10 Roy Keane v Alan Shearer

THE TOP 10

1 Alex Ferguson v Arsène Wenger

2 Alex Ferguson v Kevin Keegan

3 José Mourinho v Arsène Wenger

4 Pep Guardiola v Jürgen Klopp

5 Rafa Benítez v Alex Ferguson

6 Kenny Dalglish v Alex Ferguson

7 Rafa Benítez v José Mourinho

8 Roy Keane v Patrick Vieira

9 Roy Keane v Alan Shearer

10 Andy Cole v Teddy Sheringham

Gary's Verdict: It always seemed to be Alex Ferguson against everyone, and only a couple ever gave as good as they got. Wenger was one of them: he was smart enough to keep up with Fergie, and good enough not to be cowed by him. That has been the defining managerial rivalry of the Premier League era.

THE DEBATE

Alan: I can see why Jürgen Klopp winds other managers up. I'm not sure he quite realises what he's doing, and I'm almost certain he does not do it deliberately to annoy his peers, but there are times when he might be considered a little disrespectful: running onto the pitch to celebrate with Alisson, his goalkeeper, while the Merseyside derby was still going on is possibly the best example.

Micah: I never really had a rival, someone I relished beating out of pure spite, but there were several players I looked forward to playing against. Most of the time, they were the most difficult opponents: Gareth Bale and Ryan Giggs. It was nothing personal at all: it was simply that it was up against them that I had chance to prove how good I was, to see what I could really do against truly elite opposition.

16

THE TOP 10
FLOPS

GARY LINEKER

I was barely ever injured during my career. I think, in all the years I played in England and Spain, the longest I was ever ruled out – other than when I developed hepatitis – was about two weeks: a tweaked hamstring here, or a twisted ankle there. I was available for pretty much every game.

That all changed when I arrived in Japan for the final stop of my career, at Nagoya Grampus Eight. It is still a source of embarrassment for me, really. I had been brought in to help grow the game there, alongside two other high-profile foreigners, the German striker Pierre Littbarski and the great Brazilian playmaker Zico. A lot of our duties were away from the pitch: we went on television shows to talk about the J-League, which had just been launched, and try to turn a whole new generation of fans on to domestic football.

I did all of that, and enjoyed it; part of what appealed to me about Japan was the chance not only to experience a new culture, but also to help develop a new competition. But we were expected to play a bit, too, and there things were a bit more complicated. I featured in the first three or four games, but then managed to snap my toe. It should have been a relatively straightforward injury, but there were all sorts of complications. It healed badly, and I was constantly in agony. It got so bad at one point that I could not sleep: even the touch of the sheet on my foot was too painful to bear.

Eventually, I went to the United States to see a specialist; he told me that if I did not have an operation, the pain would last forever. The drawback was that it might well end my career. I had the operation. There was a slim chance of coming back, I was told, and I did manage to play a few more games, about eight months later, but it was not the same. My toe was fused solid. I could not take off, couldn't accelerate. My career was over. I'd only played a handful of games in Japan. It wasn't my fault, particularly, and it certainly wasn't on purpose, but I am pretty confident that all of it qualifies my time at Grampus Eight as an unmitigated flop.

THE CONTENDERS

Alberto Aquilani (Roma to Liverpool, £19m, 2009)

Andy Carroll (Newcastle to Liverpool, £35m, 2011)

Stéphane Guivarc'h (Auxerre to Newcastle, £7m, 1998)

Michael Owen (Real Madrid to Newcastle, £16m, 2005)

Robinho (Real Madrid to Manchester City, £32.5m, 2008)

Alexis Sánchez (Arsenal to Manchester United, swap)

Andriy Shevchenko (AC Milan to Chelsea, £30m, 2006)

Chris Sutton (Blackburn to Chelsea, £7m, 1998)

Fernando Torres (Liverpool to Chelsea, £50m, 2011)
Juan Sebastián Verón (Lazio to Manchester United, £28m, 2001)

ALAN SHEARER

Signing a World Cup winner, in the summer of 1998, should have been just what Newcastle needed. We had been in contention for the title for the last couple of years, and we already had a really good team in place. Bringing in someone who had been in the French squad that had won the biggest tournament on the planet that summer might have been just the thing to take us over the edge.

There was just one problem: he was a striker who did not score. The club can't say they weren't warned. Stéphane Guivarc'h had started the tournament as France's number nine, in a team that had the creative prowess of Zinedine Zidane and Youri Djorkaeff and Thierry Henry, and he still had not been able to score a goal, through the whole tournament. That, to me, is a bit of a red flag.

Still, he had played in the World Cup final, so he must have had something about him. Even so, I wasn't worried that his arrival would mean my place was under threat: it was only two years since the club had made me the most expensive player in the world, and it's not like I wasn't scoring goals. Once I saw him in training, I was absolutely certain that my place wasn't under threat.

Well, it was not quite that quick. You tend to give new signings a little bit of time to settle in, especially if they are arriving in a new country and a new league. They have to get used to their teammates, get used to their surroundings, get their heads right.

I would not have expected Guivarc'h to hit the ground running straightaway. And I don't want to be disrespectful to him but, after a few days of training, it was blindingly obvious that the club had not really known what it was getting. It wasn't one of our best signings, put it that way. He scored on his debut, and then played a handful of games more before being sold on to Rangers. He only played for Newcastle for a few months. That is not exactly a ringing endorsement.

That said, I am always wary of labelling a player a flop. Sometimes there is a problem you don't know about: I have always wondered if Fernando Torres had some sort of underlying injury that meant he was not the same player for Chelsea as he was for Liverpool. Sometimes, it depends on the team you are in: Chris Sutton looked like a world-beater for Blackburn, but then couldn't buy a goal for Chelsea – you can look a lot better depending on who you are playing alongside. There are all sorts of factors that influence how a player does. Often, if they do not live up to expectations, it is not entirely their fault.

ALAN'S LIST

1 Fernando Torres (Liverpool to Chelsea, £50m, 2011)

2 Andriy Shevchenko (AC Milan to Chelsea, £30m, 2006)

3 Juan Sebastián Verón (Lazio to Manchester United, £28m, 2001)

4 Alexis Sánchez (Arsenal to Manchester United, swap)

5 Robinho (Real Madrid to Manchester City, £32.5m, 2008)

6 Andy Carroll (Newcastle to Liverpool, £35m, 2011)

7 Stephane Guivarc'h (Auxerre to Newcastle, £7m, 1998)

8 Michael Owen (Real Madrid to Newcastle, £16m, 2005)

9 Alberto Aquilani (Roma to Liverpool, £19m, 2009)

10 Chris Sutton (Blackburn to Chelsea, £7m, 1998)

MICAH RICHARDS

Andriy Shevchenko was one of the few players I faced during my career that left me a little bit starstruck. It did not happen often: the day Patrick Vieira walked into training with Manchester City, the first time I stood in the tunnel at Anfield and saw Steven Gerrard. Shevchenko was in that class, for me. I'd grown up playing video games with him on my team, so to be sharing a pitch with him was quite hard to get my head round. He was a legend.

He didn't perform like it at Chelsea, of course. Looking back, it was pretty clear that they signed him when his legs had gone or injuries had caught up with him; that may have been the reason that AC Milan were happy to accept an offer for a player who had been their biggest star for so long. Whatever the reason, it's a shame that the impression he left in England was such an anti-climax, because he was one of the very best of his generation.

We should be careful not to write players off based on them not being able to perform for one club or in one league. I always think of Diego Forlán, who is another of those who struggled in England and always suffered a bit for it. But a decade or so after he was such a let-down at Manchester United, he was possibly the player of the tournament for Uruguay in the 2010 World Cup. It just shows that players can only show their true ability if the circumstances are right. One bad period shouldn't mean you're cast forever as a bad player. I played with Jérôme Boateng at Manchester City, another deal that didn't work out. He just seemed to be too slow on the turn to play in England. But he went to Bayern Munich and became one of the best defenders of the last ten years. He had to be in the right place, that's all.

Besides, Shevchenko might not have been at his best when he was in England, but you could still see flashes of the player he had been. On one level, I was disappointed that he was not the player I remembered from the television – or from computer games – but on another, there were moments when he would put in a clever little bit of movement, or make a really unexpected, perfectly timed run, just something to show how intelligent a player he was, and you would see why he had been so special for so long. He might have been on the way down, but he had not lost it. I don't think you can, when you are coming from that high.

MICAH'S LIST

1 Fernando Torres (Liverpool to Chelsea, £50m, 2011)

2 Alexis Sánchez (Arsenal to Manchester United, swap)

3 Andriy Shevchenko (AC Milan to Chelsea, £30m, 2006)

4 Andy Carroll (Newcastle to Liverpool, £35m, 2011)

5 Juan Sebastián Verón
(Lazio to Manchester United, £28m, 2001)

6 Chris Sutton (Blackburn to Chelsea, £7m, 1998)

7 Michael Owen (Real Madrid to Newcastle, £16m, 2005)

8 Robinho (Real Madrid to Manchester City, £32.5m, 2008)

9 Stephane Guivarc'h (Auxerre to Newcastle, £7m, 1998)

10 Alberto Aquilani (Roma to Liverpool, £19m, 2009)

THE TOP 10

1 Fernando Torres (Liverpool to Chelsea, £50m, 2011)

2 Andriy Shevchenko (AC Milan to Chelsea, £30m, 2006)

3 Alexis Sánchez (Arsenal to Manchester United, swap)

4 Juan Sebastián Verón
(Lazio to Manchester United, £28m, 2001)

5 Andy Carroll (Newcastle to Liverpool, £35m, 2011)

6 Robinho (Real Madrid to Manchester City, £32.5m, 2008)

7 Michael Owen (Real Madrid to Newcastle, £16m, 2005)

8 Stephane Guivarc'h (Auxerre to Newcastle, £7m, 1998)

9 Chris Sutton (Blackburn to Chelsea, £7m, 1998)

10 Alberto Aquilani (Roma to Liverpool, £19m, 2009)

Gary's Verdict: None of these players should be written off so easily, for all that they struggled to make their moves work. There can be all sorts of factors that go into whether a transfer is a success or not: personal problems, difficulties settling in, injury issues. They might not have lived up to expectations, but it will not have been for the want of trying.

THE DEBATE

Alan: Michael Owen was a record signing for Newcastle, the most expensive player the club had signed since bringing me back home in 1996, but he never lived up to expectations. That did not stop him going on and performing well for Manchester United afterwards, though: sometimes, it is possible to be the right player in the wrong place.

Micah: You could easily have me on this list for my time at Aston Villa, and I'm sure many fans would. The only thing I can say in my defence is that they signed me on a free transfer, at the end of my contract at Manchester City, and that there are times in life when you get exactly what you've paid for.

17

THE TOP 10
HOMETOWN HEROES

GARY LINEKER

I had been going to watch Leicester every other Saturday, with my dad and my granddad, from the age of seven. Not too long after, I was catching the bus after school on a Tuesday and a Thursday to go and train there, too. It was not just the club I supported, it was a club that shaped my life.

I had grown up in the city, but we had moved out to a little village, Kirby Muxloe, not long before I was due to go to secondary school. My parents wanted me to be able to go to a grammar school, and there wasn't one available to me in Leicester. When my dad realised that the nearest one to the village was a rugby-playing school, though, he decided that I would be miserable there. He wanted me to be able to keep playing, so he moved us back into Leicester. For a while, I lived with my grandparents, and was spoiled rotten: my grandma made the best cake you can imagine. I asked him, years later, why he had done that, and he told me that it was because he knew that I could be a player, if only I had the chance. He hadn't told me that at the time.

The connection was so strong that leaving was an incredibly difficult decision. I knew, though, that to fulfil my ambitions I had to go: Leicester were a yo-yo team then, as they were for a long time, and if I wanted to win things, if I wanted to be the best I could be, it would have to be somewhere else. I always followed their results, and I always wanted them to do well, but you get so wrapped up in your current team that the bond lies dormant, I suppose.

It was only after I retired that, gradually, the connection came back. My club was my club again. There wasn't one particular moment when I realised that I was just as much of a supporter as I had been when I was young, but by 2002 I was fully invested again. That was the year that my agent, Jon Holmes, and I got a group together to buy Leicester out of administration, to reinvigorate it, to take it back to where it belonged. Seeing that happen has provided me with some of the best sporting moments of my life. It's a reminder that all sport is better when, deep down, you really care who wins.

THE CONTENDERS

Gabriel Agbonlahor (Aston Villa)

Phil Foden (Manchester City)

Steven Gerrard (Liverpool)

Jack Grealish (Aston Villa)

Matt Le Tissier (Southampton)

Harry Kane (Tottenham)

Gary Neville (Manchester United)

Wayne Rooney (Everton)

Paul Scholes (Manchester United)

Alan Shearer (Newcastle)

ALAN SHEARER

Signing for Newcastle was going back home, of course. I was going to play for the club that I had supported when I was a kid, the club that I used to go and watch from the Gallowgate End. But there is another part of that story that is forgotten now: I was also going to a team that was challenging for the Premier League title. The previous year, Newcastle had blown a 12-point lead over Manchester United; we were legitimate contenders to win something. It was not a decision I made purely out of romance; there was ambition there, too.

In all honesty, if that had not been the case – if Newcastle had been languishing in mid-table when the offer arrived – I probably would not have signed for them, not then. I would not have jeopardised my chances of winning things just to go and sign for my club, to go back home. It could only happen because, at the time, it seemed like both things were possible. I was supposed to be the final piece of the puzzle, not just a feel-good story.

Even though we never actually managed to fulfil that particular part of the bargain, it was special playing for my team. It had been great at Southampton and at Blackburn, of course, but there was something different about arriving at the stadium where I had enjoyed my first taste of football, the place I'd gone as a fan for years, the place I'd dreamed of playing. It felt different, somehow.

I was under pressure to deliver, of course: I was the most expensive player in the world, the club's record signing, the prodigal son returning. I never felt it, particularly: I loved that status, and I loved that it was my responsibility to deliver for the people who were standing where I had once stood. I never really had a problem dealing with pressure.

But maybe that would have been different if, rather than going back home, I had never left. I think it is more difficult for players who have grown up at a club, who have come through the youth academy, who have never known anything else. They find chances harder to come by, they can be judged more harshly, and often they are weighed down by greater expectations than players who arrive with all the excitement of a new signing.

It is why, as much as I would love to put myself first, I think it has to be Steven Gerrard, a player who survived every step of the way at Liverpool, and went on to establish himself as possibly the club's greatest ever player, and certainly the best ever to come through its academy. It is a privilege, playing for the team you support, but it can also be a challenge, and he more than rose to it.

ALAN'S LIST

1 Steven Gerrard (Liverpool)

2 Alan Shearer (Newcastle)

3 Matt Le Tissier (Southampton)

4 Paul Scholes (Manchester United)

5 Harry Kane (Tottenham)

6 Gary Neville (Manchester United)

7 Wayne Rooney (Everton)

8 Phil Foden (Manchester City)

9 Jack Grealish (Aston Villa)

10 Gabriel Agbonlahor (Aston Villa)

MICAH RICHARDS

As a kid from the academy, the day you first go and join in training with a club's team is an intimidating one. You feel like you've achieved something, but you also know that the work is only really beginning. In those circumstances, it helps to have familiar faces around you, people who are feeling exactly the same way.

I was lucky enough to have that. There were a handful of players who came through Manchester City's academy at roughly the same time I did: Nedum Onuoha not long before, Michael Johnson, Stephen Ireland, Daniel Sturridge, as well as Shaun Wright-Phillips, who was kind of the standard-bearer for all of us.

In some ways, you can offer each other support. A lot of the time, you will split your time between the first team and the academy, as the club sees how you cope with the step up. If there is just one of you, you can become a target among the players still in the youth teams. People assume that because you've been moved up that you've become big time, that you're full of yourself. There can be jealousy, and it can go a long way beyond healthy competition. If there is a group of you, that effect is watered down a bit. The other players can see a bit of a pathway for them, too. You show them that it is possible.

But in others, you learn very quickly that football is a dog-eat-dog world, and you have to look after yourself, first and foremost; it doesn't matter if your mates are doing well, or if the club feels a loyalty to you, because if you're not good enough, they will get rid of you in a second.

In some cases, being home-grown means the fans put even more pressure on you. They see you as their representative on the pitch, almost, and if you're not putting the effort in, they'll call you on it. For me, it always felt like Manchester City's fans were a lot more understanding with me because they had seen me come through. They were invested in me being the best I could be, I suppose, and they stuck with me when I wasn't playing well. Occasionally, someone would ask why I was better for England than I was for the club, but I never really had the heart to point out that the players around me with England were quite a lot better at that point.

That added a type of pressure, too: I wanted to repay them for the faith they had shown in me. But my main concern was always making sure I warranted my place. That was especially difficult after the takeover, when every summer brought a new load of signings and every day seemed to bring a story about someone losing their place. The fact that you had come through the academy did not matter to the club in the slightest. You were either good enough, or you weren't. That is the beauty of football, I suppose, but it is also, deep down, pretty brutal.

MICAH'S LIST

1 Steven Gerrard (Liverpool)

2 Matt Le Tissier (Southampton)

3 Jack Grealish (Aston Villa)

4 Harry Kane (Tottenham)

5 Alan Shearer (Newcastle)

6 Paul Scholes (Manchester United)

7 Gary Neville (Manchester United)

8 Phil Foden (Manchester City)

9 Gabriel Agbonlahor (Aston Villa)

10 Wayne Rooney (Everton)

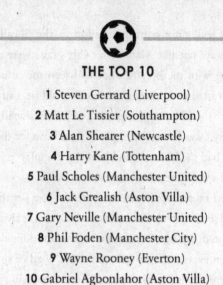

THE TOP 10

1 Steven Gerrard (Liverpool)

2 Matt Le Tissier (Southampton)

3 Alan Shearer (Newcastle)

4 Harry Kane (Tottenham)

5 Paul Scholes (Manchester United)

6 Jack Grealish (Aston Villa)

7 Gary Neville (Manchester United)

8 Phil Foden (Manchester City)

9 Wayne Rooney (Everton)

10 Gabriel Agbonlahor (Aston Villa)

Gary's Verdict: A bit of a surprise as Alan goes for Steven Gerrard to win, but it's hard to argue with that magnanimous choice. Gerrard lived out every fan's dream: not just guiding his team to a Champions League trophy, but lifting his club to the biggest victory of all almost single-handedly.

THE DEBATE

Alan: You could choose almost anyone from the Class of '92 for this list: it was not just Scholes and Neville who grew up supporting Manchester United. Nicky Butt, Phil Neville and David Beckham were all United fans, too, even if Beckham does not really count as a hometown hero.

Micah: In an ideal world, Jack Grealish would have spent his whole career at Aston Villa, just like Gabriel Agbonlahor did. They are the team he supported as a boy, and the team he loves. But there is a balance between following your heart and following your ambition: look at Wayne Rooney. He was a devoted Everton fan, but he knew he had to leave if he wanted to fulfil his talent.

18

THE TOP 10
KITS

GARY LINEKER

I like to think that it never really mattered to me what kit I was playing in. We had to do all of the promotional shoots every couple of years, of course, but whether it was a nice shirt or not was never something I considered particularly important. What was important was what you did in it, not whether you looked good wearing it.

There was one exception: I never liked wearing yellow. It was not a luck thing. We had a yellow away shirt at Tottenham while I was there, and my record was pretty good. I scored four goals against Wimbledon wearing yellow. I scored a couple on the opening day of the season wearing yellow, too. I never felt that I performed particularly badly in it. I just didn't feel it suited me.

That shirt was not an especially ugly one, but I did play in a couple of horrors. In my last couple of years at Leicester, the club introduced a green-and-yellow striped away shirt, with the name of a local brewer, our sponsor, plastered across the front. It was as aesthetically pleasing as it sounds. It's not even like they were evenly spaced stripes. They were sort of a strange double pinstripe. It was not a great look.

The kits that you remember most fondly, of course, are the ones that are most associated with happy memories. That's true, I think, of the England kits from 1986 and 1990, both of which have now achieved iconic status. What they look like is secondary, really, compared to how they make us feel, either as fans or as players. We see them and we remember the tournaments, the games, and the summer; it's those happy associations, as much as the design, that make us so fond of them. Although it probably helps that none of them were yellow.

THE CONTENDERS

Arsenal (Away) 1992/1993
Nottingham Forest (Home) 1992/1993
Blackburn (Home) 1994/1995
Manchester United (Home) 1994/1995
Wimbledon (Home) 1994/1995
Newcastle (Home) 1995/1996
Tottenham (Home) 1999/2000
Leeds United (Home) 2002/2003
Arsenal (Home) 2003/2004
Liverpool (Home) 2019/2020

ALAN SHEARER

Newcastle wore a couple of truly horrendous shirts during my time there. You're always relatively safe with the home shirt – there is a limit to what anyone is willing to do with the traditional colours of the club – but the away shirt seems to be a free-for-all. I was never especially bothered by what kit I had to wear: you don't have a choice, after all, and once you're presented with it, there is not a vast amount you can do about it.

But even so, there were one or two that I did not particularly enjoy looking at. There was a canary yellow number, in 2004, that was supposed to be our European shirt, and was especially horrible. It had the opposite problem to the famous one that Manchester United wore for a half at Southampton: that one, Alex Ferguson said afterwards, meant that his players could not see each other on the pitch. That was not a problem with that yellow kit. If anything, we could see each other too well.

Other than that, I think I got away relatively lightly. I played in a decent kit at Southampton – the Draper Tools shirt, with a chevron and the red and white stripes – and a lovely one at Blackburn, with those iconic halves. But there is, surely, no contest on this category: the best Premier League of all time is very clearly the one that became synonymous with Newcastle's Entertainers, with the black and white stripes, the buttons on the collar, and the Newcastle Brown Ale badge on the front.

I don't know what it is about that kit that makes it so special. Maybe it is because the sponsor just seems so appropriate, so local. For me, it is maybe because it is the kit that I signed for the club in:

it is the one that reminds me of what it felt like to come home. For Newcastle fans, it is maybe the memories that it brings. We had some success later on, under Bobby Robson, but that side meant so much to people in the city, people who had been following the team for years, and seeing that shirt maybe brings back all of the excitement that they felt at the time, the hope and the belief that they could be about to win the title.

That could well be true for everyone, too: that team was wonderful to watch, brave and attacking and fearless, and it seemed to resonate with people beyond Newcastle. Certain kits immediately make you think of certain games, certain moments, and if those associations are happy ones, then the kit benefits from that.

ALAN'S LIST

1 Newcastle (Home) 1995/1996

2 Blackburn (Home) 1994/1995

3 Arsenal (Away) 1992/1993

4 Leeds United (Home) 2002/2003

5 Arsenal (Home) 2003/2004

6 Manchester United (Home) 1994/1995

7 Nottingham Forest (Home) 1992/1993

8 Wimbledon (Home) 1994/1995

9 Tottenham (Home) 1999/2000

10 Liverpool (Home) 2019/2020

MICAH RICHARDS

This is not that hard to follow. I was born in Birmingham. I grew up in Leeds. But I was an Arsenal fan. My reasons were simple: I loved watching Ian Wright smiling after he had scored a goal, I loved the style and poise of Thierry Henry, and I loved the grit and power of Patrick Vieira.

There is one slight complication, one that does not really help my case. I also quite liked Newcastle. Well, I liked one thing about Newcastle: the shirt. The famous one with Newcastle Brown Ale on the front and the Granddad collar, the one that they came so close to winning the title in during the 1996 season. So, as a kid, one who was born in Birmingham and grew up in Leeds and supported Arsenal, I also proudly wore the Newcastle shirt my mum had bought me. I had some Arsenal ones, too, but that Newcastle one was so beautiful that I didn't care that they weren't my team.

I was never a particularly high-maintenance player. It did not matter much to me what the kit we were wearing looked like, though I did care about how it felt: it sounds silly, but you need to be comfortable in what you're wearing while you're playing. I found that some brands – I won't name them – fitted better than others. I never really bothered by what the pattern on the shirt was, but I looked forward to some kits more than others, just because I knew they would feel better on me.

I was the same with boots. While I was in the academy at Manchester City, a lot of the kids would make sure they were playing in the best boots they could afford: ones they had bought, initially, and then ones that their suppliers had sent them once they had done boot deals. I did not have anyone volunteering to give me boots until I was in the England team, so I spent most of the early years of my career in cheap knock-off boots, ones that we had bought for £10 or £12 in the local sports shop. I played in a Victory Shield in those boots. It didn't stop me, though: it doesn't really matter how fancy your boots are, after all, just as it doesn't matter how nice the kit looks. What matters is how good you are.

MICAH'S LIST

1 Newcastle (Home) 1995/1996
2 Leeds United (Home) 2002/2003
3 Arsenal (Away) 1992/1993
4 Nottingham Forest (Home) 1992/1993
5 Arsenal (Home) 2003/2004
6 Tottenham (Home) 1999/2000
7 Blackburn (Home) 1994/1995
8 Manchester United (Home) 1994/1995
9 Wimbledon (Home) 1994/1995
10 Liverpool (Home) 2019/2020

THE TOP 10

1 Newcastle (Home) 1995/1996
2 Arsenal (Away) 1992/1993
3 Leeds United (Home) 2002/2003
4 Blackburn (Home) 1994/1995
5 Arsenal (Home) 2003/2004

6 Nottingham Forest (Home) 1992/1993
7 Tottenham (Home) 1999/2000
8 Manchester United (Home) 1994/1995
9 Wimbledon (Home) 1994/1995
10 Liverpool (Home) 2019/2020

Gary's Verdict: At last, a title of sorts for the Newcastle team that just missed out in 1996: they might not have won the league that year, thanks to throwing away that 12-point lead over Manchester United, but no team has ever looked better in disappointment.

THE DEBATE

Alan: Quite a lot of these contenders come from the 1990s, don't they? They were obviously not quite as fitted as they are now – we wore our shirts quite baggy, looking back – but it's good to know that we all looked so good.

Micah: One of the nicest shirts I ever wore was the special edition, 1960s-style one we wore for the derby to commemorate the 50th anniversary of the Munich air disaster. It was a mark of respect to wear it, of course, but it had also been designed beautifully.

PART THREE

HALL OF FAME

1

THE TOP 10
CAPTAINS

GARY LINEKER

It's hard to pinpoint, precisely, what makes a good captain. There's no manual for it: every player has a slightly different idea of what they're supposed to do, and how they're supposed to do it.

Not everyone is an inspirational speaker, the sort of character who can lift their teammates with a few choice words or a rousing speech. For some, the key thing is being a leader on the field: making sure that your performances never dip, that all of your teammates can rely on you to turn up every game, that nobody can ever accuse you of shirking responsibility or allowing your level to dip. Some players become captains because they're liked by their teammates, but not all captains are popular. Others become captains because they're intensely disliked by their opponents. But not all captains are unpopular, either.

And what turns a good captain into a great one is an imperfect science, too. Aside from Alan Shearer – I'm not entirely sure what he's doing in this category – all of the captains on this list have won something. And in some cases, they have won lots of things. But I don't know if you necessarily have to win something to be a great captain. That is not always how it is measured.

Maybe what makes the difference is being there in the big moments: think of Vincent Kompany, such an extraordinary leader at Manchester City, who scored the goals that effectively clinched two Premier League titles, first against Manchester United in 2014 and then again, against Leicester City, in 2019. Or Steven Gerrard, central to Liverpool's Champions League triumph in Istanbul and then, a year later, in the 2006 FA Cup final.

But perhaps more than anyone else, Roy Keane and John Terry have embodied that idea of leadership in the Premier League era. They both led by example, they both lifted the players around them, they both came to symbolise their teams. Terry would, just, shade it for me: Roy always had that tendency to allow the red mist to descend, and that is the sort of trait that can cost your team in those fine, final moments. There isn't much to choose between them, though. They both won the lot, and they both won it all from the front.

THE CONTENDERS

Tony Adams (Arsenal)
Steven Gerrard (Liverpool)
Jordan Henderson (Liverpool)
Roy Keane (Manchester United)
Vincent Kompany (Manchester City)
Wes Morgan (Leicester City)
Alan Shearer (Newcastle United)
John Terry (Chelsea)

Nemanja Vidić (Manchester United)
Patrick Vieira (Arsenal)

ALAN SHEARER

What you want of a captain is fairly simple to describe, but difficult to achieve: it is someone who delivers for their team when they are needed most, someone who commands the respect not just of their teammates, but of their fans, too. Tim Sherwood, our captain at Blackburn when we won the league, more than fulfilled those criteria.

It's not for me to say whether I did or not when I was captain at Newcastle – I'll have to put myself tenth on this list – but I should probably point out that I did lift a trophy for England. The year before the 1998 World Cup, we went to France to play in Le Tournoi, a four-team dry run for the tournament: an early version of the Confederations Cup. We lost to Brazil in our last game, but we beat Italy and France, and that was enough to finish top. It's easy to laugh and point out it wasn't a major trophy, but it was a trophy, and that's more than Gary won as captain.

Everyone else on this list was a seriously impressive player, and you can't argue with what any of them delivered. Patrick Vieira was tough, nasty and incredibly talented. Nemanja Vidić won five Premier League titles. Vincent Kompany got Manchester City, and he got Manchester City fans.

During my career, I'd be lying if I said I liked Roy Keane. I'm not sure I was alone in that. We had plenty of rucks, including one at St

James's Park which ended up with him getting sent off. He clocked me smiling as he was shown the red card, and you could almost see the steam coming out of his ears. It meant I had a tricky choice at the final whistle: do I run straight off, or do I linger a bit on the pitch? I knew he'd be waiting for me. Nothing happened, in the end: our teammates got in the way as I shouted at them to hold me back, while not trying all that hard to get away.

He was a great leader, Roy, but I'd go for John Terry as the defining captain of the Premier League era. He delivered. He got angry when he had to. Managers respected him, fans respected him, and his teammates respected him. Opposition fans weren't too fond of him, but that only seemed to spur him on more. A great captain doesn't have to be loved. In a way, that's the last thing you want.

ALAN'S LIST

1 John Terry
2 Roy Keane
3 Patrick Vieira
4 Steven Gerrard
5 Tony Adams
6 Vincent Kompany
7 Jordan Henderson
8 Nemanja Vidić
9 Wes Morgan
10 Alan Shearer

MICAH RICHARDS

Vincent Kompany was almost the perfect captain. He led by example. He never let his performances dip. He put the needs of the team above himself. He made sure he worked the hardest, showed the most dedication, kept everyone in line. If training hadn't been great one day, he would ask around, find out why, put it right tomorrow.

It was, in a lot of ways, a pleasure being his deputy, but it wasn't always easy. Vincent had an elaborate system of fines for anyone who broke his rules, whether it was being late for training or having a phone on at a team dinner. The fines weren't paltry: they started out at about £5,000 and went up from there, with the money all going into a kitty, either for a Christmas party or for charity.

He had them written down on a little clipboard, and it was my job to enforce them. That made me the bad cop, and him the good one, and that never really struck me as fair. At one point, I decided to end his tyranny: he kept all of the details of the fines in a locker, secured with a padlock. So I broke in, destroyed the padlock, and mysteriously all the fines disappeared.

I would have loved to be the same sort of captain – to have that sort of authority – when I was at Villa, but there was one problem. We had joint captains: me for on-the-pitch stuff, and Gabby Agbonlahor, who knew the club inside out, for off-the-field things. My job was to get everyone going, but the problem was, by that stage, my form had disappeared completely. A captain has to be a consistently good performer: you can't have a captain whose place in the team is questioned.

Steven Gerrard is the best example of that. The Liverpool teams he played in were not always the best in the country or the best in Europe, but he lifted everyone around him. He was quite a quiet person by nature, I think, but he led by example: he made sure that, whatever pitch he was on, he was the best player on it. He set the tempo, he dominated the game. That is exactly what a captain needs to do.

MICAH'S LIST

1 Steven Gerrard
2 John Terry
3 Roy Keane
4 Vincent Kompany
5 Tony Adams
6 Patrick Vieira
7 Nemanja Vidić
8 Jordan Henderson
9 Wes Morgan
10 Alan Shearer

THE TOP 10

1 John Terry
2 Steven Gerrard
3 Roy Keane
4 Patrick Vieira
5 Vincent Kompany

> **6** Tony Adams
> **7** Nemanja Vidić
> **8** Jordan Henderson
> **9** Wes Morgan
> **10** Alan Shearer

Gary's Verdict: You can make a case for any of Gerrard, Keane and Terry. It's hard to separate the three, though Terry narrowly claims it here. The only point I'd quibble with is that Wes Morgan should be a lot higher. That's not just my Leicester bias shining through: he was the captain of the team that pulled off the greatest miracle in Premier League – and maybe football – history. To lead that team to that achievement is extraordinary.

THE DEBATE

Alan: Keane was not quite as good a player technically as the likes of Gerrard or Vieira. He was an incredible leader and a brilliant presence to have on the pitch, but he maybe did not have quite their talent.

Micah: I like Roy. I like making him feel slightly uncomfortable. I can't match what he achieved on the pitch – I have to remind him, every so often, that I was the youngest defender ever to play for England, just to put him in his place – but if I can keep on his toes in a studio, that's my job done.

2

THE TOP 10
GOALSCORERS

GARY LINEKER

Being in the right place at the right time is not as easy as it looks. That is always the accusation when a striker pops up in the last minute to score a winner, as though for the rest of the game they have just been standing around, waiting for that moment to come, and it has always seemed unfair to me.

Much of the work a striker does goes unnoticed. It is in making run after run after run into a pocket of space, and the ball never arriving. It is in moving a defence around, forcing defenders to abandon their shape, so that your teammates might benefit. Strikers are rarely in the right place at the right time by accident. They get there by design, and that design takes a lot of effort.

It is a product both of ability and mentality: the willingness to keep going even when you don't see any immediate reward. The great forwards have the attitude and the work ethic to keep getting into those positions, to keep making those runs, to keep looking for space. I don't know if that is something that can be manufactured. You either have it, or you don't.

The stereotype is that strikers are all selfish, though I wonder if that isn't quite the right word: maybe it is more to do with being self-confident. When you find yourself in that position and the odds are only slightly in your favour, do you have the belief and ability to say you will take on that responsibility?

And it is also, of course, an addiction. That is the only way to describe it: scoring goals is addictive. When you have that feeling, of seeing the ball hit the net, feeling the buzz in the crowd, you want to do it over and over again.

All of the players on this list had that addiction, just as they all had the talent and dedication to fulfil it. We've had to fine-tune the criteria a little anyway, just because there were so many players to consider: Michael Owen, Robbie Fowler, Ian Wright and Frank Lampard do not even make the Top 10.

We are judging players exclusively on what they did while they were in the Premier League, and not what they would go on to do – if the consideration was a player's entire career, Cristiano Ronaldo would have walked it – after they had left.

But what defines a great goalscorer is a little harder to pin down. Is a great goalscorer the player who scored the most goals, or the player who scored the most important ones? Does it matter what those goals helped them achieve? Is it simply a numbers game, or is there more to it than that?

THE CONTENDERS

Sergio Agüero (Manchester City)

Andy Cole (Newcastle United,
Manchester United, Manchester City)

Didier Drogba (Chelsea)

Thierry Henry (Arsenal)

Harry Kane (Tottenham)

Alan Shearer (Southampton, Blackburn Rovers, Newcastle)

Luis Suárez (Liverpool)

Cristiano Ronaldo (Manchester United)

Wayne Rooney (Manchester United)

Ruud van Nistelrooy (Manchester United)

ALAN SHEARER

It really, really won't look good if I put myself first, will it? I don't want to put myself top, but ultimately this is a category about putting the ball in the back of the net. There are other things to factor in: a player's longevity, how much they won, their goals-to-game ratio, but what makes a great goalscorer is how many goals they score. And the evidence is 260 goals in the Premier League, and that was after losing three years to injury. So I don't think I have much of a choice, do I?

The competition is tough, though. Maybe the best measure of that is the fact that Harry Kane is down in ninth. Maybe in a few years that will have changed: he still has plenty of time to score more goals, after all. But look at the players he is up against. Ruud van

Nistelrooy was an incredible goalscorer, a pure goalscorer, completely relentless.

Sergio Agüero has been one of the finest imports we've ever had in the Premier League: he was still banging the goals in at the age of 32, playing in a magnificent, title-winning Manchester City team. We've been really lucky to have a decade watching him play.

It seems strange to say it about Wayne Rooney, given that he's the record goalscorer for both Manchester United and England, but I do wonder if he perhaps was not quite selfish enough. He sacrificed himself at various times to play in a slightly deeper position; he was not always Manchester United's outright number nine. And Cristiano Ronaldo would be out there on his own if we were to judge him by his entire career; he and Lionel Messi have redefined what we think is possible in terms of goalscoring.

They have also helped to change what we expect our strikers to do. Very few teams now play with a centre-forward in the traditional sense; the role is now for an all-purpose forward, one who might drop deep or wide or help to build play. Teams look to their wingers for goals as much as the player in the middle. But if the job has changed, the remit has not. The clue is in the name: a great goalscorer means scoring goals. And there's only one winner there.

ALAN'S LIST

1 Alan Shearer

2 Sergio Agüero

3 Thierry Henry

4 Wayne Rooney

5 Ruud van Nistelrooy

6 Didier Drogba

7 Cristiano Ronaldo

8 Luis Suárez

9 Harry Kane

10 Andy Cole

MICAH RICHARDS

Andy Cole came to Manchester City as his career was winding down and mine was getting going. He always called me 'Topper', because that's what he used to accuse me of doing in training: getting overenthusiastic with my tackling and going over the top on people.

There was one session, in particular, where I crunched him during a game. He got up, looked at me, and warned me not to do it again. 'Topper,' he said. 'Do that once more and I'll embarrass you.'

I wasn't the sort to back down, though. 'You can't do it, old man,' I told him. The next time he got the ball, he shaped to shoot, feinted and dropped off into a little bit of space. I couldn't keep up: he left me on the ground. He shot and scored, obviously. He'd done what he said: he'd embarrassed me because, even in his old age, his movement was incredible. He was smarter than you, and he was better than you. He maybe wasn't the hardest worker, but he didn't need to be. He had enough quality.

Sergio Agüero wasn't the most dedicated trainer either. He wasn't lazy, particularly, he was just very laid back. It's not something you associate with Argentineans: Pablo Zabaleta worked as hard as anyone, and Carlos Tevez was so competitive in five-a-side that you basically couldn't get the ball off him.

Agüero was different. He's as nice as they come, and he was really chilled in training; at first, I wasn't even sure I could see what all the fuss was about. But then he came on as a substitute in his first game and scored a hat-trick, the first one set up by a pinpoint cross from Manchester City's marauding, talented, handsome right-back. I think you can make the case that I set him on his way. I'd love to put him first, but even with all of the things he achieved in his ten years at City – scoring more goals for one club than anyone else in Premier League history – sadly, I can't. It's goalscoring, so it has to be the person who scored the most goals. And, unfortunately, that person is Alan Shearer.

MICAH'S LIST

1 Alan Shearer

2 Sergio Agüero

3 Andy Cole

4 Thierry Henry

5 Wayne Rooney

6 Ruud van Nistelrooy

7 Harry Kane

8 Didier Drogba

9 Cristiano Ronaldo

10 Luis Suárez

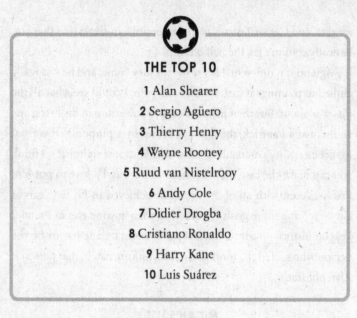

THE TOP 10

1 Alan Shearer

2 Sergio Agüero

3 Thierry Henry

4 Wayne Rooney

5 Ruud van Nistelrooy

6 Andy Cole

7 Didier Drogba

8 Cristiano Ronaldo

9 Harry Kane

10 Luis Suárez

Gary's Verdict: In the end, the numbers are telling. Both Sergio Agüero and Thierry Henry have better ratios than Alan Shearer – they scored more goals per game than he managed – but he still has to go down as the greatest goalscorer of the Premier League era just for sheer volume. He was a proper goalscorer, even if he didn't want to put himself first.

THE DEBATE

Alan: He might not have come top – despite being the leading goalscorer in history for both Manchester United and England – but the player on this list that I would most like to have played with is Wayne Rooney. He scored plenty himself, obviously, but he was just as good at creating chances for others.

Micah: I kept a couple of these in my pocket when I played against them. Ronaldo was tricky – you could never tell which way he was going to go – but I kept him quiet in at least one derby. I think I managed a clean sheet against Suárez at one point, too. But I was there for Rooney's overhead kick to win the derby: you can just see him beat me to the ball as I go to head it clear.

3

THE TOP 10
GOALKEEPERS

GARY LINEKER

My golden rule was always that, no matter what happened, no matter what they had done, you never congratulated a goalkeeper. As a striker, you never wanted to show them you were impressed.

I only ever made one exception, and that was for David Seaman. It was a game at White Hart Lane, while I was at Tottenham and he, obviously, was at Arsenal. I was no more than three yards out, absolutely certain I was about to score, and he just came out of nowhere. When the ball had gone out of play, I picked myself up and walked over to him and just said: 'Good save.' That is the highest praise I was ever going to give a goalkeeper.

It's hard to think of a position that has changed so much in such a short space of time. In Seaman's heyday – and mine – goalkeepers were thought of as almost separate from the game itself: that was true not just until the change in the back-pass rule in 1992, but for quite some time after that. Goalkeepers were not expected to be involved in build-up, to spread the ball from the back, to be able to play. They are a part of the team in a way that never used to be true.

Now, that is what marks the finest goalkeepers out: the two Brazilians on our list, Alisson and Ederson, are among the best exponents of playing out from the back in the modern game. That shift has created victims, too. There were times when David de Gea was thought of as the best goalkeeper on the planet. He was like Spider-Man; the last decade would have been much rougher on Manchester United without a player of his quality between the posts.

But his stock has fallen, just a little, and in part that is because he is not quite so comfortable on the ball as the likes of Ederson. He has not suffered as much, though, as probably the most notable absentee from this list: Joe Hart. Arguably, he was caught out by the changing nature of goalkeeping more than anybody, dropped and eventually sold by Pep Guardiola because he did not believe he was good enough with his feet to be part of his Manchester City team. What he could do with his hands, suddenly, was not the be all and end all.

THE CONTENDERS

Alisson Becker (Liverpool)

David James (Liverpool, Aston Villa, West Ham, Manchester City, Portsmouth)

Shay Given (Newcastle, Manchester City)

Jens Lehmann (Arsenal)

David de Gea (Manchester United)

Ederson (Manchester City)

Edwin van der Sar (Fulham, Manchester United)

Petr Čech (Chelsea, Arsenal)

David Seaman (Arsenal)

Peter Schmeichel (Manchester United, Manchester City)

ALAN SHEARER

That change in what we expect from goalkeepers is important. Some of the names on this list would never have been judged for how accurate they were with their feet; that was not something that anybody really thought about at the time. So we have to take that into consideration, to a degree: judging them by the standards of the time, rather than by what we would look like now.

That said, I think the top two stand out, head and shoulders above the rest. I played with David Seaman for England for many years, so I know exactly how hard he worked, and exactly how good he was. But it's hard to see past Peter Schmeichel for top spot, given everything he won for Manchester United.

It was hard to see past him full stop, as it goes: he was a big, mad presence on the pitch, and everything he did was designed to make him bigger. He was a revolutionary in his own way, too. He brought in what became known as the starfish, rushing from his line and spreading his arms and legs as wide as he could, closing down every angle. He did it at such speed, and with such size, that you always knew that if he clattered into you it would hurt.

Facing him, you knew that's what he would try and do: make himself as big as possible. In all those years of playing against him – and scoring against him now and again, too – I tried not to have a preconceived idea of what I was going to do. I wanted to stay in control, to be able to choose the best thing to do in the moment, rather than planning something in advance.

That's not to disparage the others on the list. To be around as long as Jens Lehmann was, or to make as many appearances as Shay Given, you have to be a really good goalkeeper. Maybe, in time, Alisson and Ederson will rise up the list: at the moment, they suffer a little because they haven't made that many appearances. But it is a fragile thing, being a goalkeeper: look at De Gea, who was flawless for years but has allowed mistakes to creep into his game. Rightly or wrongly, that is how goalkeepers are judged, by their mistakes. And ultimately, Seaman and Schmeichel made very, very few of them.

ALAN'S LIST

1 Peter Schmeichel
2 David Seaman
3 Petr Čech
4 Edwin van der Sar
5 Ederson
6 David de Gea
7 Jens Lehmann
8 Shay Given
9 David James
10 Alisson Becker

MICAH RICHARDS

I've got to come to the defence of Joe Hart here, and not just because he's my guy. In his prime, he was better than quite a few of these goalkeepers. He dislodged Shay Given as Manchester City's first choice, for a start. I'd say he achieved more than David James. At his peak, he was better than David de Gea, too.

There are two games that really stand out for me, both in the Champions League. He singlehandedly kept Borussia Dortmund at bay at the Etihad in 2012, and that was not a bad Dortmund team at all: they were champions of Germany, and they had Mario Götze, Marco Reus and Robert Lewandowski upfront.

And then, three years later, City went to Camp Nou to face Barcelona in the knockout stages. They lost the game and the tie, but Joe was equal to everything Lionel Messi could throw at him. Even Messi acknowledged it: I think he called Joe 'phenomenal' afterwards. That's not a bad seal of approval.

So why is he not on this list? I can't help thinking that a major part of the reason is because of the way his England career ended: the humiliation against Iceland in 2016, and then a couple of difficult years before he was finally left out of the squad for the 2018 World Cup.

By that time, he'd already lost his place at City, of course. Goalkeeping is a zero sum game: your success can only mean one of your teammates' failure. Seeing Joe and Shay compete for the same place had been really awkward, because although they were always both ultra-professional, it's the sort of thing that would be killing you inside.

Joe eventually won that battle, but Pep Guardiola had clearly decided he couldn't do what he wanted his goalkeeper to do. I was devastated for him when first Claudio Bravo and then Ederson came in to replace him. It must have really hurt him.

But watching what Ederson has done in the last few years has been nothing short of incredible. He doesn't have much shot-stopping to do, because as a rule City have the ball, but his passing is out of this world. He's not been around long enough to challenge Peter Schmeichel, Petr Čech or David Seaman for the top spot, but I've never seen a goalkeeper so good with his feet. The more important that becomes, the more likely it is that he'll go down as the Premier League's greatest ever modern goalkeeper.

MICAH'S LIST

1 Peter Schmeichel
2 Petr Čech
3 David Seaman
4 Ederson
5 Edwin van der Sar
6 Alisson Becker
7 David de Gea
8 Shay Given
9 David James
10 Jens Lehmann

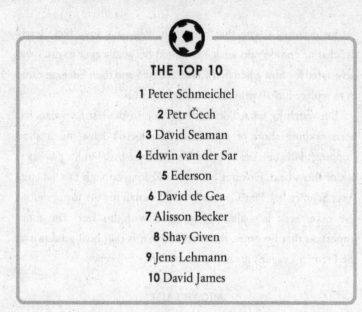

THE TOP 10

1 Peter Schmeichel

2 Petr Čech

3 David Seaman

4 Edwin van der Sar

5 Ederson

6 David de Gea

7 Alisson Becker

8 Shay Given

9 Jens Lehmann

10 David James

Gary's Verdict: A unanimous victor in Schmeichel, and agreement on who should come in just behind him. I would probably go for Čech, who had such a long and illustrious career, particularly at Chelsea, just ahead of Seaman. I don't want to praise David more than once, after all.

THE DEBATE

Alan: We talk a lot now about how players like Alisson and Ederson have changed goalkeeping, but Peter Schmeichel had just as much of an impact. He was one of the key figures of that Manchester United team, and his last game for the club was the Champions League final. It wouldn't have been the same without him.

Micah: The one thing with Seaman was that he pulled off the greatest save in my lifetime: that incredible dive backwards to deny Paul Peschisolido in the FA Cup semi-final. I have no idea how he did it. If that had happened now, in the era of social media, you would see it replayed all the time.

4

THE TOP 10
MANAGERS

GARY LINEKER

If this was purely down to what they meant to me, I would have Claudio Ranieri at number one. When people ask me the best sporting moment of my life, it's not winning the FA Cup or playing for England in a World Cup: it is genuinely the one that Ranieri gave me when he brought the Premier League title to Leicester.

Those last few weeks of that season were magical. I watched the run-in with my boys and, because Leicester was such a compelling story, they always seemed to be playing on a Sunday. We'd sit and watch together, and it was agonising. It never felt like it was getting more secure; it only got more and more tense, as though it could all fall apart at any minute.

Ranieri managed it brilliantly, though. He took the pressure off his team, he never let expectations rise too high, he always seemed to be smiling, marvelling at the improbability of it all. They weren't playing the day they won the league, but I was with my boys again, watching Chelsea play Tottenham. There were tears running down my cheeks when Eden Hazard scored that equaliser, the one that handed the league to Leicester. I cried again when they gave them the trophy.

Unfortunately, the criteria for this are a bit broader than how happy they made me. How many trophies they won has to be taken into consideration, but also their longevity: how long they survived in the cut-throat world of the Premier League. It's something that perhaps counts against someone like Carlo Ancelotti, who is the only manager in history to have won league titles in Italy, Spain, England and Germany, but has only been in charge of a hundred games or so in the Premier League.

And then there is the football they play. I would love to have had the chance to play for Jürgen Klopp or Pep Guardiola. Klopp's football can be breathtaking to watch, but as a striker, you would relish playing in that Guardiola system. His teams create so many chances for their centre-forward, when they play with a centre-forward. I'd have been able to score as many as Messi. And then there is José Mourinho, who might not be to everyone's tastes, but his record is second to none. Well, almost second to none, as we'll see.

THE CONTENDERS

Sir Alex Ferguson (Manchester United)

Arsène Wenger (Arsenal)

Jürgen Klopp (Liverpool)

Pep Guardiola (Manchester City)

Rafa Benítez (Liverpool, Chelsea, Newcastle United)

Sir Bobby Robson (Newcastle United)

José Mourinho (Chelsea, Manchester United, Tottenham)

Claudio Ranieri (Chelsea, Leicester City)
Sir Kenny Dalglish (Blackburn Rovers,
Newcastle United, Liverpool)
Carlo Ancelotti (Chelsea, Everton)

ALAN SHEARER

The best managers know about people. I'll always have Kenny Dalglish to thank for winning the Premier League at Blackburn – people will say that he had the wealth of Jack Walker behind him, but it's one thing having the money, and quite another spending it – but the one that leaps out for me, as a man-manager, is Sir Bobby Robson.

Bobby saved my Newcastle career. Things had turned for me under Ruud Gullit, and looking back there is a chance I would have left if Bobby hadn't come in when he did. He could see, straightaway, what made me tick; he knew, instinctively, how to get me enjoying playing and scoring goals again.

The first thing he did was to show me some video footage he'd compiled, to show me where he thought I was going wrong. He told me I was making life too easy for defenders, drifting into spaces where they would be happy to see me go. He told me to get into the areas where I could do damage, and he would take care of making sure the ball arrived. You could say it worked: we beat Sheffield Wednesday 8-0 in his first home game. I scored five.

That was a gift Bobby had, though, whether you were a 35-year-old veteran or a teenager just coming through. He didn't always get everybody's name right, but he knew exactly how to get the best out of you.

That was a gift that Alex Ferguson had, too. All of the managers on this list have done something special: Claudio Ranieri delivered a miracle at Leicester, Carlo Ancelotti has been sensational everywhere, Jürgen Klopp has produced Liverpool teams that play electric football, Pep Guardiola has won three Premier Leagues, José Mourinho made the country swoon when he first arrived.

But how Ferguson kept building teams, how he managed to start again after one side had peaked, was truly remarkable. He seemed to know exactly when to get rid of players, and he was ruthless enough to go through with it. He was the total package: to get the best out of all your players for that long, year in, year out, is an achievement that can't be matched. I had the chance to sign for him, of course, but turned him down to go to Newcastle. It's not something I regret. Looking at all the trophies he won without me, it's probably not something he regrets, either.

ALAN'S LIST

1 Sir Alex Ferguson (Manchester United)

2 Arsène Wenger (Arsenal)

3 José Mourinho (Chelsea, Manchester United, Tottenham)

4 Pep Guardiola (Manchester City)

5 Sir Kenny Dalglish (Blackburn Rovers, Newcastle United, Liverpool)

6 Jürgen Klopp (Liverpool)

7 Claudio Ranieri (Chelsea, Leicester City)

8 Sir Bobby Robson (Newcastle United)

9 Rafa Benítez (Liverpool, Chelsea, Newcastle United)

10 Carlo Ancelotti (Chelsea, Everton)

MICAH RICHARDS

José Mourinho had excellent taste: in his first spell at Chelsea, he tried to sign me. Manchester City had asked if they could bring Shaun Wright-Phillips back to the Etihad, and Mourinho suggested a swap deal. Shaun would return to Manchester if I went the other way.

It was tempting, the idea of playing for Mourinho, and playing in the team he had built at Chelsea. This was before City would turn into the force they eventually became, and Chelsea had won the Premier League twice in a row.

Two things stopped me. One was how comfortable I was in Manchester. I was a young man, still at the start of my career. I felt like a king. I didn't want to have to uproot my life and move to London. The second, more important, was that I was worried I wouldn't play. That regular place in the team was what I needed most at that stage. For all the pull of Mourinho, for all that he would have been able to improve me as a player, that made my mind up.

I had to wait a few years before I found the manager who would transform me. He's not on this list, though he should be: ahead of Rafa Benítez and possibly Carlo Ancelotti, too. My relationship with Roberto Mancini was brutally honest and occasionally fiery. There was at least one occasion, early on, when I tried to punch him. But after that, something clicked.

It was Mancini who taught me how to defend. It's not long since full-backs were expected to run and tackle and head the ball away, and not do a vast amount more than that. Mancini showed me the art of defending. He walked me through videos of when I should attack. He convinced me that when you went forward, you had to go forward with absolute conviction. He structured his team so that, when I chose to go, someone would cover me. He showed me that I had so much left to learn.

I listened to him, and I won him over. The only thing that ever disappointed him was my injury problems. I remember he pulled me aside in a hotel once, when I had been ruled out of another game, and asked me what was going on. 'Do you want me to buy another right-back, Micah?' he said. I told him that, whoever he bought, they wouldn't be able to do what I do. And he looked at me and said: 'I know.' He never did buy another one.

MICAH'S LIST

1 Sir Alex Ferguson (Manchester United)

2 Pep Guardiola (Manchester City)

3 José Mourinho (Chelsea, Manchester United, Tottenham)

4 Arsène Wenger (Arsenal)

5 Jürgen Klopp (Liverpool)

6 Sir Kenny Dalglish (Blackburn Rovers,
Newcastle United, Liverpool)

7 Carlo Ancelotti (Chelsea, Everton)

8 Sir Bobby Robson (Newcastle United)

9 Claudio Ranieri (Chelsea, Leicester City)

10 Rafa Benítez (Liverpool, Chelsea, Newcastle United)

THE TOP 10

1 Sir Alex Ferguson (Manchester United)

2 = Pep Guardiola (Manchester City)

2 = Arsène Wenger (Arsenal)

4 José Mourinho (Chelsea, Manchester United, Tottenham)

5 Jürgen Klopp (Liverpool)

6 Sir Kenny Dalglish (Chelsea, Leicester City)

7 Claudio Ranieri

8 Sir Bobby Robson (Newcastle United)

9 Carlo Ancelotti (Chelsea, Everton)

10 Rafa Benítez (Liverpool, Chelsea, Newcastle United)

Gary's Verdict: A fairly straightforward one, this, with a unanimous and pretty obvious winner: 13 Premier League titles; 11 manager of the year awards; two Champions League trophies; five FA Cups; the winner of 528 games. But apart from that, what did Alex Ferguson ever do in management?

THE DEBATE

Alan: Mourinho made an incredible impact when he first arrived, but over the years that has changed slightly. His last two jobs have ended in disappointment, really: he rated taking Manchester United to second as one of his greatest achievements, but I'm not sure the José that arrived in England back in 2004 would have agreed with him.

Micah: Guardiola has outstripped Mourinho now, pretty clearly: he's won three of the last four Premier League titles. It's strange to think that there was all of that worry over whether his methods would work in England. He's had just as much of an impact as Mourinho had initially, but he might be able to sustain it for longer.

5

THE TOP 10
BALLON D'OR
WINNERS

GARY LINEKER

This should be nice and easy. Just the small matter of sorting a list of ten of the greatest players into an order of best to worst, which means not only confronting the eternal debate about which of Lionel Messi and Cristiano Ronaldo is superior, but condemning one player to finishing last: something that not many of these ever did.

Of course, it's quite a statement to be in the top 10 at all, but quite how you separate them I have no idea. Just look at the players who have won the Ballon d'Or in what is, I think, best described as football's modern era – since the birth of the Premier League and Champions League in 1992 – but have not made this list: Michael Owen, Pavel Nedvěd, George Weah, Andriy Shevchenko.

How do you choose between Marco van Basten, one of the most ruthless strikers there has ever been, and the effortless imagination of Ronaldinho? Is there a debate to be had over who is the best Ronaldo: the original, Brazilian one who seemed set to transform the game before injuries halted his career, or the apparently age-defying Portuguese one? And how can you definitively choose Messi over (Cristiano) Ronaldo, when their lists of achievements are equally remarkable and the raw data of their careers, the number of goals they've scored and games they've won, would once have been unthinkable?

Whatever the answers, the simple fact that all of these players have at one point or another been voted the finest on the planet is testament to just how good they all were. The Ballon d'Or has always been the most prestigious of football's individual awards, something reserved for the true greats.

Mind you, I thought I was in with a good chance of winning one in 1986. I think I'd ticked most of the boxes: I'd finished with the Golden Boot at the World Cup that summer, and I'd signed for Barcelona almost immediately afterwards. I thought I was a shoo-in: I'd finished third in the FIFA equivalent, behind the Brazilian Careca and someone called Diego Maradona, which wasn't bad going.

They weren't eligible for the Ballon d'Or at the time – back then, it was limited to just European players – so I assumed it would be me. But it was voted for exclusively by journalists, and they had never produced an Eastern Bloc winner. For some reason, that year was chosen as the one when that would change, so everyone voted for Igor Belanov, a forward who'd helped Dynamo Kyiv win the Cup Winners' Cup that year. He didn't do very much anywhere apart from that, but still, he beat me to it. Fortunately, almost 40 years on, I've almost forgotten about it. I'm not bitter at all.

THE CONTENDERS

Roberto Baggio

Luís Figo

Kaká

Lionel Messi

Rivaldo

Ronaldo

Cristiano Ronaldo

Ronaldinho

Marco van Basten

Zinedine Zidane

ALAN SHEARER

I thought I had a chance of winning the Ballon d'Or at one point, too. I'd done pretty much everything I could in 1996: I'd finished as top scorer in the European Championships that summer, and I'd broken the world transfer record when I signed for Newcastle a few months later. In the end, I finished third, behind Matthias Sammer – the German captain – and Ronaldo.

I was up for the FIFA equivalent, too, the World Player of the Year award. There was a glitzy awards show to announce who had won it; I turned up wearing this horrendous suit. I genuinely went thinking I might win it. I came third in that one, too: this time it was Ronaldo and George Weah ahead of me. It's good that I took it well, though. There was a gala dinner afterwards, but I was in such a bad mood about not winning that I decided not to go.

Funnily enough, even though Ronaldo beat me to that award, he might not have moved to Barcelona if it wasn't for me. Bobby Robson had taken the job and made me his first choice to play upfront. It was tempting, not only to work with Bobby but to play for Barcelona, but I decided not to go. I was happy in England and, not long after, the offer from Newcastle came in.

What a result that was – for Barcelona. They got Ronaldo from PSV Eindhoven instead, and he was sensational, a striker of pure ability. For a few years, before the injuries took his edge off, he was the best player in the world.

You could say that about pretty much anyone on this list. Nobody wins the Ballon d'Or by accident. It's almost impossible to put them in any sort of order: how can you put any of these players at number 10? Roberto Baggio could play anywhere. Rivaldo and Luís Figo could just glide past players. Ronaldinho made everything look effortless. Zinedine Zidane was the best player I ever played against. Marco van Basten was the complete centre-forward.

There's nothing between the top two, either. We have been so lucky to watch Lionel Messi and Cristiano Ronaldo in their prime over the last, what, 15 years? Getting to the top is one thing; staying there for as long – delivering week in, week out – as they have is quite another. They have a hunger and desire that I'm not sure anyone can match.

And the standard they have set is beyond anything we have seen before. It used to be that scoring one goal every two games was considered exceptional. They have made that look ordinary. They've taken goalscoring to another level: it is impossible to emphasise enough how much dedication that has required from both of them. You could toss a coin on them, really. I'd put Messi top, but it really wouldn't bother me either way. You can't argue with either. We have been blessed to see both.

ALAN'S LIST

1 Lionel Messi

2 Cristiano Ronaldo

3 Ronaldo

4 Zinedine Zidane

5 Marco van Basten

6 Ronaldinho

7 Kaká

8 Luís Figo

9 9 Rivaldo

10 Roberto Baggio

MICAH RICHARDS

There was only one time in my entire Manchester City career that I wasn't exactly devastated to be told that I was missing out on a game, and that was when Manuel Pellegrini told me that he thought Pablo Zabaleta might be the better bet to go up against Lionel Messi and Barcelona at Camp Nou.

Earlier that season, we'd played Bayern Munich in the group stage. Pellegrini had pulled me aside a couple of weeks before and told me that he'd studied the video and come to the conclusion: I was the man to deal with Franck Ribéry and Arjen Robben, Bayern's alternating wingers. It was a hiding to nothing. Playing against players of that quality is not a pleasant experience. You can't get near the game. You're far too busy thinking about tracking them. It becomes nothing but a running exercise. And if I'm honest, I didn't want another one in Barcelona, spending a night watching Messi sail away from me. I was happy to let Zabaleta take that one.

Even Pellegrini admitted as much before the game. He said he would not tell us how to defend Messi, because there is no way to defend Messi. He spends all of his time in no man's land: those little bits of space that aren't the territory of the full-back or the central defender or the defensive midfielders. He forces you to make choices all the time; he takes you into places you do not want to be. And then he gets on the half-turn, and at that point, you have no chance.

The only thing that can help is numbers: Pellegrini's strategy was to make the winger his first point of contact when he picked the ball up out wide. That way, he would not be able to expose the full back quite so quickly. There is a limit to how effective that, or anything, can be. Messi's quite possibly the greatest of all time, after all. He wouldn't be Messi if he was easily stopped.

He has to be top, just ahead of Cristiano Ronaldo, but I do wonder whether that might have been different had Ronaldo, the Brazilian Ronaldo, not been plagued by injury when he was at his peak. People perhaps do not realise just how good he was: he was the first twenty-first-century player, a one-man strike-force, and the most influential player of his generation. Everyone from Zlatan Ibrahimović to Romelu Lukaku lists him as their biggest inspiration. Messi and Cristiano have changed what we thought was possible, but so did Ronaldo, and his true prime only lasted three or four years.

MICAH'S LIST

1 Lionel Messi

2 Cristiano Ronaldo

3 Ronaldo

4 Zinedine Zidane

5 Ronaldinho

6 Kaká

7 7 Marco van Basten

8 Rivaldo

9 Roberto Baggio

10 Luís Figo

THE TOP 10

1 Lionel Messi

2 Cristiano Ronaldo

3 Ronaldo

4 Zinedine Zidane

5 Ronaldinho

6 Marco van Basten

7 Kaká

8 Rivaldo

9 Luís Figo

10 Roberto Baggio

Gary's Verdict: You wonder how much Lionel Messi and Cristiano Ronaldo have driven each other on, to what extent the competition between them has helped them reach new heights. Both are remarkable, and there's few players who deliver in the big moments like Cristiano, but most players tend to lean toward Messi, and I'd go along with that. I try to judge players by the joy they bring, and nobody brings as much joy as he does. Even on his quiet days, he does a handful of things that bring a smile to your face, and leave you asking how he did it. I never thought anyone would get close to Diego Maradona, but he did. He's the greatest to have drawn breath since I stopped playing.

THE DEBATE

Alan: Messi against Ronaldo is the greatest debate in modern football, but it's almost impossible to say which one comes out on top. That they stand out even in a list with all these other players shows how good they are, and how much they have changed what we think is possible. I'm not sure anyone will be able to match them for a long time.

Micah: I have to go with Messi. I never did manage to play against him, but I did play against Ronaldo, and to be honest I got the better of him. That was at the start of his career, of course, when he was still learning his trade at Manchester United, but I never found him too much of a problem.

6

THE TOP 10
STRIKE PARTNERSHIPS

GARY LINEKER

Nobody could wish for a better strike partner than Peter Beardsley. I was fortunate enough to play alongside some wonderful strikers – Graeme Sharp, at Everton, stands out – but none of them came close to Peter. Not for me, anyway. I think my record when we played together for England was a goal a game.

He was a wonderfully bright player, incredibly unselfish and hugely creative. He produced an almost endless supply of chances for me. But the best thing, by a long way, was that he didn't want to be in the box. He did most of his damage outside. And that gave me free rein over everything inside the penalty area. For a striker, that's gold-dust. It's quite a selfish instinct, but it's how I worked. I wanted space in the box, and Peter provided me with that.

It is quite unusual, now, to see a pair like that. They're another facet of the game that I played that seems to be dying out, as teams prefer to play with three forwards: either what we now know as a false nine and two wingers – often playing on their non-natural sides – or with a central striker flanked by two attacking midfielders.

No strike-force sums up that approach better than Sadio Mané and Mohamed Salah for Liverpool. They both take up that modern role of wingers who aren't strikers, and yet they're the ones who have supplied the bulk of Liverpool's goals. Salah, in particular, seems to have an insatiable thirst for scoring, that attitude that once he's scored one, he immediately wants another one. He had a goal put up in his garden so that he could practise finishing at home. It's clearly worked, given his record.

But it feels strange to talk about them and not about the third member of that front-line, Roberto Firmino. He is the one who knits it all together, who creates the space for Mané and Salah to exploit, who makes everything work. That is the blueprint most teams follow now – think Neymar, Lionel Messi and Luis Suárez for Barcelona – and it seems to have heralded the end for the old-fashioned strike pairing.

We have chosen to ignore that trend, though, and go for those 'outdated' partnerships. It may seem obvious what makes a pairing a success: the end result. The ones we remember are the ones that scored a lot of goals together. But those goals don't always have to be equally shared. They don't necessarily have to lead to a lot of trophies, though of course they often do. And the precise nature of the chemistry that makes them work so well is a difficult thing to pin down. Do you need different strengths? Do your styles have to contrast? Do you even need to like each other?

THE CONTENDERS

Sergio Agüero and David Silva (Manchester City)

Dennis Bergkamp and Thierry Henry (Arsenal)

Andy Cole and Dwight Yorke (Manchester United)

Eiður Guðjohnsen and Jimmy Floyd Hasselbaink (Chelsea)

Harry Kane and Son Heung-min (Tottenham)

Sadio Mané and Mohamed Salah (Liverpool)

Kevin Phillips and Niall Quinn (Sunderland)

Cristiano Ronaldo and Wayne Rooney (Manchester United)

Alan Shearer and Chris Sutton (Blackburn)

Daniel Sturridge and Luis Suárez (Liverpool)

ALAN SHEARER

The best partnerships are the ones you do not have to work at. I had a few like that during my career: Chris Sutton and Mike Newell for Blackburn, Les Ferdinand for Newcastle, Teddy Sheringham for England.

Some of those were more easily explained than others. Mike Newell wanted to drop deeper when we didn't have the ball. Teddy Sheringham did his best work almost playing as a number 10. Chris Sutton was happy to do that extra bit of running, to drop into midfield when we were out of possession while I occupied the central defenders. From that point of view, they were all perfect. My main priority was that I wanted them to create chances for me, and they did.

Les Ferdinand was a bit different. There was a feeling that we couldn't play together when I joined Newcastle, and in fairness we only played one full season together. But it worked spectacularly. We both missed a couple of months that season, but we still managed to score 49 goals between us. That's not bad going, is it? In fact, you can make the case that I should have been in this list twice.

The worry was that we were both goalscorers, and that one of us would end up taking precedence over the other. It didn't turn out like that. The key thing was that, between us, we had a bit of everything: we were good in the air, we were technically good, we had a bit of pace. That's crucial. A partnership can be great even if one player scores more than the other – Thierry Henry and Sergio Agüero were more prolific than Dennis Bergkamp and David Silva – but, between you, you have to be good at every aspect of the game.

You need a good understanding, too. Not just of your own games, but of the team's. Chris Sutton wasn't necessarily my favourite strike partner, but we had that. We were both ideally suited to how that Blackburn team played. We had two incredible wingers, Jason Wilcox and Stuart Ripley, who got up and down and got crosses into the box. That's what both me and Chris wanted, and we thrived off the supply line.

We weren't especially close, but I'm not sure that's important. I liked Chris, and we were friends, but we didn't socialise. You don't have to be best mates: it seems accepted now that Mané and Salah are not pals, but that's not stopped them. Andy Cole and Teddy famously didn't get on, but they did not let that impact their performances when they played together at Manchester United.

That said, the best pairing of the Premier League era were good friends: Cole and Dwight Yorke. Cole could have been in there for his partnership with Peter Beardsley at Newcastle, too, He scored a phenomenal number of goals, and that was without taking penalties.

I have never quite understood strikers who don't want to take penalties, but how good his record was without them shows just how good a finisher he was.

ALAN'S LIST

1 Andy Cole and Dwight Yorke (Manchester United)

2 Cristiano Ronaldo and Wayne Rooney (Manchester United)

3 Dennis Bergkamp and Thierry Henry (Arsenal)

4 Sergio Agüero and David Silva (Manchester City)

5 Harry Kane and Son Heung-min (Tottenham)

6 Sadio Mané and Mohamed Salah (Liverpool)

7 Alan Shearer and Chris Sutton (Blackburn)

8 Daniel Sturridge and Luis Suárez (Liverpool)

9 Kevin Phillips and Niall Quinn (Sunderland)

10 Eiður Guðjohnsen and Jimmy Floyd Hasselbaink (Chelsea)

MICAH RICHARDS

The general rule, as a defender facing a proper strike partnership, is that you take responsibility for the player who is most suited to you. The centre-back who's better in the air will take the target man; the quicker defender will look after the Jamie Vardy-type, the one playing on the shoulder, looking to make those runs in behind.

Most of the time it works. But only most of the time, because occasionally you run into an attack that doesn't really fit the criteria. Normally, you have one quick striker and one strong one. Daniel Sturridge and Luis Suárez didn't really fit that mould, though. They could both run in behind. They could both go deep. They were both technically brilliant.

Most of all, they both asked you questions. They made you do things you didn't want to do. You can't man mark them, not really, because they move into areas that defenders don't want to be in so, if you follow them, you're out of position. If you do as you're told and stick with one player, not giving them any time to get the ball and turn, your whole shape disappears.

But then dropping off, giving them that extra yard, didn't work, either. You can't give players that good that sort of space in dangerous areas. They'd spread the play, pick a pass, start to unravel your defence. So that was out, too. It was impossible to know how to play against them. You could just about defend them in the air, but that was about it.

You'd take up good positions, get in a space to block off a line or an area, and think you'd shut something down. And then they wouldn't run there: they were smart enough to go somewhere else. You'd be thinking you'd done well to close the door, but it would turn out they were going into a different house. With both of them, that was fatal: one touch from Suárez, in particular, was often enough to cause all sorts of problems. A quick touch, a little bobble, and he'd be gone.

You can't underestimate the work ethic they needed to be that dangerous. Strikers are asked to do a lot more now than they used to be, I think. They have to be involved in play in a way that wasn't the case a few years ago: not just making those runs and dropping deep to pick up possession, but leading the press, too. They have to work.

MICAH'S LIST

1 Andy Cole and Dwight Yorke (Manchester United)

2 Dennis Bergkamp and Thierry Henry (Arsenal)

3 Cristiano Ronaldo and Wayne Rooney (Manchester United)

4 Sergio Agüero and David Silva (Manchester City)

5 Sadio Mané and Mohamed Salah (Liverpool)

6 Alan Shearer and Chris Sutton (Blackburn)

7 Daniel Sturridge and Luis Suárez (Liverpool)

8 Harry Kane and Son Heung-min (Tottenham)

9 Kevin Phillips and Niall Quinn (Sunderland)

10 Eiður Guðjohnsen and Jimmy Floyd Hasselbaink (Chelsea)

THE TOP 10

1 Andy Cole and Dwight Yorke (Manchester United)

2 Cristiano Ronaldo and Wayne Rooney (Manchester United)

3 Dennis Bergkamp and Thierry Henry (Arsenal)

4 Sergio Agüero and David Silva (Manchester City)

5 Sadio Mané and Mohamed Salah (Liverpool)

6 Harry Kane and Son Heung-min (Tottenham)

7 Alan Shearer and Chris Sutton (Blackburn)

8 Daniel Sturridge and Luis Suárez (Liverpool)

9 Kevin Phillips and Niall Quinn (Sunderland)

10 Eiður Guðjohnsen and Jimmy Floyd Hasselbaink (Chelsea)

Gary's Verdict: I'm not sure playing in a squad with four top-class strikers would have suited me. I wanted to play all the time; having to rotate in and out with three other players would have really frustrated me. But even with Teddy Sheringham and Ole-Gunnar Solskjær pushing them, Dwight Yorke and Andy Cole stood out as the definitive partnership, not just for that great, treble-winning Manchester United team, but in the Premier League era.

THE DEBATE

Alan: Thierry Henry was so elegant, the way he ran with the ball, but I'd put Cristiano Ronaldo and Wayne Rooney just below Yorke and Cole. Rooney could play however you wanted, could do whatever you wanted. He could play. He could fight. He couldn't be bullied. Put him with Ronaldo and his drive and technique, and it was something special.

Micah: What Yorke and Cole won means they're top, but I'd say Bergkamp and Henry run them close. Bergkamp made everything look so effortless. His touch and his vision with Henry's perfect finishing? That's everything you need in a partnership. Ronaldo was so gifted – he could twist you up left, right and centre – and he was unpredictable. You didn't know what he was going to do. But while he was in England he still had that slight showboat streak.

THE TOP 10
CHAMPIONS

GARY LINEKER

Even I wouldn't try to pretend that the Leicester City team that won the Premier League were the greatest team English football has ever seen. Certainly not when you compare them to the greatest teams of the last 25 years: the Manchester United side that won the treble in 1999, Arsenal's Invincibles of 2004, or Pep Guardiola's record-breaking Manchester City of 2018 and 2019.

There are many ways to achieve success. There is no one specific recipe. At Arsenal and Manchester United – and I suppose at Manchester City, under Guardiola, and Liverpool, with Jürgen Klopp – it came through stability, enabling a visionary manager to shape the team and the club as he wanted.

At Chelsea, though, it is quite the opposite. José Mourinho won the league in his first two seasons, had a year of disappointment, and then he was packed off. He came back, won it, and barely lasted another few months. Antonio Conte was the same. But you can't really argue with results: five Premier League titles since 2005. The model works for them.

But there are also many different ways to assess it. The best players and the best managers obviously migrate to the biggest clubs, the ones that can pay the most money, and the teams that end up getting the most points. Those are the teams that go on to dominate the league, to end the season going unbeaten or setting record points tallies.

Once in a while, though, a team comes along that does it a different way. And it's that, I think, that makes Leicester stand out. They were not as good a team as some of their predecessors or successors as champions, of course. But they had a much better story: not just where the team had come from, having only just avoided relegation the previous season, but what the players had come through.

It was not just Jamie Vardy, signed for a million pounds only a couple of years after he left non-league football, but people like N'Golo Kanté and Riyad Mahrez, both of whom had been overlooked by teams in France and had to work their way up through the second division. The manager, too, had been written off as too nice to win trophies. There was a reason Leicester were 5,000-1 to win the title. That they managed to overcome it makes them, in my biased eyes, the greatest champions the Premier League has ever had.

It still makes me emotional to think about it. What was remarkable about it was that it was not just Leicester fans who were enthralled by it. It was everyone: the whole world was obsessed with this city that normally nobody really knows how to spell or how to pronounce, and the whole world fell in love with this football team. That is far more special, to me, than what all of the other, wonderful teams on this list achieved.

THE CONTENDERS

Blackburn Rovers (1995)

Arsenal (1998)

Manchester United (1999)

Arsenal (2004)

Chelsea (2006)

Manchester United (2008)

Manchester City (2012)

Leicester City (2016)

Manchester City (2018)

Liverpool (2020)

ALAN SHEARER

Blackburn and Leicester are, by a long way, the two smallest clubs ever to win the Premier League title, but there is one key difference. Everybody saw Blackburn coming. The same could not be said, not by a long shot, for Leicester. They knew our intentions. We were signing big players and, in Kenny Dalglish, we had an outstanding manager. We were not exactly a surprise package.

That was the dream the club had sold us: that little Blackburn Rovers could compete with the big boys, and we all believed it. There were certain ways in which the club was not quite elite: we did not own our own training ground, and we had to wash our own kit, for a start. I still remember my first day, going back into the dressing room and chucking my dirty kit on the floor, and all of the other players looking at me as if to say: 'And who do you think will be picking that up?' They must all have thought they'd brought in a proper big-time player, too good to do his own washing.

But everything was in place, on the pitch, for success. The season before we won the league, we had been right in the mix; in fact, you can make a case that we should have done a little better. We weren't like Leicester in 2016: we were under intense pressure to win the league, to make all of the investment worth it. We were desperately trying to stave off Manchester United, who had been slowly chipping away at our lead for months. Alex Ferguson had tried all of his tricks, and we'd done all we could to blank it out.

It all came down to the final day: we were at Anfield, and Manchester United were at West Ham. It was beyond nerve-wracking. We were petrified. Kenny was trying to tell us to stay calm, but the pressure was huge. Even so, we managed to go a goal up at Anfield, while United were drawing at Upton Park. The fans were letting us know what was going on, and at some point we just seemed to crumble.

Liverpool equalised, and then took the lead. There is a story that their fans were supporting us that day, to stop Manchester United winning the league, but that's not how I remember it: Anfield wanted Liverpool to win. In the end, we fell over the line. We lost, but United couldn't score in London. It was at that point that the fans stayed to applaud us, though really I think they were just applauding Kenny. That was definitely the highlight of my club career; it's up there with being captain of England as the highlight of everything I did as a player.

ALAN'S LIST

1 Leicester City (2016)

2 Blackburn Rovers (1995)

3 Manchester United (1999)

4 Arsenal (2004)

5 Manchester City (2012)

6 Manchester City (2018)

7 Liverpool (2020)

8 Chelsea (2006)

9 Arsenal (1998)

10 Manchester United (2008)

MICAH RICHARDS

The way Manchester City won the league in 2012 still seems quite surreal to me. There will never be a moment like that again: almost the last kick of the season, and the title changing hands from one side of a city to the other. There is a reason the time of Sergio Agüero's goal – 93 minutes, 20 seconds – is so special to City fans.

I'm not sure that achievement is always put in the right context. Obviously it was history being made: Pep Guardiola's teams, in particular, have gone on to set new records and to turn the club into the dominant force in English football, but we will always be the ones who got the ball rolling, the ones who won the FA Cup and the Premier League, the ones who started the era.

But it is quite often dismissed as simply being about money, that what Manchester City did was buy a load of the best players – and keep the odd right-back around – and that it was inevitable that they'd win the league sooner or later. It doesn't quite work like that, though.

You have to remember the teams we were up against: the Manchester United of Alex Ferguson, the Arsenal that Arsène Wenger had built, a Chelsea team that was good enough that year to win the Champions League. No matter how good the players you have are, no matter how much money you have spent, getting past all of them for the first time in almost 50 years is an incredible feat.

That is not to say that we were necessarily better than all of these other teams, of course. Manchester United in 2008 had Cristiano Ronaldo just entering his peak years, about to become one of the two best players in the world and, maybe, in history. Liverpool, in 2020, not only handled the pressure of a 30-year wait for the title but the pressure that they had come so close the year before. Manchester United won the treble in 1999. Arsenal went unbeaten a few years later. And, of course, Guardiola's City have played some of the best football this country has ever seen, getting the sort of points totals we thought were impossible.

But what makes a title special is the story behind it, and deep down I still cannot believe I was involved in what happened in 2012. Even if I was only a substitute.

MICAH'S LIST

1 Leicester City (2016)

2 Arsenal (2004)

3 Manchester City (2012)

4 Blackburn Rovers (1995)

5 Chelsea (2006)

6 Manchester United (1999)

7 Liverpool (2020)

8 Manchester City (2018)

9 Arsenal (1998)

10 Manchester United (2008)

THE TOP 10

1 Leicester City (2016)

2 Blackburn Rovers (1995)

3 Arsenal (2004)

4 Manchester City (2012)

5 Manchester United (1999)

6 Chelsea (2006)

7 Manchester City (2018)

8 Liverpool (2020)

9 Arsenal (1998)

10 Manchester United (2008)

Gary's Verdict: You have reached the correct decision. Leicester were so unlikely to win the league that I tweeted that I'd present *Match of the Day* in my underwear if they held on to do it. I thought there was absolutely zero chance of it happening, but it did. It was agony over the last few weeks, waiting to see if they could, and it wasn't great appearing topless on television, but I would do it all over again.

THE DEBATE

Alan: There is something extra special about going the whole season unbeaten. Every few years there is a team that gets close to matching what Arsenal did in 2004, and they always fall short. It may never be done again, you know. If you look at the teams that we have had who have not quite managed it, that shows you just how difficult it is.

Micah: I think I would rather go unbeaten for a whole season than set a record points total. You can make the case that the Invincibles are not quite as good as Guardiola's Manchester City because they didn't get near 100 points, but the mental strength it takes not to lose a game over the course of a campaign is unbelievable.

THE TOP 10
DEFENDERS

GARY LINEKER

Defenders should never be the centre of attention. They are the game's bad guys. That is their job. Football is about creating joy, not destroying it. It's about scoring goals, not preventing them.

Increasingly, that's not just the way retired strikers think: it's how coaches see it, too. It's interesting that this list of the ten greatest central defenders of the Premier League era includes only one who is still in action: Virgil van Dijk, who had such a transformative effect on Liverpool. The rest all belong to the recent – and sometimes more distant – past. So, too, do most of those who might have a claim to a place among their number: Jamie Carragher, Ledley King and Sol Campbell.

There is no question that the art of defending has changed. I'm certain that most attacking players from my era would score goals if they played today: not because they were more talented, but because the game has been tilted so much in their favour. Partly that is because the playing surfaces are so much better: it's no longer the case that pitches are covered in mud by October, frozen solid in winter and then bare earth by spring. But largely it is because defenders can no longer kick lumps out of them. There are times when that shift feels like it has gone too far, as though tackling itself is slowly being outlawed, but for the most part it is to the benefit of the game.

What makes so many of these defenders stand out is that they would have thrived in whatever era they played in. They were all tough, uncompromising, ruthless. But they were also, without fail, wonderfully gifted players, boasting the composure and the technical ability to play the ball out from the back.

Some of them do not always get the credit that they, even as defenders, deserve. Some of them know it, too. Marcel Desailly, one of the finest of all time, was a guest on the BBC's coverage of a World Cup a few years ago. We were watching a game and discussing why it seemed to be that there was more affection and appreciation for Thierry Henry in England than in France.

Marcel thought about the question. 'Well, you have to remember that in France they have seen some of the finest players of all time,' he said, with complete seriousness, as he outlined the standards Henry was expected to live up to. 'They've had Zinedine Zidane, Michel Platini, Marcel Desailly.'

THE CONTENDERS

Tony Adams (Arsenal)

Ricardo Carvalho (Chelsea)

Marcel Desailly (Chelsea)

Rio Ferdinand (West Ham, Leeds United, Manchester United)

Vincent Kompany (Manchester City)
Gary Pallister (Manchester United)
Jaap Stam (Manchester United)
John Terry (Chelsea)
Virgil van Dijk (Southampton, Liverpool)
Nemanja Vidić (Manchester United)

ALAN SHEARER

It's difficult to nominate individual central defenders as the greatest ever, for the simple reason that defending is about partnerships. Gary Pallister was a brilliant defender, but he was improved even further by the fact he played alongside Steve Bruce. Gary was the better player – more comfortable on the ball – but the fact that he had Steve next to him, as reliable a player as you will ever find, enabled him to shine.

Of course, some partnerships are a bit more lopsided than that one. Strikers and defenders quite often will have a running conversation through the game: it can be funny, it can be friendly, it can be the complete opposite of both. During one game against Chelsea, Marcel Desailly came over and asked me why I never came to stand next to him; why I always seemed to prefer single out Frank Leboeuf, his partner in defence. I was perfectly honest with my answer: why would I go and stand next to Marcel Desailly when I could have a much easier afternoon standing next to Frank Leboeuf? I reminded him of that little comment the day I turned him and put one in from 30 yards at St James's Park, but he was right. As a striker, you would not go up against someone like Desailly unless you had to.

Like all the great defenders, Desailly could play. The same was true of John Terry, even if it was generally thought that Rio Ferdinand was the more cultured player. Both had incredible passing ranges, both were comfortable in tight spaces.

What stood out about Tony Adams, though, was his more traditional qualities. He was a leader. He was an organiser. He could tackle. He was happy on the ball, too, but what stood out about him when you came up against him was how tough he was. I didn't like playing against him, or against that famous Arsenal back-line full stop. There was no Frank Leboeuf in that team. To avoid Adams, you had to deal with Martin Keown or Steve Bould. The level of aggression was something else. On the rare occasions you got the better of them, the only problem was getting past David Seaman, waiting behind them.

You always came away from meetings with Arsenal, and Adams in particular, with a few reminders. I had cuts above my eyes, cut lips, broken noses as little souvenirs of our encounters, and I am sure he did too. The game was tough then in a way that maybe it isn't now. But Tony always shook hands at the end of it. You left the battle on the pitch, and went to nurse your bruises over a drink in the players' lounge.

ALAN'S LIST

1 Tony Adams (Arsenal)

2 John Terry (Chelsea)

3 Rio Ferdinand (West Ham, Leeds United, Manchester United)

4 Virgil van Dijk (Southampton, Liverpool)

5 Vincent Kompany (Manchester City)

6 Nemanja Vidić (Manchester United)

7 Marcel Desailly (Chelsea)

8 Jaap Stam (Manchester United)

9 Gary Pallister (Manchester United)

10 Ricardo Carvalho (Chelsea)

MICAH RICHARDS

It upsets me to see the art of defending slipping out of the game. I admire how teams like Manchester City play out from the back, obviously, but the aspect of football I always liked the most was one-on-one defending: an attacker and a defender going mano a mano. It gave me more satisfaction to clear a shot off the line or stop a forward in their tracks with a perfectly timed tackle than it did to score a goal. It gave you that sense of triumph, that feeling that you could look these great players in the eye and say: 'I own you.'

There are not enough players left who think like that. Too few are coached in the finer points of defending, and that is a shame. The game has changed, without question, but I am not convinced it is for the better. You see too many defenders being caught out because they are being asked to do things that they aren't really able to do.

The very best, of course, can do both, though I think there are times when elegance can play tricks on you. Our eyes can deceive us. Ricardo Carvalho did not look quite as smooth on the ball as either John Terry or Rio Ferdinand, say, but even if he was not quite as stylish, he was no less of a defender: cultured and composed, tough and quick, and with a massive haul of trophies and medals to prove it.

Vincent Kompany was so good with his feet that the first time I saw him – in a pre-season game between Manchester City and Hamburg – he was playing as a number 10. He was doing all these tricks and flicks, showing off his talent. We signed him off the back of that, and at first he played in midfield. It was only after he struggled in one game, as he was battling an injury, that he was moved into defence. As soon as he got there, you realised that was where he belonged. He was imperious, immediately. He is the best I have ever played alongside, other than Rio Ferdinand and John Terry.

Rio made playing for England easy. As well as being a Rolls-Royce of a player, he was a real talker: he would walk you through the game as a full-back, giving you all the benefit of his experience. But while they were both as good as each other defensively, and while they were both great on the ball, I would have to give it to Terry because he was more of a threat at the other end. He scored 41 goals for Chelsea, which is a superb return for a central defender. If you watched an individual game, Rio's style would probably stand out more. But Terry's effectiveness at the other end gives him the slightest edge.

MICAH'S LIST

1 John Terry (Chelsea)

2 Rio Ferdinand (West Ham, Leeds United, Manchester United)

3 Tony Adams (Arsenal)

4 Vincent Kompany (Manchester City)

5 Virgil van Dijk (Southampton, Liverpool)

6 Nemanja Vidić (Manchester United)

7 Jaap Stam (Manchester United)

8 Gary Pallister (Manchester United)
9 Ricardo Carvalho (Chelsea)
10 Marcel Desailly (Chelsea)

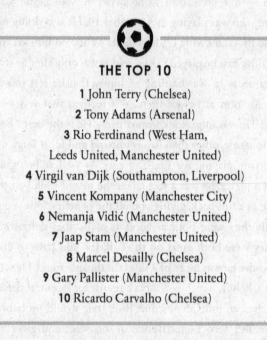

THE TOP 10

1 John Terry (Chelsea)

2 Tony Adams (Arsenal)

3 Rio Ferdinand (West Ham,
Leeds United, Manchester United)

4 Virgil van Dijk (Southampton, Liverpool)

5 Vincent Kompany (Manchester City)

6 Nemanja Vidić (Manchester United)

7 Jaap Stam (Manchester United)

8 Marcel Desailly (Chelsea)

9 Gary Pallister (Manchester United)

10 Ricardo Carvalho (Chelsea)

Gary's Verdict: Suitably, it's as tight a finish as you can imagine: only a narrow offside between John Terry, Tony Adams and Rio Ferdinand. Terry takes it, though, because Micah has been swayed by his goalscoring record. Which kind of proves my point that football, when it comes down to it, is about scoring goals, not stopping them.

THE DEBATE

Alan: Virgil van Dijk had such an impact at Liverpool, and how much they struggled in his absence showed how important he is. The question for him will be how much the injury that ruled him out of the 2020/21 season affects him in the future. My major injuries eventually cost me just a little bit of pace. If the same happens to him, he will have to adjust his game.

Micah: Van Dijk could end up higher on this list by the time he has finished. He has got absolutely everything. He can spray passes as well as John Terry, read the game as well as Rio Ferdinand, and he is as dominant in the air as Adams.

THE TOP 10
WINGERS

GARY LINEKER

There was no real mystery about why I was so prolific for England. Behind me, seeing passes nobody else could, I had Peter Beardsley. And at either side, for several years, I had John Barnes and Chris Waddle. For a striker, it was paradise.

Barnes and Waddle could not have been more different in terms of their style. John was elegant. He wasn't rapid, necessarily, but he seemed to glide past defenders with the utmost ease. He made it all look so effortless. And then, of course, he had that wand of a left foot to deliver the ball, invariably putting it in exactly the sort of place that his striker would want it.

For quite a lot of his career, he was dogged by this idea that he never quite managed to play at the same for level for England as he had for Liverpool. It always seemed unfair to me. The landscape of international football has changed a lot since then: this was before the collapse of the Soviet Union and the demise of the former Yugoslavia. There were not quite so many smaller nations involved in qualifying for major tournaments. As a rule, games were a little tighter. Often, the closest thing we had to an easy game was someone like Turkey.

For John, that meant that the calibre of opponent he was facing was higher than he would have been used to. With Liverpool, he could do ten magical things every game; for England, up against the best right-back in Spain or France or Germany, maybe that would only be three or four. That's what created the impression he was not quite as good for his national team as his club, but it did not take into account the context.

Waddle's style was very different – he had this floppy, funny look with the ball at his feet – but no less effective. His delivery was exceptional. The most important thing for a forward is knowing when the ball is coming, and where it is going. Movement, and timing, are the crucial things in scoring goals. With Chris, you could be sure not only of when he would play it, but where he would put it.

He was one of the reasons I signed for Tottenham when I left Barcelona, as it happens. I was really looking forward to playing alongside him at club level; our relationship was so good for England that I was confident we would be able to replicate it – even improve it – in the league. Spurs seemed to be just as excited. They told me they wanted to build the team around both of us. Perfect, I thought. I signed on, wondering what sort of damage we would do together. And then, within a few days of me arriving, Spurs went and sold him to Marseille.

THE CONTENDERS

Gareth Bale (Tottenham Hotspur)

David Beckham (Manchester United)

Ryan Giggs (Manchester United)

David Ginola (Newcastle, Tottenham Hotspur)

Eden Hazard (Chelsea)

Marc Overmars (Arsenal)

Stuart Ripley and Jason Wilcox (Blackburn Rovers)

Cristiano Ronaldo (Manchester United)

Raheem Sterling (Liverpool, Manchester City)

Chris Waddle (Sheffield Wednesday)

ALAN SHEARER

I've cheated a little bit here. It wouldn't really have been fair on either Stuart Ripley or Jason Wilcox to include one and leave the other out. I genuinely could not choose between them. And besides, part of what made the Blackburn team that won the Premier League so effective was that we did not have just one hardworking, energetic, creative winger. We had two.

Playing in a team with both of them was dreamland for any centre-forward. They were not particularly alike as characters – Stuart was too bright for all of us, all coolness and common sense, while Jason was the class clown, a practical joker – and they'd arrived at Blackburn at different stages of their career. Jason had come through the youth team, while Stuart had been bought, for reasonably big money, from Middlesbrough.

But they both had the same job. Kenny Dalglish, the manager, knew exactly what he needed to do to get the best out of me. He needed two wingers putting quality balls into the box for me to attack. Or, I suppose, for Chris Sutton to go for in the unlikely event that I couldn't get there. And they were perfect for that.

They were both proper, old-fashioned wingers. They worked up and down the flanks all day, Jason on the left and Stuart on the right, helping out in defence and then tearing forward in attack. I think for both of them those were the best four years of their careers; they worked so hard that I'm not sure they could have kept it up over a longer period than that. But I will always be grateful to them, because their supply was a big part of the reason that I scored so many goals at Blackburn.

Wingers like that have become a bit of a dying breed now. We could quite easily have thrown the likes of Sadio Mané and Mohamed Salah into this list, but while they both occupy the same positions and spaces as wingers traditionally did, they do not really play as wingers. That has been one of the biggest consequences of the shift from most teams playing a 4-4-2, as they did 20 years ago, to most lining up in some variation of a 4-3-3. Instead of wingers, teams tend to have all-purpose forwards, whose first instinct is to come inside, rather than put their head down and tear towards the byline. Salah and Mané are among the best in the world at that, though they have some way to go before they catch the two best examples: Cristiano Ronaldo and Lionel Messi.

ALAN'S LIST

1 Ryan Giggs (Manchester United)

2 Cristiano Ronaldo (Manchester United)

3 Chris Waddle (Sheffield Wednesday)

4 Stuart Ripley and Jason Wilcox (Blackburn Rovers)

5 David Beckham (Manchester United)

6 David Ginola (Newcastle, Tottenham Hotspur)

7 Gareth Bale (Tottenham Hotspur)

8 Raheem Sterling (Liverpool, Manchester City)

9 Eden Hazard (Chelsea)

10 Marc Overmars (Arsenal)

MICAH RICHARDS

I'd been up against Arjen Robben for about 20 minutes when I had to have a long, hard chat with myself. It was not the first time I'd done that – just taken myself a side for a minute in the middle of a game to go over some hard truths – but it was probably the most urgent. It was my England debut, and he'd had me on a bagel, which is like having someone on toast, but just a touch classier.

I told myself that he wasn't bigger than me, he wasn't quicker than me, and that he wasn't even necessarily more agile than me. So why was he ripping me to shreds? I'm not sure I ever found an answer, other than wondering if maybe the easiest solution was for him to go and play on the other wing and make someone else's night a misery.

What made Robben so special was how quickly he could change directions. He had this amazing ability to chop one way, drawing you in, and then while you were still reacting to cut back the other way. There wasn't really a way to defend against it. He could move his feet quicker than your brain could send a signal to your body.

We never, really, saw the best of him in the Premier League, which is why he did not make the top 10: he was outstanding whenever he did play, but injuries limited how much of a long-term impact he could have. That Chelsea team had another great winger, as it goes, one who could easily have made this list, too: Damien Duff. He was an absolute baller. He did not have Robben's trickery, but he was so direct. There was no faffing about. He was going to run at you, run by you, and create something.

Gareth Bale was similar, in that sense, though if anything he was quicker and stronger than Duff. But what really made the difference with Bale – what made him the toughest direct opponent I ever faced – was how fit he was. After about 70 minutes, you would expect him to start getting tired. As a defender, you are definitely getting tired. But he didn't. He just kept on going. He would be running as fast in the 92nd minute as he was in the second. There was not much you could do about that, either, really. He might not get you early on, Bale, but he would get you eventually, because he would just keep coming.

MICAH'S LIST

1 Ryan Giggs (Manchester United)

2 Gareth Bale (Tottenham Hotspur)

3 Cristiano Ronaldo (Manchester United)

4 Eden Hazard (Chelsea)

5 David Beckham (Manchester United)

6 Marc Overmars (Arsenal)

7 Raheem Sterling (Liverpool, Manchester City)

8 David Ginola (Newcastle, Tottenham Hotspur)

9 Chris Waddle (Sheffield Wednesday)

10 Stuart Ripley and Jason Wilcox (Blackburn Rovers)

THE TOP 10

1 Ryan Giggs (Manchester United)

2 Cristiano Ronaldo (Manchester United)

3 Gareth Bale (Tottenham Hotspur)

4 David Beckham (Manchester United)

5 5 Chris Waddle (Sheffield Wednesday)

6 Eden Hazard (Chelsea)

7 Stuart Ripley and Jason Wilcox (Blackburn Rovers)

8 David Ginola (Newcastle, Tottenham Hotspur)

9 Raheem Sterling (Liverpool, Manchester City)

10 Marc Overmars (Arsenal)

Gary's Verdict: Ryan Giggs is the player who, for a long time, made me feel old. Strange as it seems, our careers crossed over. My final game for Tottenham was at Old Trafford. Manchester United had this blisteringly quick, technically dazzling young winger playing for them. Even during the game, he caught my eye: you could tell, straightaway, that he would turn out to be a real player. Given that he won 13 Premier League titles, that probably wasn't too bad a prediction.

THE DEBATE

Alan: Raheem Sterling has benefited so much from working under Pep Guardiola. There was a point in his career when his finishing was a real weak point, but you can see from his goal return over the last few years at Manchester City that he has put the hours into improving it. A modern wide forward – rather than winger – needs to have that side to their game.

Micah: I still think there is more to come from Raheem. His final ball has got a lot better, but I'm not sure he is as devastating as he can be in every single game. That's the next step in his development. If he can do it, he has the talent to get further up this list.

10

THE TOP 10
DEAD BALL
SPECIALISTS

GARY LINEKER

It would never even have occurred to me to take a free-kick, all through my career. I might have taken a quick one every now and again, after I'd been fouled, but I never had any desire to demand the ball in a promising position and try to dip one over or curl one around a wall. I knew my abilities but I also knew my limitations, and one of them was that I wouldn't have been able to kick the ball quite that far. Not the balls we played with, at any rate: I might have stood a chance with the modern ones. But we played with heavy old things, ones that soaked up the water from the mud baths of pitches that we played on. You needed a fair bit of power to strike them.

I barely ever took a set-piece of any description, in fact. I had a few games playing as a right-winger in my very early days at Leicester, and so I guess I would have taken a corner or two, and a handful of throw-ins. But later on, playing upfront, my job was to be in the middle, waiting for a chance. That was how I liked it, too. I wouldn't have wanted to be 25 yards out, sizing up a free-kick; all I cared about was scoring goals, and I figured my chances of doing that were better if I was in the box, hoping for a deflection or the goalkeeper to spill the shot. Taking the free-kicks themselves was better left to the specialists.

There has never been a greater dead-ball specialist than David Beckham, of course. Even if you discount all of the goals he scored, he was exactly the sort of player you needed, as a forward, to have taking your set-pieces. What matters, in those situations, is being able to time your run to meet the ball as it comes in. Beckham's delivery was so precise and so reliable that you would have been able to do that with ease: you knew the ball was coming, you knew where he would put it, and you knew that he could get it to you in whatever way you needed.

I could never have done what he did, but I do like to think I contributed to one of the most iconic free-kicks of all time. If you watch the footage of Paul Gascoigne's free-kick in the 1991 FA Cup semi-final, you'll see me run over to have a word with him beforehand.

People often ask me if I was demanding to take it, but that's not what happened. It was so far out: I could never have kicked it that far. I was a bit worried that he couldn't either. He seemed to be sizing it up to bend it, and I wanted to tell him not to: it wouldn't work, because of the distance. All I did was tell him to blast it instead.

That was exactly what he did. Because he was Gazza, of course, he decided that he could bend it as well: that was what made the shot unstoppable. It was one of his great moments, but I like to think I helped, just a little.

THE CONTENDERS

David Beckham (Manchester United)

Kevin De Bruyne (Manchester City)

Ian Harte (Leeds United)

Matt Le Tissier (Southampton)

Dimitri Payet (West Ham United)

Laurent Robert (Newcastle United)

Wayne Rooney (Everton, Manchester United)

Cristiano Ronaldo (Manchester United)

James Ward-Prowse (Southampton)

Gianfranco Zola (Chelsea)

ALAN SHEARER

What separates good players from great ones is that the truly outstanding are pretty much good at everything. Every player has different attributes, obviously. It's the manager's job to blend all of that into a team, to make sure that one player's strengths compensate for another's weaknesses, to try to make the whole as complete as possible.

But some players are complete all by themselves. Laurent Robert and David Beckham make the point quite nicely. Robert had all the talent in the world. His left foot was unbelievable. From a set-piece, he had that ability to whip the ball in, with pace, to a specific part of the box. That's what you want as a striker: to know the ball is going to go where it is supposed to be going, pretty much every time. When he got it right, it was basically impossible to stop.

There was nothing wrong with Laurent's attitude particularly; he wasn't a difficult player to have around or anything. But he did not especially like doing the dirtier side of the game: all the tracking back, the dropping into position, the helping out with defence. It was something every player sees a lot during their career: what makes the difference, a lot of the time, is not how good a player can be, but how hard they are prepared to work.

Beckham was the opposite. He had that same knack: he could get a ball up and down, and do it with this incredible whip and speed. The free-kicks that we all remember are the ones that he scored: the goal against Greece for England, and dozens of strikes for Manchester United.

But what made him stand out for me was the quality of his delivery, both from set-pieces and from out on the right wing. He was a dream to play alongside, because he was so reliable with his crossing. There's at least one of my goals, against Germany in Euro 2000, that comes to mind immediately as being a result of his delivery.

That wasn't fate; he hadn't been born like that. He was so good because he never stopped working. That was what meant that he made more of his talent than someone like Laurent; it was what put him on a different level. He did not just hone his special skills, he did the same with every part of the game. He tracked back, he helped out, he put the hard yards in. He was brilliant, but he was brilliant because he worked.

ALAN'S LIST

1 David Beckham (Manchester United)
2 Matt Le Tissier (Southampton)
3 Cristiano Ronaldo (Manchester United)

4 Kevin De Bruyne (Manchester City)

5 Gianfranco Zola (Chelsea)

6 James Ward-Prowse (Southampton)

7 Wayne Rooney (Everton, Manchester United)

8 Laurent Robert (Newcastle United)

9 Ian Harte (Leeds United)

10 Dimitri Payet (West Ham United)

MICAH RICHARDS

Meeting David Beckham was the first time I was star-struck. The first time I was called up by England, I was only 18. I had only been a professional for a little more than a year. I was a kid from Chapeltown, in Leeds, and I was playing for a Manchester City team that were nothing like they are now. We were rubbish. And yet there I was, walking into the Grove, the hotel outside London where the squad used to gather, playing alongside David Beckham, the biggest superstar in the game.

And he looked every inch the star, too. When I wear a tracksuit, it's always not quite the right fit: it's a bit baggy here or a bit too tight there. It's just a tracksuit. You're not meant to look like you're going to some glitzy premiere.

Not Beckham, though. I don't know whether he'd had it tailored or something, but it was like he was wearing different clothes to the rest of us. Better clothes. It fitted him like a glove. He looked smart. He obviously thought about it: he had the base layer underneath, but with one sleeve just rolled up enough to show off whichever watch he was wearing. On the other side, there was just a little flash of his sleeve of tattoos.

Given that status, you might have expected him to be horrible, but he was the total opposite. He was the nicest guy you could imagine. That is not always true of the top players: plenty of them are lovely, but not all of them. And often, with the nice ones, you're not really sure how to take it, just because it's so unexpected.

But what really stood out about Beckham was how hard he worked. He was towards the end of his career when I played with him: he had already played for Manchester United and Real Madrid; he was already a celebrity in his own right. He could place a ball on a sixpence, and he could do it any way he wanted: he could whip it or he could fizz it or he could loft it. He had done it all a million times. He was still staying behind after training to practise his free-kicks, though, trying to get better, trying to get the most out of all of his talent. That's a powerful example to a young player training with him for the first time: that is how hard you have to work to get that level.

MICAH'S LIST

1 David Beckham (Manchester United)

2 Dimitri Payet (West Ham United)

3 Cristiano Ronaldo (Manchester United)

4 Matt Le Tissier (Southampton)

5 Gianfranco Zola (Chelsea)

6 Kevin De Bruyne (Manchester City)

7 James Ward-Prowse (Southampton)

8 Wayne Rooney (Everton, Manchester United)

9 Ian Harte (Leeds United)

10 Laurent Robert (Newcastle United)

THE TOP 10

1 David Beckham (Manchester United)

2 Matt Le Tissier (Southampton)

3 Cristiano Ronaldo (Manchester United)

4 Kevin De Bruyne (Manchester City)

5 Gianfranco Zola (Chelsea)

6 Dimitri Payet (West Ham United)

7 James Ward-Prowse (Southampton)

8 Wayne Rooney (Everton, Manchester United)

9 Laurent Robert (Newcastle United)

10 Ian Harte (Leeds United)

Gary's Verdict: Of all the players I wish I could have played alongside, Beckham is probably the top of the list. I can't imagine how many goals I would have scored from his delivery, whether it was from free-kicks or from his crosses. He would be a blessing for any striker at all to have in their team. It is maybe too easily forgotten because of just how famous he became, but he was a really special player.

THE DEBATE

Alan: I'm not sure Dimitri Payet scored enough from free-kicks to warrant a place on the list, to be honest. He was only in the Premier League for a couple of seasons, too: one memorable goal is not enough to get past someone like Ian Harte, who was maybe less spectacular but his delivery was so consistent.

Micah: The free-kick Dimitri Payet scored for West Ham was as good as any I've seen: whipping the ball high, away from goal, and then seeing it bend back in at an impossible angle. But playing against him was not as difficult as it should have been: as soon as he didn't have the ball, he switched off. He was only interested when he could attack. He came alive, then, but the rest of the time he drifted out of games.

11

THE TOP 10
MIDFIELDERS

GARY LINEKER

We've done the best goalkeepers, we've worked through the finest central defenders and we've identified the greatest goalscorers of the Premier League era. So it is only right that we should afford midfielders the same honour, isn't it?

If only it was quite so simple. It is much harder to compare and contrast midfielders, especially in the modern game, because the roles they are asked to play are so different. How do you say, for certain, that N'Golo Kanté is better than Kevin De Bruyne, when the jobs they do for their team have about as much in common as Virgil van Dijk and Mohamed Salah?

Midfielder, as a category, is almost too broad. Perhaps it would have been easier to do separate lists for defensive midfielders, attacking midfielders and box-to-box midfielders, rather than grouping them all together under one banner.

That is a relatively new phenomenon, though. The outstanding midfielder during my career was Bryan Robson. He did a little bit of everything: he was as combative as Roy Keane and as dynamic as Steven Gerrard, although he did not quite have the same ability to score from long range. When I was coming through, breaking into the Leicester team and then playing for England, he was the player I admired the most.

He was a force of nature, Robson. There was one game, against Manchester United, when our manager at Leicester told me before the game that, when they won a corner, instead of hanging about on the halfway line waiting for a counterattack, my job would be to track back and sit on the edge of the box to mark him. I looked at him completely baffled: 'Me? Really?'

I did as I was told, though, and as soon as they got their first corner, I duly trotted back and stood next to him. Bryan looked at me and said: 'What are you doing?' 'Marking you,' I said. 'You're marking me,' he answered. 'You?' He was smiling, and with good reason. The ball came in, he burst past me, jumped, met the ball, and hit the bar.

A few minutes later, the same thing happened. I went back to mark him, he pushed me out of the way, got to the ball and scored. He was laughing as he ran back to the centre circle. It was at that point that the manager called me over and said that, next time they won a corner, I was to hang about on the halfway line, waiting for a counterattack.

THE CONTENDERS

Kevin De Bruyne (Manchester City)

Fernandinho (Manchester City)

Steven Gerrard (Liverpool)

Paul Ince (West Ham, Manchester United, Liverpool)
N'Golo Kanté (Leicester City, Chelsea)
Roy Keane (Manchester United)
Frank Lampard (West Ham, Chelsea, Manchester City)
Paul Scholes (Manchester United)
Yaya Touré (Manchester City)
Patrick Vieira (Arsenal, Manchester City)

ALAN SHEARER

Some players make no secret of their combative streak. Patrick Vieira was like that: he could play with the best of them, but he let you know he was there. The same was true of Roy Keane: we did not get on while we were playing, and we had several running battles, but Roy did not hide who he was. He was tough and he was ruthless. He was quite like Paul Ince, his predecessor in that Manchester United team, in that way. Paul was loud and vocal, a real leader, but he also had a nasty streak. He was not afraid to kick you at all.

There aren't too many left of that ilk in the modern game, but the one who stands out is Fernandinho. He is the master of the tactical foul: the clever little trip that stops the opposition launching a counter-attack against Manchester City. It is the same role as Keane and Ince played, but fit for the stricter game we see now. Put it this way: there was nothing particularly tactical about Roy Keane when he fouled you.

And then some players are just as canny, just as dirty, but they hide it better. There is no better example of that than Paul Scholes.

He was a wonderful player, Scholes, with an incredible passing range and a brilliant shot, but he was also a silent assassin. Everyone knew about his tackling, which was not exactly his strength: every so often he would throw in one of the worst tackles you can imagine.

But there were countless little things about his game that you didn't see. He was always a quiet, no-nonsense sort of person away from the pitch, and he was exactly the same on it. He had no qualms at all about leaving a leg in or putting his foot through you or giving your ankles a bit of a stamp. They weren't always the sort of fouls that drew attention, but you always knew you'd been in a game with him. He didn't really mind if he hurt you. That was probably what made him the player he was, the fact that he could combine this sumptuous ability with a really dirty streak. In fact, it may be what marks out the truly great midfielders. They have to be able to express themselves, of course, to have the ability to make an impact on the game. But before they do that, they have to win the battle for control of the midfield, and that takes just a little bit of grit.

ALAN'S LIST

1 Roy Keane (Manchester United)

2 Steven Gerrard (Liverpool)

3 Paul Scholes (Manchester United)

4 Frank Lampard (West Ham, Chelsea, Manchester City)

5 Patrick Vieira (Arsenal, Manchester City)

6 N'Golo Kanté (Leicester City, Chelsea)

7 Yaya Touré (Manchester City)

8 Paul Ince (West Ham, Manchester United, Liverpool)

9 Kevin De Bruyne (Manchester City)

10 Fernandinho (Manchester City)

MICAH RICHARDS

Fernandinho did not make a strong first impression. The first time he trained with us at Manchester City, straight after he'd arrived from Shakhtar Donetsk, he struggled. And when I say struggled, I mean struggled: pre-season is hard work physically, and after one session he was so tired he was sick.

We knew about him when he signed, of course, but he wasn't exactly a big name. We weren't quite sure what to expect, and this didn't seem to be a great start. You could tell that among the rest of the squad there was a little bit of worry: what have we signed here? We didn't think he'd be able to cut it in the Premier League.

And then we got the balls out, and we realised that there was nothing to worry about at all. He was unbelievable. He might have a reputation as a tough, defensive, smart midfielder, but you don't captain Brazil unless you can play. And Fernandinho can play.

Yaya Touré arriving, a few years before, was different. He had been a star at Barcelona, and in a way it was his arrival that really signalled that Manchester City were going to a different level. At first, he seemed a bit cold, a bit distant, as though he was doing us a favour by playing for us. He was, at that point, bigger than the club he'd joined, and you have to remember that he is up there with the best players the Ivory Coast has ever produced: only Didier Drogba really compares to him. He is a king at home, and he's used to being treated as such.

In one of his first games, though, I had a go at him: he wasn't tracking back, and I asked, in what was probably not the most polite tone, if he might like to consider doing a bit of work and maybe run around a bit. Some players of his profile would have objected to being called out like that, but Yaya didn't. From that point on, I think I had his respect.

He was as good a goalscorer as Frank Lampard and as good a passer of the ball as Paul Scholes. He could play deep, he could play box-to-box, he could play as an attacking midfielder. He could play centre-back, too, just like he did at Barcelona. He could run games and he could win games, as he did in the FA Cup final in 2011. He carried us to the title in 2014 almost singlehandedly. He scored 20 goals that season, all from midfield. To me, he is the single most gifted player Manchester City have ever had.

MICAH'S LIST

1 Steven Gerrard (Liverpool)

2 Paul Scholes (Manchester United)

3 Roy Keane (Manchester United)

4 Patrick Vieira (Arsenal, Manchester City)

5 Yaya Touré (Manchester City)

6 Frank Lampard (West Ham, Chelsea, Manchester City)

7 Kevin De Bruyne (Manchester City)

8 N'Golo Kanté (Leicester City, Chelsea)

9 Fernandinho (Manchester City)

10 Paul Ince (West Ham, Manchester United, Liverpool)

THE TOP 10

1 Steven Gerrard (Liverpool)

2 Roy Keane (Manchester United)

3 Paul Scholes (Manchester United)

4 Patrick Vieira (Arsenal, Manchester City)

5 Frank Lampard (West Ham, Chelsea, Manchester City)

6 Yaya Touré (Manchester City)

7 N'Golo Kanté (Leicester City, Chelsea)

8 Kevin De Bruyne (Manchester City)

9 Paul Ince (West Ham, Manchester United, Liverpool)

10 Fernandinho (Manchester City)

Gary's Verdict: Not much in this one at all, but Steven Gerrard takes it. That is probably about right. If we ran a list on attacking midfielders, Scholes would probably win it. Keane would take the crown for defensive midfielders. But Gerrard was an all-round, all-action midfielder, one who could do a bit of everything: he could win a battle, but he could also win a game.

THE DEBATE

Alan: You have to have a place for Kevin De Bruyne on the list. He maybe does not have that combative streak that some of the others do, but in terms of pure ability, he is up there. Some of his through balls are exquisite, but the way he crosses the ball is extraordinary. He is a striker's dream.

Micah: I saw Frank Lampard up close for England, and the way he timed his runs was incredible. I'm not sure there's ever been a more dangerous midfielder in terms of goalscoring. He was probably the most prolific player on this list – to be Chelsea's all-time leading goalscorer as a midfielder is remarkable.

THE TOP 10
EUROS TEAMS

GARY LINEKER

Football seems to produce more than its fair share of underdog stories. There is one that is close to my heart, of course, but it feels like they happen more frequently in football than they do in most other sports. As a rule, it seems to me that in rugby, cricket and basketball, the better team generally wins. In football, though, it is not quite so straightforward. Maybe it is because goals are so rare, and therefore so significant, that the ball can break the way of an unfenced team, and they can spend the rest of the game trying to hang on.

The European Championships, particularly, produces that kind of story surprisingly often. Even allowing for the presence of the greatest European player of his generation, Portugal's win in 2016 fits the pattern. So, too, does Greece's victory – on Portuguese soil – in 2004. They were not, by any stretch of the imagination, a great team to watch. They would have gone into the tournament with barely any expectation at all. And yet, because these things can be a bit arbitrary, a combination of a defined style of play and a little bit of luck was all they needed.

The most famous example of all is Denmark, a team that was not even supposed to be in the tournament in 1992. They only stepped in at the last minute, when the collapse of Yugoslavia forced the country to abandon: the apocryphal story has it that the players were called in off the beach. They had a couple of weeks to prepare and then they were straight into it. Maybe that helped. The big teams, the countries that are expected to compete for trophies, are all under pressure. That can be counterproductive. Denmark, in contrast, had no pressure at all – they were the ultimate example of a team just being glad to be there.

They are still the exception, though: we have seen plenty of era-defining teams win the Euros, too. Nobody encapsulates that better than Spain, the first country to win consecutive tournaments, in 2008 and 2012, with a World Cup in 2010 thrown in for good measure. Luis Aragonés, their coach for the first of those victories, was my manager at Barcelona for a season. He was always so animated: he would always gather us together before a game, get us into a huddle and then make us shout 'Vamos, Muchachos!' We did it at the tops of our voices, and I was not especially comfortable with it – I was never much of a shouter.

I could be useful to him at times, though. Towards the end of the season, it became clear that Barcelona wanted Mark Hughes to leave, and Mark wanted to go: he was very young, and his move to Spain had not quite worked out. The fans had turned on him a bit, and his style of play did not work well there.

But neither of them would make the first move, so I was called in as a mediator. We went backwards and forwards for ages, the club saying he could stay if he was happy – emphasis on the if – and Mark saying he was happy, but he would go if the club wanted him to leave. In the end, I stopped translating, told Mark that the club wanted him gone, and told Luis that Mark wanted to leave, and that they really should sort it out between themselves.

THE CONTENDERS

France (1984)

Netherlands (1988)

Denmark (1992)

Germany (1996)

France (2000)

Greece (2004)

Spain (2008)

Spain (2012)

Portugal (2016)

Italy (2020)

ALAN SHEARER

We quite often talk about how pressure has affected England over the years: the weight of expectation that hangs over the players before every tournament, the impatience of trying to end the 50-year wait for a trophy. Hopefully reaching the final in Euro 2020 will have lifted it a little, but it shows that even very good players can struggle to perform at their best when the stakes are so high, when the entire country is willing you to do well.

But England is not the only team that has had to deal with that. For a long time, Spain had exactly the same problem: they had won the Euros in 1964, but they had been in the wilderness ever since. In a way, actually, they had probably performed even worse than England – we made a couple of semi-finals, in 1990 and 1996, but the Spanish had been nowhere, despite having two of the biggest clubs in the world and a pretty reliable supply of top-class players.

Winning the Euros in 2008 changed all that. The greatest teams are the ones that are good at everything: solid at the back, inventive in midfield, deadly in attack. They do not always win, of course: you look at the Greece team that won the Euros in 2004 and there is no way to describe them other than boring. They were dreadful to watch. They weren't inventive, and they weren't deadly. But they were extremely difficult to beat, and that was enough – they beat Portugal twice during the tournament, on home soil, which is no mean feat. It was the same with Portugal in 2016: they finished third in their group, and were quite lucky to do that, and only managed to win one game in 90 minutes throughout the tournament. And yet they went on to win it.

But Spain were a cut above both. That was a team that dominated international football for six or seven years, and in a lot of ways they set the bar for what it takes to be a truly great international team. They played that wonderful, attractive, passing football, making their opponents dizzy with the way they used the ball, and they did it all under that pressure, that expectation, that so often proves a team's undoing. To play like that when you had all that history weighing on you takes guts, but most of all it takes talent. That was what made the difference for Spain: for the first time in 40 years, they had so much talent that nothing could stop them. They ticked every box: they had a defence marshalled by Carles Puyol, a midfield of Xavi and Andrés Iniesta, and then David Villa and Fernando Torres up front. They were the definition of a great team.

ALAN'S LIST

1 Spain (2012)

2 France (2000)

3 Spain (2008)

4 France (1984)

5 Netherlands (1988)

6 Germany (1996)

7 Italy (2020)

8 Portugal (2016)

9 Denmark (1992)

10 Greece (2004)

MICAH RICHARDS

What is really impressive about Denmark's win in 1992 was that they managed to get all of the players back in time to make the tournament. They would all have been called up at short notice; they were, supposedly, all on the beach when they were contacted and told to report for duty.

Getting them together would, in my experience, have been easier said than done: after a long season, you don't necessarily want to be told to cut your holiday short and go and play football, even if it is for your country. It is different at senior level, but I know that with the under-21s, you would quite often find that players had unfortunately turned their phones off when the unexpected call came, or they were in places where there weren't any direct flights for a few days, or they just happened to be out of signal.

I do sometimes wonder if those sorts of difficult circumstances can make a team greater than the sum of its parts: look at how Denmark responded to the terrifying loss of Christian Eriksen at Euro 2020. Greece were awful to watch, but you could not question their commitment or their desire. They had all of that in abundance, even if none of their players were exactly superstars. If you think about Portugal in 2016, too, they lost the player that made their team tick early on in the final: the thing that I remember most from that game is the sight of Cristiano Ronaldo prowling around on the touchline, barking instructions at the players on the pitch, after he'd been taken off injured. It was like he had taken over from the manager for the rest of the game. But it fitted, because he was the player that the rest of the team followed; he was their leader, whether he was playing or not.

Losing their big star should, really, have been the end of Portugal's chances. France, their opponents, would definitely have fancied their chances as soon as he left the pitch, especially on their own turf. But losing him seemed to galvanise the rest of the players. Maybe they wanted to win it for him. Maybe they wanted to show that they could win it even without him. Either way, they found something within themselves, they dug in, and they managed to win it with a goal from a completely unexpected player: Eder, who was really just a journeyman striker. That is the mark of champions, I suppose – that you rise to the occasion, and you meet the challenge.

MICAH'S LIST

1 Spain (2008)

2 Greece (2004)

3 Spain (2012)

4 France (1984)

5 Italy (2020)

6 Portugal (2016)

7 Denmark (1992)

8 Netherlands (1988)

9 Germany (1996)

10 France (2000)

THE TOP 10

1 = Spain (2012)

1 = Spain (2008)

3 France (1984)

4 France (2000)

5 Greece (2004)

6 Italy (2020)

7 Netherlands (1988)

8 Portugal (2016)

9 Germany (1996)

10 Denmark (1992)

Gary's Verdict: Well, then, it's definitely Spain, but it's almost impossible to separate the two of them: not just because they were largely the same team, with many of the same players, but because they won both in such considerable style. So maybe this time we should allow ourselves to have joint winners.

THE DEBATE

Alan: It would be the 2012 team for me: that was Spain in their pomp, at their absolute best, destroying a really good Italy team in the final. It was their last hurrah, really – they were knocked out of the World Cup very early a couple of years later – but what a way to sign off.

Micah: I had to go for 2008 as the high point of Spain's reign, just because the first trophy is always the hardest, especially when you have gone so long without one. The pressure is intense. That was the start of everything that came afterwards. Plus they had a fully fit, fully firing Fernando Torres; by the time 2012 came around, he was not quite the same player.

13

THE TOP 10
WORLD CUP TEAMS

GARY LINEKER

My dad had a regular card game that would go on for hours. Days, sometimes. He and a group of friends would gather in our front room every so often and sit there, playing Kalooki. Sometimes, the singer Engelbert Humperdinck would be among their number, strange as that is to say. They would pay my mum to make tea and coffee and snacks. I would hang around, watching my dad play, in the hope that he would slip me a bit of money when he was winning. Going to bed was always disappointing, but it had to happen. There were times when they played for 48 hours straight.

I only ever saw that game grind to a halt once, and that was the day that England played Brazil at the 1970 World Cup, the game with the Jairzinho goal and that gravity-defying Gordon Banks save. That was the magic of that Brazil team. They were good enough to interrupt my dad's card game.

That was the first World Cup I really remember, and that Brazil team stands out to me even now. Their display in the final, swatting aside Italy in Mexico City, remains in my eyes the single greatest performance by any team in any World Cup final. Like so many others of my generation, that Brazil side captivated me.

Not all World Cup winners since have lived up to them, but we do have a tendency to underestimate some teams that have won it. Take the West Germany side that we lost to in the 1990 semi-final. They were, from front to back, incredibly strong, led by the core of the Inter Milan team at the time: Lothar Matthäus, Andreas Brehme and Jürgen Klinsmann. They were a side worthy of a little more respect than they are sometimes given; in many ways, it is an impressive achievement that we ran them so close in the semi-final – not only taking them to penalties, but coming within the width of the post of beating them long before that. Maybe we were not such a bad team, either. We were certainly an attacking one: our midfield three was Chris Waddle, David Platt and Paul Gascoigne. There is no holding player there.

It was not quite up to the level of the one that led Spain to the ultimate trophy two decades later, of course. That was a beautifully balanced side, built around Xavi and Andrés Iniesta and Xabi Alonso, one that played wonderful football. They were the sort of team, I think, that might have interrupted a few card games, too, the sort of team that made you want to stop what you were doing and watch.

THE CONTENDERS

Brazil 1970

Italy 1982

Argentina 1986

West Germany 1990

Brazil 1994

France 1998

Italy 2006

Spain 2010

Germany 2014

France 2018

ALAN SHEARER

Talent is not always enough. It is not always the case that the team with the most gifted players wins the World Cup. It does not always come together: injuries might take their toll or a player might get sent off or a referee might make a single bad decision. Any team that wins a major tournament is, by definition, special. But sometimes it is the most solid team, or the most efficient, or the most hardworking that comes out on top. And they all, regardless of ability, need just a little bit of luck, too.

There are two World Cup winners that stand out as the most obviously talented teams of their eras. One of them misses out on the top spot because they are before mine and Micah's time: the Brazil team of 1970. The first World Cup I remember watching in any great detail was Mexico in 1986 – Gary might have mentioned what happened in it once or twice – when I was 15. I have snatches of memories from Spain in 1982, but nothing clear or complete.

The other, though, is very much of my era. Spain went from having very little success at all on the international stage – ranking alongside England as one of the great underperforming countries in football history, always near but not quite there – to dominating the game: winning the Euros in 2008 and 2012, and picking up the World Cup in between. They had some remarkable talent in that side, of course, but they were also unbelievably solid and incredibly efficient: it worked because, as well as the brilliance of Xavi and Andrés Iniesta and Xabi Alonso, they had finishers of the quality of Fernando Torres and, particularly, David Villa. It's no coincidence that they have dropped off in the last few years: the style of play is pretty much the same, but without that cutting edge, they cannot get past the most well-organised defences.

The best way to judge how good they were, though, is how much they changed the game. That Spanish style became the way everyone wanted to play for a few years, and even now we still see a lot of the ideas they either introduced or made popular being used at the highest level of the game, Pep Guardiola's Manchester City being probably the best example.

That is not true of a lot of the teams that have won the World Cup. For most, it is a month where everything comes together: the talent of the players and the game plan of the manager and a momentum that gathers strength through the tournament. For Spain, it lasted a lot longer. It led them to three consecutive trophies, making them possibly the best international team of all time, and influenced the way the game was played across the world for years after that.

ALAN'S LIST

1 Spain 2010

2 Brazil 1970

3 France 1998

4 Italy 2006

5 Germany 2014

6 France 2018

7 West Germany 1990

8 Argentina 1986

9 Italy 1982

10 Brazil 1994

MICAH RICHARDS

The first thing we asked Nigel de Jong when he came back to Manchester City after the 2010 World Cup was obvious: what on earth had he been thinking? We maybe didn't put it quite as politely as that, but he certainly didn't live that challenge on Xabi Alonso down. He kicked him in the chest, in a World Cup final, and somehow managed not to get sent off for it. That challenge wasn't a red card. It was a five-game ban.

He knew it, too; he was fully aware of how lucky he'd been not to be dismissed. I think Howard Webb, who was refereeing the final that year, came out later and admitted he'd got it wrong, or that if he'd had a clear view of it he wouldn't have just booked him. Either way, I think De Jong could not quite believe that he'd been able to stay on the pitch.

Even so, he was not especially apologetic about it. Nigel's game was physical and it was tough and loved a scrap; it's what made him such a great player. So when we asked him to tell us what was going through his mind as he planted his foot right next to Xabi Alonso's heart, he looked us straight in the eye and just said: 'I was in battle.' In his mind, that probably justified just about anything at all.

The reason that tackle resonated so much – apart from just how bad it was – was that it seemed the only reasonable way of stopping that Spanish team. They were by far the best team on the planet for about six years; nobody in that tournament, certainly, came close. All you could do to try to close the gap was to intimidate them out of the game. It speaks volumes for just how good they were that it didn't work; even with De Jong in battle mode, they kept on playing their football, passing the ball around, and they got their rewards when Andrés Iniesta scored in extra time to claim the trophy.

It's easy to think the teams that mean the most to us personally were the greatest of all time. I will always have a special place in my heart for the Brazil team from 1998 because that is the first World Cup I remember, the summer that I discovered not just Ronaldo but Dunga, the midfielder, who seemed to dominate every game he played. But looking back, I can recognise that Spain were a cut above even most other World Cup winners. Because of the way they played, their victory was not just a win for their country, but for a whole style of play.

MICAH'S LIST

1 Spain 2010

2 France 1998

3 Brazil 1970

4 France 2018

5 Italy 2006

6 Brazil 1994

7 Germany 2014

8 Argentina 1986

9 Italy 1982

10 West Germany 1990

THE TOP 10

1 Spain 2010

2 Brazil 1970

3 France 1998

4 Italy 2006

5 France 2018

6 Germany 2014

7 Argentina 1986

8 Brazil 1994

9 West Germany 1990

10 Italy 1982

Gary's Verdict: A clear win for the Spain team of 2010, then. I think we'd all say that 1966 is our favourite World Cup victory, even if we were not old enough to remember it – or even old enough to be alive when it happened – but Spain, for me, comes a close second. They were such a good team that I was desperate for them to win it that year. And they were so good that, perhaps, they were always going to do exactly that.

THE DEBATE

Alan: The France team that won it on home soil in 1998 – taking Brazil apart in the final – was ridiculous. Zinedine Zidane is the best player I ever came up against, bar none, and then you had Thierry Henry, Marcel Desailly and Youri Djorkaeff around him. Patrick Vieira was only a substitute; that is how good they were.

Micah: The player that I loved from that France team in 1998 was Lilian Thuram. I wasn't a right-back as a kid, but as soon as it became clear that's where I was going to play, he was the example I set for myself. You rarely ever saw him beaten: he was quick, strong, brave, great in one-on-ones and he scored twice in a World Cup semi-final. That's not bad going.

14

THE TOP 10
FULL-BACKS

GARY LINEKER

There is a good chance that this list will date quite a lot quicker than some of the others, because I have a feeling that, in a few years' time, Trent Alexander-Arnold might sit very clearly at the top of it. There is a wealth of great full-backs in England at the moment, but not one of them is quite as good – or even the same type of player – as the Liverpool defender.

That, maybe, is part of the reason: he is not really a defender. Stuart Pearce was probably the defining full-back of my generation, and though he liked to go forward, he was also utterly uncompromising, and as hard as nails. I remember one of his free-kicks hitting me, during a game against Nottingham Forest, in what is probably best described as a personal area. He walked over as I lay writhing on the ground, looked at the fans, all of whom were enjoying my discomfort, and just started laughing.

It was that which made his heartbreak at missing a penalty in 1990, and redeeming himself at Euro 96, so emotional; for it to mean so much to a man that tough made what he went through, the bad and the good, all the more moving. His penalty against Spain is one of my favourite sporting moments of all time. You could almost see Stuart getting rid of all the demons that had accompanied him for six years.

Trent, on the other hand, is a midfielder who happens to be playing at right-back. He was a midfielder as a young player, and it may well be that he goes on to play in midfield again. He may do even more damage there, such is his vision and his technique and his passing range. Not that finding himself playing at right-back stops him using all of the weapons at his disposal. He somehow manages to be Liverpool's playmaker, the player who makes the team tick and the system work; I'm not sure that's something that has ever been said of a full-back, certainly in this country, before. I do not get a vote, of course, but he would be close to winning it already in my mind, which is ridiculous, given his age. Give it a few years, though, and he may well take it unanimously.

THE CONTENDERS

Trent Alexander-Arnold (Liverpool)

César Azpilicueta (Chelsea)

Ashley Cole (Arsenal, Chelsea)

Patrice Evra (Manchester United)

Denis Irwin (Manchester United)

Lauren (Arsenal)

Graeme Le Saux (Blackburn Rovers, Chelsea)

Gary Neville (Manchester United)

Stuart Pearce (Nottingham Forest)

Kyle Walker (Tottenham, Manchester City)

ALAN SHEARER

What teams look for in a full-back has changed. It may have changed more than any other position on the pitch, in fact, and in an incredibly short space of time. The full-backs I played alongside, and the ones I came up against, were all steady, tough and reliable. There were a few who liked to get forward – I have a few goals to thank Graeme Le Saux, who I played alongside at Blackburn, for creating with a burst down the left – but their main job was always to defend. When a team did have an attacking player on one side of the defence, that was always balanced out on the other: so, at Blackburn, we had Graeme on the left and Henning Berg on the right. I don't think even Henning would describe himself as an attacking right-back.

Pretty much everyone fitted that mould. The two full-backs in that iconic Arsenal defence, Lee Dixon and Nigel Winterburn, were primarily there to shut down opposing wingers. Stuart Pearce was an incredible left-back for England and for Nottingham Forest, and he was a threat from set-pieces, but he was not the sort of overlapping full-back you see now. The players who filled those positions at Newcastle, Warren Barton and John Beresford, were good footballers, but they were there to defend, not to attack. The same could be said, really, of Gary Neville and Denis Irwin, the two in that great Manchester United team.

That has changed, of course: Trent Alexander-Arnold is probably the outstanding modern full-back: he is almost Liverpool's chief playmaker, despite playing in a position that's never really been associated with that role. I think we may well come to see him as a player who has changed his position forever.

But he will have to have quite a career to surpass the player who is, certainly, England's greatest ever left-back, and possibly the best full-back the country has ever produced: Ashley Cole. He may not have been the best-loved player in the Premier League during his career, and that might influence how he is seen now, but everyone who played either with or against him would know just how good he was. He had absolutely everything: he could pass, he could cross, he could tackle, he could defend one-on-one, he could run all day, he was quick, and he was a little bit nasty, when he needed to be. He was an athlete, he was as smart as they come, and he was brave: he was never afraid to be isolated against a winger. His positioning was perfect. No matter who he was playing for, and no matter how much he was being booed by the fans, there were not many wingers who ever got the better of him.

ALAN'S LIST

1 Ashley Cole (Arsenal, Chelsea)

2 Denis Irwin (Manchester United)

3 Patrice Evra (Manchester United)

4 Stuart Pearce (Nottingham Forest)

5 Graeme Le Saux (Blackburn Rovers, Chelsea)

6 Trent Alexander-Arnold (Liverpool)

7 Gary Neville (Manchester United)

8 César Azpilicueta (Chelsea)

9 Kyle Walker (Tottenham, Manchester City)

10 Lauren (Arsenal)

MICAH RICHARDS

If this is meant to be a joke – a Top 10 full-backs list that doesn't have me on it – then it's backfired, because I wouldn't have selected myself anyway. It's enough for me that I built a career out of being a full-back despite never actually having played there before getting into first team at Manchester City. I played right-back for England when I'd only played in the position 30 or so times, at most. It takes talent to learn on the job that fast.

The first time I played in the position, it was my home debut, against Charlton. Stuart Pearce had come down to watch me in the academy, and he'd always told me that he 'liked the look' of me. He brought me up to train with the first team, and I think he wanted to see what I could do, but had no particular position to play me in. We had a settled central defence, and it's a real risk putting a kid into central midfield in a Premier League game. So right-back it was.

Manchester City had a good run of home-grown full-backs at that point: Nedum Onuoha was a couple of years ahead of me, and Kieran Trippier a couple of years behind. I was – and am – good friends with Nedum, the Chief, but he was a rival, too. He was the golden boy: smart and eloquent and a great player. I think what gave me the edge, apart from his occasional injuries, was that Manchester City were not especially good when we were coming through. We didn't have the ball all the time. It didn't matter how well you did in attack, because the bulk of your work was defending. And when it came to one-on-ones, nobody could get past me.

That was maybe what meant that Trippier never quite made it at City. His delivery was outstanding: he could put a ball on a sixpence, even when he was a youth team player. But he was not quite as quick or as strong as I was: I remember him being absolutely ruined by Emmanuel Adebayor in training once. At the time, that was what mattered.

That has all changed now. That change happened incredibly quickly, too: it was only under Roberto Mancini that anyone started to coach me to put crosses into specific areas. If you contrast that with what we see full-backs doing now, especially Trent Alexander-Arnold, they are a crucial part of every team's attack. All of the top sides have full-backs whose crossing is flawless: Trent, Trippier at Atlético Madrid, Reece James at Chelsea. Whether they can defend or not is not quite as important as it used to be.

MICAH'S LIST

1 Ashley Cole (Arsenal, Chelsea)

2 Patrice Evra (Manchester United)

3 Lauren (Arsenal)

4 Kyle Walker (Tottenham, Manchester City)

5 César Azpilicueta (Chelsea)

6 Trent Alexander-Arnold (Liverpool)

7 Gary Neville (Manchester United)

8 Denis Irwin (Manchester United)

9 Graeme Le Saux (Blackburn Rovers, Chelsea)

10 Stuart Pearce (Nottingham Forest)

THE TOP 10

1 Ashley Cole (Arsenal, Chelsea)

2 Patrice Evra (Manchester United)

3 Denis Irwin (Manchester United)

4 Trent Alexander-Arnold (Liverpool)

5 Lauren (Arsenal)

6 César Azpilicueta (Chelsea)

7 Kyle Walker (Tottenham, Manchester City)

8 Stuart Pearce (Nottingham Forest)

9 Graeme Le Saux (Blackburn Rovers, Chelsea)

10 Gary Neville (Manchester United)

Gary's Verdict: Quite right too that it is Ashley Cole: he won everything as a player, including about a million FA Cups, and he always turned up in big tournaments for England. He was one of the few who kept Cristiano Ronaldo quiet whenever he faced him, too. A consummate full-back, and maybe the best the country has ever produced. So far, at least.

THE DEBATE

Alan: As long as Micah's not on this list, that's all that matters. I'm certain that Pablo Zabaleta should have had a place, though: it made such a difference to Manchester City actually having a halfway decent right-back for the first time. It's no surprise that it was when he replaced Micah full-time that they started to dominate.

Micah: Lauren is not the first player you think of when Arsenal's Invincibles are mentioned, but he was pure class as a player. Azpilicueta is the same: he may not be the most spectacular, but he does everything incredibly well. He's dangerous going forward and he's solid at the back: that's still what makes the ideal full-back. Just like me, really.

15

THE TOP 10
ALAN SHEARER GOALS

GARY LINEKER

As England captain, I tried to make sure that I welcomed new players joining up with the squad for the first time. Nothing especially ceremonial: just to say hello, ask them how they were doing, make sure they were settling in. Most of those encounters were so ordinary that I do not remember them particularly.

Only one sticks in my mind: Martin Keown. He was sitting in the dressing room when I came in before training. I said hello to a couple of more familiar faces, and then walked over to Martin. 'Good morning,' I said, in what I am sure was a friendly voice. He looked up, stared at me, and just said: 'Why?'

Meeting Alan cannot have been quite that strange. I don't remember him querying whether it was the morning or not, for one thing. The impression he made in training was quite striking, though. You could see, straightaway, that this kid had something special. It was not just his technique – he could strike a ball so cleanly – or his strength. His hold-up play was exceptional, and he was great in the air. He had it all. But most importantly, he had those things that mark out the players who will go all the way. What made Alan different was his mentality, his drive, his leadership. That is what it takes to be a top-class player, and especially a top-class striker, and it was obvious from the first time you saw him that Alan had it.

There was just a hint of a natural rivalry between us, because we played in the same position: he wanted my place, and I was in his way. In the end, of course, our paths crossed only relatively briefly. I was coming towards the end of my career, and he was just at the start of his. We played just one half of one game together for England, in a game against France, and we were only together for one squad, in the European Championships in 1992. That proved to be the last time I represented my country, and by that stage it was clear that Alan was there as my successor. He took that opportunity with aplomb. In a way, I suppose, it worked out for the best. I am glad he was born when he was, and not a decade or so earlier. I felt much happier handing over to him than I would have done having to compete against him.

THE CONTENDERS

Crystal Palace v **Blackburn**, 1992

Blackburn v Tottenham, 1995

Newcastle v Wimbledon, 1995

Newcastle v Tottenham, 1996

Newcastle v Arsenal, 2000

Newcastle v Aston Villa, 2001

Newcastle v Everton, 2002

Manchester United v **Newcastle**, 2002

Newcastle v Chelsea, 2005
Newcastle v Portsmouth, 2006

ALAN SHEARER

What a goal looked like never interested me in the slightest. A scrambled tap-in from a yard out and a 30-yard screamer gave me the exact same amount of joy: all I cared about, really, was scoring goals. I don't think I would be able to identify a favourite. They all count the same, as they say, and to an extent they all feel the same, too.

But there are some, maybe, that I am a little prouder of than others. You can probably split them into two categories. There are some that are better goals from a technical point of view. Prime among them, to me, would be the volley I scored against Everton: that was as sweet a connection with the ball as you can possibly hope for. That it was from range – that it looked spectacular – is less significant to me than the fact that it was an absolutely flawless volley. You do not get many that fall to you as perfectly as that in your career, and you do not catch many as well as that, either.

The only one that rivals it, really, is a goal I scored against Aston Villa a year earlier, a side-footed volley back across the goal and into the far post. What makes that one special is who it came against: a finish like that would always be a source of pride, but to do it against Peter Schmeichel made it even better. That is a big factor in every goal you score; it feels a bit different to do it against the very best teams and the very best players: there is a goal I scored against Chelsea, getting the better of Marcel Desailly, which I enjoyed more than I would have if I had been up against, for example, Frank Leboeuf.

And then there are the goals that might not be so artistic, but that mean something more than normal. In my last season, the quest to break Jackie Milburn's record for Newcastle had become a big story. He had scored 200 goals, and I was closing in on him. But the closer I seemed to get, the harder it seemed to be to score goals.

That all changed against Portsmouth, in February 2006. I scored my 200th goal for the club in the first half, in front of the Leazes End. The second wasn't bad, but it was not especially beautiful – a back-heel from Shola Ameobi, and a toe-poke through the goalkeeper's legs – but it is the greatest feeling I've had on a pitch, really. To go ahead of Jackie, who had been one of my dad's heroes, and to do it by scoring in front of the Gallowgate End at St James's Park, the place where I used to go and watch Newcastle play, felt absolutely perfect. It was not the best goal I ever scored. It was not the most technically challenging or the most aesthetically pleasing. But it was the one that meant the most to me.

ALAN'S LIST

1 **Newcastle** v Portsmouth, 2006
2 **Newcastle** v Everton, 2002
3 **Newcastle** v Aston Villa, 2001
4 **Newcastle** v Chelsea, 2005
5 Crystal Palace v **Blackburn**, 1992
6 Manchester United v **Newcastle**, 2002
7 **Blackburn** v Tottenham, 1995
8 **Newcastle** v Tottenham, 1996
9 **Newcastle** v Wimbledon, 1995
10 **Newcastle** v Arsenal, 2000

MICAH RICHARDS

The only word I can use to describe Alan, as a player, may not even be a word. To me, he was just the perfect bagsman. He struck the ball as pure and as sweet and as hard as anyone. He had that air of a player who will score every time he shoots, a player born to score goals.

Our paths did not cross during his career. His last season for Newcastle – in 2005/2006 – was my first for Manchester City. We have worked out, though, that we shared a pitch for exactly 14 minutes. We played Newcastle at the Etihad in February that season, and Alan started. I came on for Joey Barton late on: he had played brilliantly that day, but he had also asked to be allowed to leave the club, so he had been getting booed relentlessly all afternoon. By that stage, we were already 3-0 up. All I had to do was keep Shearer in my pocket and see the day out.

The idea of being on the same pitch as him was a little bit ridiculous to me. I was just a kid, barely out of the academy, and he was the former England captain, one of the best strikers the country had ever produced. I would never say it to him, really, but it felt like an honour to be playing against him.

I was not besotted with football when I was growing up. I wasn't one of those kids who was watching it on television all the time. I loved playing, obviously, but I wasn't absorbing all of the facts and the figures and the statistics from a young age. Gary and Alan laugh at my memory, at how much I don't seem to remember, but that's why: I wanted to play football more than I wanted to read about it, or even to watch it.

Alan was one of the few things that cut through. I remember watching the Newcastle team of him and Les Ferdinand when I would have been five or six and being blown away by how powerful they were, how deadly, how attacking that whole side was. So when I found myself on the same pitch as the player I had watched – the one I had seen scoring all of those goals, doing that iconic celebration – it was a little bit surreal. That now I share a studio with him, and get to point out where his analysis is wrong, is even stranger.

MICAH'S LIST

1 Newcastle v Everton, 2002

2 Newcastle v Aston Villa, 2001

3 Manchester United v **Newcastle**, 2002

4 Newcastle v Chelsea, 2005

5 Newcastle v Arsenal, 2000

6 Blackburn v Tottenham, 1995

7 Newcastle v Tottenham, 1996

8 Crystal Palace v **Blackburn**, 1992

9 Newcastle v Portsmouth, 2006

10 10 **Newcastle** v Wimbledon, 1995

THE TOP 10

1 Newcastle v Everton, 2002

2 Newcastle v Aston Villa, 2001

3 Newcastle v Chelsea, 2005

4 Manchester United v **Newcastle**, 2002

5 Newcastle v Portsmouth, 2006

6 Crystal Palace v **Blackburn**, 1992

7 Blackburn v Tottenham, 1995

8 Newcastle v Arsenal, 2000

9 Newcastle v Tottenham, 1996

10 Newcastle v Wimbledon, 1995

Gary's Verdict: This is one category in which I think we have to accept that Alan finishes top. It's no surprise that it is so competitive – he did, after all, score quite a lot of goals – and even though it is that brilliant goal against Everton that claims it, if the strike that broke Jackie Milburn's record is Alan's favourite, who are we to argue?

THE DEBATE

Alan: These are just Premier League goals, but if I could throw an England one in, it would have to be the second against Holland at Euro 96. I scored in the semi-final against Germany, too, and I scored in World Cups, but that was the best night I experienced playing for my country, and the noise that the crowd made when that goal went in still sends shivers down my spine.

Micah: The goal against Everton is vintage Shearer, isn't it? It's technically perfect, it's spectacular, and ultimately he just hits really, really hard. You have to be good to connect with a ball like that. I'm not sure about the defending, though. Someone needs to close him down, there, if you ask me.

16

THE TOP 10
GREATEST PLAYERS
OF ALL TIME

GARY LINEKER

Let's finish with the most difficult category of all. Almost impossible, in fact. Who is the greatest player ever to lace a pair of boots?

Judging players you have only seen on video is hard. I wonder how much that influences our discussions on just who is the greatest of all time: even at my ripe old age, it is hard to compare players I only saw snatches of – Pelé, Alfredo Di Stéfano, even George Best – with those I am much more familiar with.

I played against one figure on this list, of course, in Maradona. He was always the bar for me, the player anyone would have to surpass if they were to be a serious contender to be the greatest player of my lifetime.

He is not the only one I had personal experience of: Johan Cruyff coached me at Barcelona, too. Our relationship was not always the easiest. Often, he played me out on the right wing, a position he would have known I did not like and was not my strongest, because I think he had decided he wanted me out of the club. He messed me around on purpose, as far as I can tell, and it all came to a head during a *clásico* against Real Madrid.

It was late in the season, and we had to win to have any chance of overhauling them to win the league. My record against Madrid was good: as well as a hat-trick on my debut, I'd scored a couple of winners against them, too. I had a reputation as a bit of a bogeyman for them. But that day, he put me on the bench. As the clock ticked down, our need for a goal got ever more desperate. We had to score, and still he didn't put me on. Soon the whole stadium was singing my name, challenging Cruyff to play me. Still nothing. Ten minutes left. Five minutes left. 'Lineker, Lineker' coming down from the stands. He did not even tell me to warm up. Eventually, I snapped a little. I turned to him and told him that he didn't have the courage to put me on, not now that it would look like changing his mind. I was right. I stayed on the bench. We drew. They won the league.

I have met Messi, too, thanks to my relationship with Barcelona, and it is him that I would put above everyone else as the greatest footballer ever to have lived. The charge against him is always that, unlike Maradona or Pelé, he has never won the World Cup. I find that deeply unfair. He has been lumbered in a sub-par Argentina team, for a start. But more importantly, nobody ever asks why Maradona did not help Napoli win the European Cup three times. Nobody ever points out that Pelé did not play, week in and week out, against the best teams in the world in Europe. It is true, of course, that the World Cup is the one great hole on Messi's CV, but I think everything else he has done, the absurd consistency over the course of his career, more than makes up for it.

THE CONTENDERS

Franz Beckenbauer

George Best

Cristiano Ronaldo

Johan Cruyff

Diego Maradona

Lionel Messi

Pelé

Michel Platini

Ronaldo

Zinedine Zidane

ALAN SHEARER

The mark of a top-class striker, for decades, was scoring a goal every two games. That was not necessarily what you aimed for – as a striker, you wanted to score as many as you could, every game – but it was the bar you needed to pass. If you averaged one in two, you were a good player. You were doing your job. It was the players who scored more than that who stood out: when I was coming through, I knew that Jimmy Greaves had scored loads of goals. Everybody knew that Pelé had scored loads of goals.

But nobody has ever scored goals in the sorts of volumes that Lionel Messi and Cristiano Ronaldo have. I am not old enough to have seen Pelé play: like almost everyone else, my knowledge of him comes from videos, grainy footage from the four World Cups he played in. I watched Diego Maradona, though I can't honestly say that all of my memories of him are desperately happy. But I feel genuinely privileged to have lived through the era of Messi and Ronaldo.

Between them, they have completely changed what we think of as possible. Just the sheer numbers of goals they have scored have been unprecedented. With both Pelé and Maradona, you have to take into account the way the game was played at the time: both would have been kicked ruthlessly and relentlessly, in a way that no modern player is expected to endure. And the pitches they were playing on were, quite often, terrible; a contrast to the perfect turf that Messi and Ronaldo have been fortunate enough to play on.

But all of that is offset by the fact that we know the quality of opponent that Messi and Ronaldo have scored against so consistently – so ridiculously consistently – for the last 15 years, and counting. The numbers they have put up cast everyone else into shade. They have taken the game, and particularly goalscoring, to new levels. And that is before we even get on to the types of goals they score: they can both hurt you in any number of different ways.

It is no disrespect to everything Pelé and Maradona achieved to suggest that the greatest player of all time has to be between Messi and Ronaldo. Personally, I would plump for Messi: the main argument against him seems to be that he has never won the World Cup – whereas Maradona and Pelé both did, and Ronaldo helped guide Portugal to the European Championship in 2016 – but everything else he has achieved, to me, more than makes up for it.

ALAN'S LIST

1 Lionel Messi

2 Cristiano Ronaldo

3 Pelé

4 Diego Maradona

5 Johan Cruyff

6 Ronaldo

7 Zinedine Zidane

8 George Best

9 Michel Platini

10 Franz Beckenbauer

MICAH RICHARDS

The numbers tell one story. The amount of goals scored by Lionel Messi and Cristiano Ronaldo make it easy to say they are the two greatest players ever to have graced the game, but bear with me a second, because I think you can make a case for Ronaldo – the Brazilian Ronaldo, the original Ronaldo – to have had more impact than either of them.

There has never been another striker like him. I know I joke about bursting onto the scene, but he was the originator of bursting onto the scene. He was a one-man attack. Literally, too: it was Ronaldo who brought an end to the old idea that you always had to play with two strikers. Not if one of them could do everything, you didn't: he was lightning quick, strong as a bull, he could dribble in the same tight spaces as Messi, and he was as good in the air as Cristiano Ronaldo. There was not a flaw in his game.

And his numbers were pretty special, too: almost a goal a game at PSV Eindhoven, almost a goal a game at Barcelona, and then a season and a half at Inter Milan when he made the best league in the world look easy. He carried Brazil to the World Cup final in 1998, and then he went one better and led them to victory in 2002. What's most impressive, though, is that victory came after he had started to suffer with injuries. That is the case against Ronaldo, really: that while Messi and Cristiano Ronaldo have sustained their level for years, his peak was only really three or four seasons. After that, his knees gave out, and he was never quite the same player again. That is something I can sympathise with, of course.

But even after the injuries, he was world class. He got 68 goals in 97 league games in his first three seasons at Real Madrid – those are hardly the statistics of a player who was finished. His iconic hat-trick at Old Trafford in the Champions League came after he was, in theory, past his peak. That alone tells you how high his peak must have been.

So much of this is tied up with what these players mean to you, of course. You're always going to build up the players who were special to you when you were a child, the players that you first fell in love with watching. A lot of it is down to who your own personal favourite is: I'm sure, if I was older, I'd say Pelé or Johan Cruyff or Franz Beckenbauer. But though Ronaldo was my era – I remember asking for his shirt from the 1998 World Cup, and being devastated when my mum said no – I genuinely believe he deserves to be in this conversation. He might only have taken the world by storm for four years. But he did enough in that short spell to last a lifetime.

MICAH'S LIST

1 Lionel Messi

2 Ronaldo

3 Cristiano Ronaldo

4 Diego Maradona

5 Pelé

6 Zinedine Zidane

7 Johan Cruyff

8 Michel Platini

9 George Best

10 Franz Beckenbauer

THE TOP 10

1 Lionel Messi

2 Cristiano Ronaldo

3 Pelé

4 Diego Maradona

5 Ronaldo

6 Johan Cruyff

7 Zinedine Zidane

8 George Best

9 Michel Platini

10 Franz Beckenbauer

Gary's Verdict: It has to be Messi, as much for his longevity as anything else. The problems Maradona had outside the pitch meant that his peak only lasted for three or four years. What matters, ultimately, is not which of the two got the highest, but who stayed around at the top for longest, and that has to be Messi.

THE DEBATE

Alan: There cannot have been many better individual performances at a tournament than Michel Platini helping the French to win the European Championships in 1982: he scored in every game, got two hat-tricks in the group stage, and ended up with nine goals. Not too bad, given that France only played five games in the tournament.

Micah: Cristiano Ronaldo might be the most effective goalscorer of all time. He maybe does not have the same sort of magic as either Messi or the Brazilian Ronaldo, but he is absolutely relentless. And he is never injured, too. That is remarkable, given how long his career has lasted already. It means that he could yet keep going for another three or four years, putting up numbers that maybe nobody else will ever be able to match.

ACKNOWLEDGEMENTS

Finally, we reach a section of the book where we are all in absolute agreement – this is the one part where there is no need whatsoever for any debate.

Everything that *Match of the Day: Top 10* has become over the last couple of years – a podcast, a show and now a book – is, first and foremost, because of those listeners, viewers and readers who tuned in. That so many people like hearing us argue about football is proof, really, of how much people like arguing about football. We know you didn't always agree – that's the fun of it.

The success of the show is also a fitting tribute to all the people who have made it possible. At Goalhanger Films, special thanks go to Tony Pastor, Harry Lineker, Jon Gill, Paul King, Vasco Andrade, Izzy Reid and Joey McCarthy for turning the idea into a reality, and for giving us all the information we need to tell each other why we're wrong. At BBC Sport and Match of the Day, we are all indebted to the vision and the interest of Marc Vesty, Richard Hughes, Matt Smith, Garry Miller and Steve Rudge.

We're grateful, too, to the team of commentators and observers at the BBC, who helped to compile the lists for more than two dozen of the subjects in this book – though we still can't believe some of your choices – and to Ian Wright, who debated them so passionately during the first series.

This book, meanwhile, would not have been possible without the skilful touch of Rory Smith, the guiding hand of Nell Warner, the eagle eye of Steve Tribe and the expert control of Albert DePetrillo. This is one subject that we could not possibly turn into a top 10: we would all just have to agree that everyone is ranked as joint first.